GENTLEMAN OF WIT AND FASHION

The Extraordinary Life and Times of George Selwyn

GEORGE AUGUSTUS SELWYN

A Gentleman of Wit and Fashion:

The Extraordinary Life and Times of
GEORGE SELWYN

∽∽∽∽∽∽

by

OSCAR SHERWIN

TWAYNE PUBLISHERS, INC.   NEW YORK

To

NANCY and JIMMY

CONTENTS

CHAPTER 1

THE KING OVER THE WATER

A DARK-HAIRED, DARK-EYED YOUNG BLADE IN
a grass green suit and pink waistcoat takes leave of his old
aunts and acquaintances and sets out in a stage coach to
Oxford. He has letters of recommendation to Doctor Richard Newton of Hart Hall (Hertford College) where he is
to be admitted. As soon as he gets there, he is introduced
amongst a parcel of honest, merry fellows who think themselves obliged in point of honor and common civility to
make him damnably drunk and carry him, as they call it,
a corpse to bed. The next night he is treated as civilly again
and for three or four nights afterwards. This glorious way
of living being new to him, it confirms the notion he has
conceived upon throwing away his satchel—that he is no
longer a boy but a man at his own disposal and at liberty to
follow his own inclination.

He immediately dons a stiff silk gown which rustles in
the wind, a flaxen tie wig or a long natural one which
reaches down below his rump, a broad bully cocked hat or
a square cap of above twice his usual size with a gold
tassel.

He then swears to a great volume of statutes, which he
has never read, and to observe a thousand customs, rights,
and privileges, which he knows nothing of and with which,
if he does, he cannot honestly comply. He subscribes to the
thirty-nine articles of religion and thinks himself sufficiently
absolved from them by kissing his thumb instead of the
book.

As a Gentleman Commoner, he receives and expects a
good deal of civility. He dines with his college head, the

Reverend Doctor Newton, and with the smart young gentlemen in the other colleges. He is made free of the Bodleian
Library, taking the usual oath not to embezzle the books.
He is welcomed at the various clubs and is impressed by
what he hears there. He gives a private ball where he meets
the young ladies of beauty and *l'esprit,* who talk with him
sitting upon large oaks and "breathing the evening fresco."
He is on good terms with his tutor and for some time after
his matriculation regales the College in the Common Room
before he goes down.

In this manner the undergraduate career of George
Augustus Selwyn—generally called George or "Bosky" Selwyn—begins.

He is the youngest son of Colonel John Selwyn, a
shrewd, silent man, humane and reckoned honest. If he is,
he does great honor to his cause, for he makes his court
and his fortune with as much dexterity as those who deem
virtue the greatest impediment to worldly success. He goes
into the Guards, fights at Malplaquet, and escapes without
a scratch. He then purchases a colonelcy for £7000, but
after the Peace of Utrecht and the fall of Marlborough, he
has to sell out. His military career closes, and he becomes
a civilian and a courtier. He holds various positions: Groom
of the Bedchamber to George II, Treasurer to the Queen
and Princesses, and also member of Parliament for Gloucester from 1734–1751. He marries his cousin, the full-
lipped, boyish Mary Farrington.

She is one of the brilliant group of women who are in
attendance at the young court in Leicester Fields and at
Richmond. It is a gay, intriguing court, distinguished by the
vivacity and frailty of its women. Queen Caroline of
Anspach is bright and clever, and she likes bright and
clever people about her. George, on the contrary, is not in
the least bright or clever and prefers for the most part dull
German women. Wit and vivacity puzzle him. But Caroline's women in waiting—Molly Lepell, Mary Bellenden
(charming, lively, soft as down), Mary Selwyn (they are
mostly Marys), and Mrs. Howard—are all witty, clever, and
handsome.

We can imagine boyish Mary Selwyn shrieking with laughter when the Queen's chaplain protests against the altarpiece before which he has to read prayers and which happens to be a naked Venus of the Dutch school. John, Lord Hervey, calls Mrs. Selwyn a simple, cunning woman and says she spies for Sir Robert Walpole. But this is a characteristic Hervey touch. Mrs. Selwyn is witty, she is clever. Is she purer and better than some of the Court women? Horace Walpole believes not. He says: "I remember to have heard forty years ago—" But forty years' old hearsay evidence is not of much value, especially when it comes from Walpole's pen. Mary Selwyn may not be spotless, but nothing is proved against her.

There are three children: Albinia, John, and George, who is born at Chislehurst on August 11, 1719. John is a delicate and amiable creature, the comfort of his parents. Albinia is married to the Hon. Thomas Townshend, has five children, and dies young.

The Selwyns have a country seat at Matson in the county of Gloucester, a manor in Chislehurst, and a town house in Cleveland Court, St. James.

At the age of nine George Selwyn goes to Eton. Dr. Bland is headmaster and later Dr. George, who marries Bland's daughter. Dr. George is a prodigious Greek scholar, can read a newspaper off into Greek, and knows the Greek for every English word except "mutton-cabobbed." But he is also pompous and affected—foolish, proud, unmannerly and brutal. He is known as Dionysius the tyrant. He tells a learned lady who quotes Latin to him that he would lay her on the block for her false quantities if she were one of his pupils.

Horace Walpole is a schoolfellow at Eton and one elegant youth of thirteen, with a sharp nose and chin, broad pale brow and large eyes, whose name is Thomas Gray. There is little, however, to attract Selwyn to Gray and Walpole. Walpole is quiet, highly strung, and fond of books. So is Gray, who regards the other boys at Eton as so many little victims playing about in the sunshine regardless of their doom. Selwyn, on the contrary, is full of health and high spirits and not in the least bookish. Thus he forms his own alliances and triumvirates.

In the list of 1732 his name appears in the fifth form near the end. After this it disappears. For the next few years he lounges contentedly around the house at Cleveland Court, St. James, or at Matson. On one occasion he sees the Duchess of Portsmouth, Charles II's mistress, at Goodwood House and marvels at the well-preserved appearance of the old lady. Finally in 1739 he goes to Hart Hall, Oxford.

What decides Selwyn to go to Oxford rather than Cambridge we do not know. It is a curious choice for one who is Whig by descent on both sides of the family. All good Whigs—men like Walpole and Gray and Mason—go to Cambridge. Oxford is Tory and somewhat Jacobitish, Cambridge is effusively Hanoverian. Jacobitism dies slowly at Oxford, partly for the reason that it is a lost cause, but principally for the reason that Whiggery colors the other University.

Freshmen are drawn from the very quarters where Jacobitism still reigns triumphant. "I am a Tory," says one of them, "and all my family have been Tories. My grandfather lost his estate against Oliver Cromwell; my father was a great sufferer for King James II, and I myself had my head broke in defence of Dr. Sacheverell before I was eight years old." One so trained is ready to sit down at his first introduction to his tutor and toast the Young Pretender six bumpers deep.

Twenty years before Thomas Warton the First preaches his famous sermon upon the text: "Justice heareth all things, hopeth all things, endureth all things, restoreth all things"— a rank Jacobite sermon in which there are several obscure hints at restoration but no direct political reference. Men praise it as the boldest and most guarded sermon ever heard at Oxford. The Masters wave their caps to the preacher as he passes through them out of church, and his health is drunk in every Common room.

On the 28th and 29th of May, 1715, the first day being the anniversary of the birthday of the new sovereign, the people of Oxford with oak boughs in their hats run up and

down the streets shouting—"King James III, the true King—
No Usurper—The Good Duke of Ormond!" and healths are
everywhere drunk suitable to the occasion. The streets are
brilliantly illuminated and the windows of Whigs broken.
The students actually besiege Oriel College and demand
out of it two young gentlemen remarkable for their zeal
for the Protestant succession. Then they break fresh windows, gut the houses of dissenters, and pull down the
chapels of Anabaptists and Quakers.

When an officer of his Majesty beats up for volunteers,
he is hissed at by the scholars and finds little encourage-
ment. Which irritates him to such a degree that he declares
Oxford is the most devilish, hellish place that ever he has
come near. "Ay, 'tis certainly Hell."

Matters come to such a pass that George I sends a troop
of horse with swords in hand to overawe disaffection. About
the same time, he presents to the University of Cambridge
a munificent donation of books. On which the following
epigram by an Oxonian is circulated—

> The King, observing with judicious eyes,
> The state of both his Universities,
> To Oxford sent a troop of horse; and why?
> That learned body wanted loyalty.
> To Cambridge books, as very well discerning,
> How much that loyal body wanted learning.

This is immediately answered—

> The King to Oxford sent a troop of horse,
> For Tories own no argument but force;
> With equal sense he books to Cambridge sent,
> For Whigs admit no force but argument.

But in 1715 it is more than good sport to be a Jacobite;
it is good policy. You can, for example, be converted (gently
and unobtrusively) by the gift of a deanery or a bishopric
or by court preferment or by being sent as ambassador to
the Turks or the Dutch. Sir Robert Walpole knows how to
arrange these little things. Again, in 1715, the Hanoverians
are not yet very comfortable upon the English throne. Nobody really likes these German people. Anything may hap-

pen. But in 1739 nothing has happened except that Walpole has bribed, coaxed, and manoeuvred England into loyalty to the Georges. Picturesqueness is fast becoming the only striking quality attached to Jacobitism.

Its adherents have often the laugh of the Hanoverians, but they have nothing else. "James the third and eighth," proclaims a preacher in the chapel of St. John's College. But it is not treason; he is only giving out his text and it is this—"But the tongue can no man tame." Oxford dons have only tongues, Oxfordshire noblemen have swords. Will they use them for the Stuarts?

There is much cry and little wool, a great deal of toasting the King over the water in the Virgilian-mottoed and rose-engraved glasses, but no going out to fight for him. We see this in the '45 when Bonnie Prince Charlie and his wild Highlanders march to Derby. What does Oxford do? The answer is, exactly nothing. That is not quite accurate, however, for on the authority of the Reverend Mr. Mason, a Whig and a Cambridge man (*Dr. Johnson*: "Mason is a Whig, Sir." *Mrs. Knowles,* not hearing quite distinctly, "A prig, Sir, did you say?" *Dr. Johnson;* "No, Madam, a Whig. but he is that too." And so he is), Oxford holds infernal orgies while the poor Highlanders are being slaughtered in the North.

But Oxford Jacobitism, futile and ineffective and exaggerated in report as it is, is preferable to the soulless political conformity that falls upon the University in later Georgian days. (In all fairness we must admit that disaffection is not so vehement as has been represented. A violent and lastingly bitter campaign is waged against Oxford by Whig pamphleteers, journalists, and even poetasters, and the government is fed with highly colored stories of Oxford's preparations for treason: ten thousand scholars ready to rise—four or five times the entire strength of the University. In fact the University occupies no place in the Pretender's conspiratorial plans. Oxford in its own way is loyal to the dynasty but *loathes* its ministers. Attacking them implies disloyalty to the King who has appointed them. Besides petulance rises with loss of preferment.)

One or two vigorous Jacobites of the academic kind remain. Such is Tom Warton the Second, scholar and buffoon, a little, thick, squat, red-faced man with an utterance like the gobble of a turkey cock. Tom is a Tory like his father and never allows the Whigs to have the last word.

CHAPTER 2

TOASTS AND SMARTS

IT WAS TILL OF LATE A CUSTOM FROM TIME immemorial for one of the family at Oxford, the Terrae Filius, to mount the rostrum at certain seasons and divert an innumerable crowd of spectators with a merry oration in the Fescennine manner dealing with the public and private lives of those drest in authority. If a venerable head of a college were caught snug abed with his neighbor's wife, or shaking his elbows on a Sunday morning, or flattering a prime minister for a bishopric, or coaxing his bedmaker's girl out of her maidenhood, the hoary old sinner might expect to hear of it from the lay pulpit at the next act of commencement. Or if a celebrated toast and a young Fellow were seen together at midnight under a shady tree, billing like two turtle doves, to him it belonged, being a poet as well as an orator, to tell the tender story to the spectators in a melancholy ditty adapted to pastoral music.

(Something like this jovial solemnity were the famous saturnalian feasts of the Romans at which every scullion and skipkennel had the liberty to tell his master his own, as the British style it. Who, says one of them, helped the chambermaid to make the beds one day when his lady was a-visiting? Or whose lady kissed Damon the butler behind a hogshead of falernian when her husband was hunting the boar? Or who lost five thousand sesterces at play and mortgaged his estate to pay it?—'Twas all water language at these times and no exceptions were to be taken.)

But these times alas! are no more. Some of the men endowed with Christian courage enough to rebuke wicked-

[16]

ness in high places, have used the old gentlemen too roughly and run their Christian patience quite out of breath. And so they have put an entire stop to the practise.

Well may a Terrae Filius swell with rage, for a twilight is fallen over Oxford. Dons drowse and drink in common rooms, professors lecture to empty benches, or better do not lecture at all, students fuddle their time away in taverns and coffee houses, and clergymen preach mechanically to yawning and indifferent congregations. Nothing matters. Little is taught to the ordinary undergraduate except some formal logic and as much classical scholarship as is necessary for the making of Latin verses. The professor of Modern History, to salve his conscience, employs a deputy who will wait on gentlemen in their own apartments. Hardly anyone uses the Bodleian Library. Many days pass without there being a single reader, and it is rare for more than two books to be consulted. Examinations are a farce. They are held in private, and candidates choose their own examiners who never fail to be their old cronies and toping companions.

> E'en Balaam's ass,
> If he could pay the fee would pass.

Professorships are given away as pensions and sinecures to anybody that can make a good bid for them without any respect to his abilities or character in general. A profligate debauchee is chosen professor of moral philosophy and a fellow who has never looked upon the stars soberly in his life, professor of astronomy. There are history professors who never read anything to qualify them for their position, but Tom Thumb, Jack the Giant Killer, Don Bellianis of Greece, and such like valuable records. There are likewise numberless professors of Greek, Hebrew, and Arabic who scarce understand their mother tongue, and not long before a famous gamester and stock jobber is elected Margaret professor of divinity.

The teaching Fellows regard teaching as a painful interlude. They live like drone bees on the fat of colleges—they are too rich and too idle. When any person is chosen fellow of a college, he immediately becomes a freeholder and is settled for life in ease and plenty. He enjoys himself and is dead to the world, for he molders away in a supine and regular course of eating, drinking, sleeping, and cheating the juniors.

Journal of a Senior Fellow:

Monday 9. Turned off my bedmaker for waking me at eight. Consulted my weather glass. No hopes of a ride before dinner.

10. After breakfast transcribed half a sermon from Dr. Hickman.

11. Went down into my cellar.

1. Dined alone in my room on a sole . . . Sat down to a pint of Madeira. Mr. H. surprised me over it. We finished two bottles of port together and were very cheerful.

6. Newspaper in the Common Room.

7. Returned to my room, made a tiff of warm punch, and to bed before nine. . . .

The great majority of Fellows enjoy the benefits of their Founders until it is possible for them to take a living and a wife. Everybody looks for preferment and greedily watches the failing health of an incumbent. At times not content with overgrown fellowships for life, they augment them with good livings, which, according to statute, are untenable together. Compelled by regulation to celibacy, they do nevertheless marry, on the principle that you can hold anything if you hold your tongue.

Each college has its own particular house of call. (Baliol's favorite haunt is a dingy, horrid, scandalous alehouse, fit for none but draymen and tinkers.) Pastor Moritz, coming late one night into Mitre Tavern, sees a great number of clergymen, all with their gowns and bands on, sitting round a large table, each with his pot of beer before him. These reverend gentlemen sit all night discussing theological and other topics till when early morning draws near, Mr. M— suddenly exclaims, "Damn me, I must read prayers this morning at All Souls!" . . .

"Oh, Lord, Madame," says Ape-All, "why, he is a Fellow of a College—that is to say, a Rude, Hoggish, Proud,

Pedantic, Gormandizing Drone—a dreaming dull Sot that lives and rots like a frog in a ditch and goes to the Devil at last, he scarce knows why."

College heads are as bad. Dr. Dunster of Wadham is "Louzy," as well as a Whig and a rogue. Dr. Mill of St. Edmund Hall is accused of small peculations. Dr. Hall of Pembroke is an admirer of whining, cringing parasites, and a strenuous persecutor of truly honest men. Dr. Meare of Brasenose is never noted for learning or anything else, and his successor is a mere hocus-pocus. Dr. Gibson of Queen's is crazed and hastens his end by drinking drams. And his predecessor, Dr. Lancaster, is a soft, sneaking, designing person, a smooth-boots, and an old hypocritical, ambitious, drunken sot.

Professors are indiscreet. Dr. Shippen of Brasenose is charged with a scandal which not even marriage can excuse. Dr. Keill at fifty marries an Oxford bookbinder's daughter, a handsome girl whose name has already been associated discreditably with his. Bishops are scarcely more judicious. Hough is no sooner promoted from Oxford to Lichfield than he secures a swinging fat wife. White Kennet has three wives—"such a strong inclination have ye Low Church Tribe to *Flesh and Bloud.*" No wonder that he proves a perfect weathercock and that his daughter marries a coachman instead of the clergyman whom the Bishop proposes. Bishop Milles is rash enough to court at Bath a young beauty of seventeen. Bishop Crewe is a digamist in compliance with the fashion of the age. Tanner's first wife, herself a Bishop's daughter, is a short, squab dame, remarkable for drinking brandy. But that does not deter the Bishop from marrying two more.

The scandal is prodigious enough to submerge even a Terrae Filius. A proctor dies of hard drinking which he calls "corruption of the lungs." A Gentleman Commoner is drowned in a well; it makes it all the harder that he is heir to £15,000 a year. One Browne falls backwards into a boiling vat in the brewing house at Queen's. A young lady disguised as a Gentleman Commoner passes some time at Hart Hall undiscovered, and three young scholars fall upon a barber for protecting his maid against them. An All Souls Fellow shoots a constable, and it is supposed that the offender is of ye Whiggish party. Jackson, the head cook of Merton, lives to eighty-seven, though a sad old drunken rogue. His two sons are clergymen, but they are not ornaments of the Church. The second butler of All Souls dies with his bottle and glass before him—"a very great lifter, indeed, a downright Sot." An octogenarian Manciple of Queen's is famed for eating, drinking, fawning, cringing, indulging his vices, and heaping up pelf. And one Mrs. Meads poisons her husband with apple dumplings and is burnt to ashes at Green Ditch.

One Don's way of writing is to have a bottle of ale, brandy, or wine stand by him, and every three or four lines he will drink thereof. The fellows of St. John's value themselves for having the best single and double coll in the University. A Doctor of Divinity, striving to make his way through Radcliffe Square, reaches the Library, a rotunda without railings, and unable to support himself except by keeping one hand upon the building, he continues walking round and round until rescued by a friend. Kegs of brandy and other cordials crowd Christ Church meadow when the ice is frozen for skating. When John Scott breaks through into a ditch and on scrambling out, a brandy vendor recommends him something warm, "None of your brandy for that young man," cries another as he sweeps past, "he never drinks but when he is dry." That which contributes to the death of the Savilian Professor of Astronomy is drinking late on Saturday night at his own house where he entertains with wine and punch the Vice Chancellor, Sir Tom Gifford, and others.

The young people of the College trace a similar pattern of virtuous conduct. They have "cocking" and horses and gaming and drinking at taverns and making believe to be fine gentlemen from London. Freshmen in new suits of drugget, prim ruffles, bob-wigs, and brazen hilted swords soon take to swaggering at coffee houses. The transformation of these foplings is miraculous. A great many of them come to the University with their fathers (rusty old country farmers) in linsey-wolsey coats, greasy sunburnt heads of hair, clouted shoes, yarn stockings, flapping hats with silver hat bands, and long muslin neckcloths run with red at the bottom. A month or two afterwards we meet them with bob-wigs and new shoes, Oxford cut. A month or two more after this, they appear in drugget clothes and worsted stockings, then in tie wigs and ruffles, and then in silk gowns, till by degrees they are metamorphosed into complete smarts, and damn the old country putts, their fathers, with twenty foppish airs and gesticulations.

Richard Graham finds Oxford a very pleasant place. The buildings are "mighty ancient and venerable," if not inferior to those in the modern style. The college beer is much praised though not up to that of Will Blackwell's brewing. His new friends are smart. His chamber he'd like the better if the chimney didn't smoke so much. His college tutor is somewhat high and repellent. But before long he writes to his sister Lucy—"You must not think, dear sister, that they keep us at our books from morning to night. Our days are much at our own disposal . . . Some are mighty bookish, and some are mighty idle . . . I would rather be a bookworm than a dunce, but I do not see the need to be either." Presently he is writing to his father for money. The Head of the College fears that the boy "is touching pitch—touching pitch,"—and trouble follows.

Edward Gibbon enters Magdalen as a gentleman commoner. During the first week he constantly attends lessons in his tutor's room, but as they appear equally devoid of profit and pleasure, he is at once tempted to try the experiment of a formal apology. The apology is accepted with a smile. He repeats the offence with less ceremony; the excuse is admitted with the same indulgence. The slightest motive of laziness or indisposition is allowed as a worthy impediment. He spends fourteen months idly and unprofitably in a round of college business, Tory politics, personal anecdotes and private scandal, and deep potations. As soon as he leaves Magdalen College his taste for books begins to revive.

Shenstone, the poet, a quiet, practical sort of man, is

invited to a sober little party which amuses itself by reading Greek and drinking water. Here he continues for a while
but is soon seduced from this symposium to a very different
party, a set of jolly, sprightly fellows, most of them west
country lads, who drink ale, smoke tobacco, pun and sing
bacchanalian catches the whole evening. Their pious orgies
generally begin with—

> Let's be jovial, fill our glasses,
> Madness 'tis for us to think,
> How the world is rul'd by asses,
> And the wisest sway'd by chink.

He is so far captivated with the social disposition of these
young people that he begins to think them the only wise
men and to have a contempt for every degree of temper-
ance and sobriety. Some gentlemen commoners, however,
who are his countrymen and who consider the above-
mentioned as very low company (chiefly on account of the
liquor they drink) good naturedly invite him to their party.
They treat him with port wine and arrack punch, and now
and then when they have drunk so much as hardly to distinguish wine from water, they conclude with a bottle or
two of claret. They keep late hours, drink their favorite
toasts on their knees, and in short are what is called "bucks
of the first head."

This world of port wine and arrack punch, of toasts
and coffee houses and taverns, is George Selwyn's world at
Oxford. It is the world of the gentleman commoner, of
the young exquisite with the golden tuft in his velvet cap,
excusing him from chapel and lecture.

George is a college smart. Every morning between ten
and eleven he comes in his academical undress to Lyne's
coffee house, after which he takes a turn or two upon the
Park or under Merton Wall while the dull regulars, the
"slow" fellows are at dinner in their hall (according to
statute). About one he dines alone in his chamber upon a
boiled chicken or some pettitoes, after which he allows himself an hour at least to dress in to make his afternoon
appearance. (If he feels strong enough he blows a tune on

the flute.) Then smelling very philosophically of essence, with his hair just wired by the friseur and his cap trimmed to the smallest size, he escorts a fair charmer to Magdalen Grove, to Merton or Paradise Gardens and back again.

George carries his snuffbox—everyone with any pretensions to be a gentleman must—and a large comb of tortoise shell or mother of pearl with which he combs his peruke as he walks with and talks to the lady.

In Merton Walk there are smirking beaus and smiling belles, laughing and jesting and repartee, soft compliment and whispered assignation, tap of snuffbox, rattle of fan. The back door of Merton College is shut up. It is too much frequented by young scholars and ladies on Sunday night.

Then supper, and finally George turns to the less refined pleasures of the night. He is seen one of the group round the table at the Mitre or the Tuns, loud in his song, deep in puns, put, or cards, whence he staggers home to his college, a toper all night as he trifles all day.

Next day he goes to the Burlace Club at the King's Head Tavern where as usual a fine woman is pitched upon for the toast of the year. Miss Molly Wickham of Garsington is chosen Lady Patronness, and the Master of Baliol is the first clergyman present. (Though George is not of their passionate persuasion, the keen set Oxford blades will scramble for a fresh country girl like aldermen at a city feast for the first cut of a venison pastry.)

An Oxford toast is such a creature as we now describe:

She has impudence—therefore she has wit;
She is proud—therefore she is well bred;
She has fine clothes—therefore she is genteel;
She would fain be a wife—and therefore she is not a whore.

Grave dons lay down their pipes for her society. One Miss Buckenden cannot go down to Nuneham without the trees being invited to rush into the flood to meet her while the laggards (the gouty oaks), we suppose, are exhorted to

Peep o'er their fellows' heads to view the fair,
Whose name upon their wounded barks they bear.

Logic is abandoned, taverns and churches deserted for her.

On dull afternoons George and his schoolfellows mount the towers and ring the bells for hours together. Accidents often happen in bell ringing, some students being struck, or falling down and breaking a leg and arm. Bell ringing is a fashionable exercise; so are riding and hunting.

Once or twice in the year, for diversion, George gallops up to town with his quarterage in his pocket and in a few days squanders it away in tavern, pleasure resorts, theatre.

The town swarms with Bookwits. "Ha! George!" says Jack accosting our smart. "Is it you? How long have you been in town?"—"Two hours."—"How long do you stay?"—"Ten guineas."—"If you'll come to Venable's after the play is over, you'll find Tom Latine, Bob Classic, and two or three more who will be very glad to see you. What, you're in town upon the sober plan of your father's? But hearkye, George, if you'll call in, I'll tell your friend Hams to prepare for you. So your servant, for I'm going to meet the finest girl upon town in the green boxes."

George goes out all right and eats and drinks and pays better than any nobleman.

There are other worlds besides that of George Selwyn— those of John Wesley and George Whitefield. There is also a sort of flying squadron of plain, sensible, matter-of-fact men confined to no club but associating occasionally with each party. They anxiously inquire after the news of the day and the politics of the times. They have come to the University in their way to the Temple or to get a slight smattering of the sciences before they settle in the country. They are a good sort of young people and perhaps the most rational of the College. But with what contempt does our smart look down on them, and on the ragged servitors and half-starved scholars with their unpowdered hair, woollen gloves, patched gowns, and dirty shoes, as he passes by with a tripping gait and jaunty dangle of his cloudy amber-headed cane.

The Principal of Hart Hall is the Reverend Richard Newton, and there is no more vigorous head of a college at Oxford. Newton is "founder mad." After a good deal of trouble he obtains a charter for his Hall, and it becomes

Hertford College. But Newton is more than a pious founder. He is a strict disciplinarian. Several times George Selwyn is shut up in the Round-house by the proctor.

In a rare moment, or to avert the gaze of Dr. Newton, Selwyn translates as an exercise Cicero's letters to Atticus but makes great use of the Abbé Mongault's excellent version and commentary. His translation, as it goes on, is shown to Pope to correct, and Pope commends but advises him, as he proceeds, to look a little oftener at the original.

This spurt of studious zeal expended, George makes a dizzy round of the various Oxford clubs, the Arcadian Society in the Angel Inn, the Punning Club, Witty Club, Handsome Club, the Banterers (whose members talk at a venture, lie, and prate what nonsense they please), the Freecynics, a kind of Philosophical Club, who have a set of symbolical words and grimaces unintelligible to any but those of their own society. Finally, as a guest, he attends a meeting of the finest geniuses and beaux esprits of the University, the Poetical Society at the Three Tuns. They nominate a place of meeting upon these two provisos: that the owner keep good wine and a pretty wench at the bar, both of which are allowed to be indispensable.

The rules are strict: 1). That no person be admitted a member of this society without letters testimonial, to be signed by three persons of credit, that he has distinguished himself in some tale, catch, sonnet, epigram, madrigal, anagram, acrostic, tragedy, comedy, farce or epic poem.

2). That no person be admitted a member of this society who has any visible way of living or can spend 5 shillings, it being an established maxim that no rich man can be a good poet.

3). That no member do repeat any verses without leave first, had and obtained from Mr. President.

4). That no tobacco be smoked in this society, the fumigation thereof being supposed to cloud the poetical faculty and to clog the subtle wheels of the imagination.*

---

* "Dr. Crassus is hereby given leave to enjoy the free use of tobacco. Provided nevertheless that he smoke in a corner of the room so as not to offend the rest of the company."

The members being met and Mr. President having assigned the chair, three preliminary bumpers pass round the board. Dr. Crassus, in pursuance of the power granted to him, retires to a snug corner of the room where a little table is placed for him with pipes and tobacco. He is glazing his pipe with a ball of superfine wax, when he alarms the room with a sudden peal of laughter which draws the eyes of the assembly towards him and makes all of them very solicitous to know the conceit which occasions it. The doctor, however, is not for several minutes able to do it, the fit continuing and growing louder and louder. At last when it begins to subside, he makes an attempt to reveal the cause of his mirth thus: "Why, gentlemen," says he, "Ha! ha! ha!—why gentlemen, I say, the prettiest epigram, ha! ha! ha! I cannot tell you for my life. I have made, I say, the prettiest epigram upon this ball of wax here, ha! ha! ha!—that you ever heard in your lives. Shall I repeat it, Mr. President?"

"By all means, doctor," says he, "nobody more proper to open the assembly than Dr. Crassus."

Then the doctor composes his countenance, and standing up with the ball of wax in his right hand, pronounces the following distich with an heroic emphasis—

"This wax, d'ye see, with which my pipe I glaze,
Is the best wax I ever used in all my days."

"Ha! ha! ha! how d'ye like it gentlemen? Ha! ha! ha! Is it not pretty, gentlemen?"

"Very pretty, without flattery, doctor," say they all. "Very excellent, indeed." Upon which the doctor smiles pleasantly and lights his pipe.

By this time their poetical blood begins to circulate and several members repeat their extemporary verses with great fluency and applause, always first clearing their throats with a glass of port and a loud hem! (During the first part of the evening their thoughts are somewhat gloomy and run upon elegies and epitaphs upon living as well as dead men, but George finds they brighten up as the night advances

and the bottles increase. They begin with satire and funeral lamentations, but end with love, sweetness, and song.)
Exempli gratia:

Upon old Jo. Pullen of Maudlin Hall

> Here lies Jo. Pullen
> Wrapt up in woollen.

Upon Jacob Bobart, Keeper of the physic gardens

> Here lies Jacob Bobart
> Nail'd up in a cupboard.

On the Cook of St. John's College

Here lies the honest Cook of our College
Who chorus'd us of £800 to my knowledge.

On Mr. Russell of Merton College

> Here lies count Russell
> Who made a damn'd bustle.

On Doctor G——'s back door

Within upon her back is laid
A chopping, strapping chambermaid.

On the lady Jades and Dr. Fr——n

Jades tires and kills all animals that ride her
From baboon Tom to the Oxonian spider.

An Author's Epitaph. Written by himself.

Here lies the Author of the APPARITION,
Who dy'd, God wot, but in poor condition—
If reader, you would shun his fate,
Nor write, nor preach for church or state,
Be dull, exceeding dull, and you'll be great.

Sonnet of an Italian Poet

> I've lost my mistress, horse, and wife,
> Such are the ills of human life,
> 'Tis well it was no worse.
> My mistress was grown lean and old,
> My wife ugly and a scold. . . .
> . . . I'm sorry for my HORSE.

"Mr. Selwyn, as our guest, please favor us with one of your effusions." Our smart, in canary colored pantaloons, rises:

> Epigram on the discovery of a pair of shoes
> on a lady's bed.
>
> Well may suspicion shake its head,
>   Well may Clorinda's spouse be jealous,
> When the dear wanton takes to bed
>   Her very shoes,—because they're fellows.

"Very, very good, indeed." A nodding of noses.

> To Mr. Townshend, the stone cutter, now Mayor.
> By Dr. Crassus
>
> Mr. Mayor, the famous stone cutter,
> Hang out your lights, for by G—d, I'm in the gutter.

"You must suppose, gentlemen," says the Doctor, "that I am going home late, and drunk, in a dark night, and so fall into the kennel or gutter." Upon which he laughs and fills another pipe.

But by now the bowl is flowing and the gownsmen poets are heated.

> Prithee, fill me the glass,
>   'Till it laugh in my face,
> With ale that is potent and mellow.
>   He that whines for a lass
>   Is an ignorant ass,
> For a bumper has not its fellow.

A fresh colored country lad breaks in with a Jacobean song—

> Your domineering, swaggering blades,
>   and Cavaliers that flashes,
> That throw the Jugs against the walls,
>   and break in peeces glasses—
>
> When Bacchus round cannot be found,
>   they will in merriment,
> Drinke ale and beere, and cast off care,
>   and sing with one consent:

I cannot go home, nor I will not go home,
    it's long of the 'oyle of Barly;
  Ile tarry all night for my delight,
    and go home in the morning early.

"And go home in the morning e-a-r-L-Y." (This is Dr. Crassus's cheery voice repeating the chorus.) Then on to,

Come, come, come, let us drink
    And give a loose to pleasure,
Fill, fill, fill to the brink,
We know no other measure.
What else have we to do,
In this our easy station,
    But what we please pursue
And drink to our Foundation.

What Class in Life, tho' ne'er so great,
With a good Fellowship can compare?
    We still dream on at our old rate
      Without perplexing care.

Whilst those of Business when oppressed
    Lye down with Thoughts that break their Rest,
      And then, then, then,
    Rise to toil and slave again,
      An easier round of Life we keep,
    We Eat, we Drink, we Smoke, we Sleep,
      And then,
          then,
             then,
    Rise and do the same again.

Finally, with bobbing red faces, jugs high and hoarse voices—

THE JOLLY GOWNSMAN
(An excellent new Ballad)

I.

Of all the vocations,
Trades, crafts, occupations,
    Which men for a living find,

It must be confessed
The gownsman's the best,
   To captivate woman kind.

II.

No trouble we know
From friend or from foe,
   All pamper'd in plenty and ease;
We sleep, eat, and drink,
Of no studies e'er think
   But how the fair ladies to please.

III.

The statesman's a drudge,
And we do not grudge
   His actions that soar to the sky,
All day he plans schemes,
Thinks of them in his dreams,
   And his lady neglected lies by.

IV.

Pray what is the soldier,
Whose spirits grow bolder,
   At the sound of the trumpet or drum?
Worn out in the wars,
And patch'd o'er with scars,
   Can he bear a campaign at home?

V.

The lawyer all day
Seeks after his prey,
   And jaded snores all the long night,
The wrinkled physician,
Is he in condition
   To do a Young lady right?

VI.

The loud country squire
Whose whole heart's desire
   Consists in an hoop and an hollow,

Whilst he's feeding his hounds,
Or tilling his grounds,
　　Alas! jolly Madam lies fallow.

VII.

But we of the gown
In Fair Oxford town,
　　Who lead a fat College life,
Although we can't wed,
In our kind neighbor's bed,
　　We may lie with our neighbor's wife.

(P.S. We forgot to take notice that Mr. Grosvenor, Secretary of the Club, has been ordered to return to Mr. Curll, the printer, a letter of thanks in the name of the members for his kind present of an excellent book, entitled, "The Pleasures of Coition, or the nightly sports of Venus," and desire him to print the said letter.)

CHAPTER 3

"AND WHEREAS . . ."

Thursday (1740)

"DEAR GEORGE,—I AM DISPOSED ONCE MORE TO pay your debts, which is what you have no pretensions to ask. Let me know what your Oxford bills amount to, that they may be paid first, and I will remit the money to you; but don't always expect to be answered next post, for I have too much business to answer all letters next post, and yours is of a nature that I think does not merit punctuality. I am yours,   J. S.
"To Mr. Geo. Selwyn,
  at Hart Hall, Oxon."

To which George replies:

"SIR—I am sensible, I have been very careless and indiscreet in contracting so many debts, and frankly own that many, if not most of them, have been unnecessary. But nothing grieves me so much as that you should think it indifferent to me whether you are pleased or displeased with what I do. No son in the world can be more convinced than I am of your great affection for me, and of your readiness to comply with every reasonable desire I have had, particularly this of your condescending to pay my debts so quickly, though amounting to so great a sum. However, I beg to observe to you, that those in London do not amount to so much by half as Mr. Goodchild has set forth, and before they are paid I shall be glad of an opportunity to remonstrate against some articles.
"I shall be ready to wait upon you whenever you command me, and, for what is past, beg you will only remember it when you find it repeated.
                    I am, &c., &c.,
                              GEORGE SELWYN."

Is not this a very proper letter? Is there not something manly and sensible about it? If you were a father with a son at Oxford, and about to pay his debts, would you like to get from him just such a letter? Of course, you would, if you did not notice that the letter is endorsed—"Copy of a letter sent to my father penned by Dr. Newton, 1740."

For some reason or other, in 1741, Selwyn leaves the University and goes abroad. It is not the Grand Tour, for he never strays far from Paris. He is invariably in want of money. He finds it difficult to make both ends meet on £220 a year. He is in extreme want of clothes. He writes to his London agent—"If I cannot obtain any assistance from my father in such a necessity as this I shall really think it a very hard case . . . for if I was obliged to live in a more frugal manner than I have done since I have been in Paris, I do not know whether living in a cave might not be just as agreeable. I am conscious of having neglected to write my family in Cleveland Court a great while, but it has not proceeded from any indifference or want of affection, but really a want of knowing what would be most proper to say to them in my present circumstances."

The parent again relents and the prodigal returns to his father's house in Cleveland Court, and no doubt, is received with open arms.

In 1745 he is back at Hertford where he again diverts himself. He is "Bosky" to his friends and comrades, and no frolic is complete without him. But his career at Oxford terminates abruptly and the coffee houses, the Clubs, and Magdalen Walks know him no more. Towards the end of May, 1745, something happens, something so serious that he immediately leaves Oxford for London until the storm blows over. But the storm does not blow over. Dr. Newton removes his name from the book of Hertford College, although he generously allows the fiction to go forth to the world that it is Selwyn's own desire.

"The Principal having signified to me," writes the Bursar of Hertford in June, "that it was your desire that your name should not be continued in the book of my office longer than the end of this quarter, I beg leave to acquaint you that it is left out according to your request, and that there is due to the House £5, 11s., 6d., and to myself for coal 8s., in all £5, 19s., 6d." At the end of July George Selwyn is publicly expelled from the University, and all and singular the scholars are warned not to have anything to do with that abandoned person. (Selwyn has been under discipline for some disorderly conviviality at the "Angel." The disturbance plays a part in his expulsion from Oxford, but it seems to have no connection with the following episode.)

"The crimes wherewith George Augustus Selwyn, late of Hertford College, Gentleman Commoner, standeth charged, are these (viz.):

1. That drinking at a tavern in company with several young noblemen and gentlemen of the University at the house of one Charles Deverelle, an unlicensed seller of wines near St. Martin's Church in the city of Oxford, he did impiously affect to personate the Blessed Saviour and did ridicule the Institution of the Holy Sacrament.

2. That he did pour red wine into a cup or chalice and did cause the said Charles Deverelle to drink the said wine in the said cup or chalice, saying: 'Drink this in remembrance of me'—or words to that effect.

3. That making signs as though he was blooding at one of his arms, he did apply the neck of a bottle of wine into the said arm, from whence the said wine gently flowed into the cup or chalice. Whereupon he was heard to say, 'It bloods freely,' and that upon the refusal of one of the company to drink out of the said cup or chalice, he addressed himself to the person refusing, making use of these words, 'Here's my body, *Hos est corpus meum*—you know what it is in Greek—' or to that effect. . . .

"And whereas George Augustus Selwyn, late of Hertford College, Gentleman Commoner, hath been accused and convicted . . . of certain Facts betokening a Habit of mind abandon'd to the most horrible impiety . . . and in order, as far as in them lies, to punish the author of such abominable profaneness and to secure the morals and religious principles of the youth committed to their care, from being corrupted by so wicked an example we . . . do hereby pronounce Decree and declare that the said George Augustus Selwyn for and on account of the said crimes so alleged and proved against him ought to be deprived of all and singular the Rights and Privileges of our said University both now and hereafter; and that he ought to be utterly expell'd and banish'd from our said University and never henceforward to be permitted to enter and reside within our said University or the precincts of the same. And we do accordingly by these presents so deprive, expell, and banish him the said George Augustus Selwyn!

"Read and Unanimously passed in a full Committee of the University of Oxford on Monday the twenty-ninth of July, 1745."

2.

"Damn the University," writes Sir William Maynard (a disagreeable cub) to Selwyn his friend, "I wish they were both on fire, and one could hear the proctors cry like roasted lobsters." Another, Thomas Streatfield, does not "wonder at your having a dispute with the University, for I observe they bear a hatred to every man of more merit than themselves." And Lady Susan Leck gives her opinion in a postscript: "P. S. I cannot help casting my eyes on that part of your letter where you seem to think the people of Oxford had principles. This really astonishes me, for you must know that they never had any human or divine—party only governs."

Fortified by these sentiments, Selwyn is prepared to move heaven and earth to get the decree of expulsion annulled. He has wild thoughts of going to law. He consults his Oxford friends about it, but they dissuade him. There is no appeal to the King or to his judges. Selwyn's short and inglorious career at Oxford is over.

CHAPTER 4

SORDID DETAILS—
PICQUET AND MACCO

THERE IS MUCH TO FORGIVE IN THIS YOUNG
man of twenty-six. He has spent his money, wasted his
time, and been expelled from the University without a
degree. His parents are not at all in a forgiving mood; they
find it easy to withstand his fascinations. But still we wish
his parents forgive him. It is very questionable if his father
at least ever does so. Colonel John Selwyn dies in November, 1751. It is said that his death is hastened by that of
his favorite son John in June of the same year, which is
probably true, and by the conduct of his second son,
George, which we must hope is not true. Certainly after the
death of his brother, George is in a very tender and
chastened mood. He is not reconciled to his mother for
some years after this. But he is forgiven enough to be
made the heir of Matson, which is substantially a free
pardon.

He is a young man of fashion. How can he be other
than that? His parents are Court people. They move in a
select sphere where everybody knows everybody else and
where nothing matters but birth. George is born into this
world and makes himself very much at home in it. He and
his friends are never serious. They can be if they take the
trouble, for none of them are in the least stupid, but they
do not take the trouble. It is not their style to be serious.
They talk of horses and women and cards and keep serious
things like politics for letters to their uncles and aunts.

Now young men of fashion must live. How does George find an income sufficient to support him in his arduous career? His father is not a rich man. It is true that by adding one to one he has attained a competent fortune. But he is not particularly anxious to grant a large yearly allowance to the spendthrift George. He knows too well where it will go. At this point, however, we stumble upon what is regarded as a beautiful dispensation of Providence: the sinecure system. In these days there is never much trouble about younger sons or poor relations. The Army or Navy being exhausted, there is always the Civil Service—always the chance of obtaining by influence a Place (the word deserves a capital), the salary attached to which is good and the duties of which are none at all.

Observe the practise. The younger son is appointed to the Place at an adequate salary with leave to appoint a deputy. The deputy, an obscure person, does all the work, and takes all the worry for a very modest remuneration. And the balance of the salary goes to the placeman.

The Selwyn family calmly enjoy numerous and well paid sinecure places. They make a brave show in the Docquet Book of Privy Seals: John Selwyn senior, John Selwyn junior, George Selwyn, Henry Selwyn, William Selwyn, H. C. Selwyn—they are all there, some of them occurring several times. And now we see whence our young man of fashion obtains some at least of his funds.

On March 1, 1740, George Selwyn, then nearly twenty-one, is nominated to the not very distinguished office of Clerk of the Irons and Surveyor of the Meltings at the Mint—£27 a year. This is not much to a young man of fashion. But the salary of a post is not at all a conclusive indication of its real value. There are perquisites—rights, franchises, privileges. And thus the profits of Selwyn's inconsiderable place are brought up to £52 a year. In addition to this he has an allowance from his father which amounts to £220 per annum. And when Colonel Selwyn dies, George is left Matson, the Castle and manor of Ludgershall in Wiltshire, two other houses, and annuities of about £300. He inherits besides a mysterious estate

(200,000 acres) in North Carolina, lost in the loss of America. (No doubt it is this estate which makes George so fervent a supporter of Great Britain in the War of the Revolution.)

George Selwyn is now a man of means and property. But nevertheless he adds to his income by accepting other and better Places. He is appointed Paymaster of the Works (£400 a year), Surveyor General of Crown Lands (£800 a year), and Clerk of the Crown and Peace and Registrar of the Court of Chancery in the Island of Barbadoes, an inconsiderable trifle snapped up by John Selwyn, the grant being for John Selwyn's own life and for the lives of his two sons and "the life of the longer liver of them."

One must apologise to the Man of Fashion for lingering so long over the sordid details of his yearly income. But, really, it is important, for Selwyn happens to come upon the town at a time when of all things it behooves a man to stand well with his bankers. You may be a jolly good fellow (as Selwyn is), but unless you can afford to lose a few hundred guineas of an evening with equanimity, you miss the real joy of life. For it is essentially a time of play. Everybody plays at cards or dices or otherwise gambles from her ladyship of Walmoden at St. James's down to the idle apprentices in Mr. Hogarth's graveyard (q.v.).

Most of all the clubmen play; they have no other diversion. They do not sit down after dinner and drowse over a pipe and a newspaper or talk fatuously about politics in the smoking room. They draw forth the card tables, light the candles, and play piquet or macco till dawn. Lucky is he who finishes the night even or a winner. It is far more common for a young gentleman to rise from these tables broke or utterly undone. There are always kind friends who make "arrangements," knowing that their own turn may come next. In a week the young gentleman is again playing merrily and we hope winning back all that he has lost.

Now in this matter George Selwyn is essentially a clubbable man. He loves the gaming table and devotes to it a goodly portion of his life. No doubt he can and does indulge his passion at home and in the houses of his friends.

But he probably loses and wins more money at his club than anywhere else. His first and favorite club is White's in St. James's Street.

It is a club of men of fashion and leisure. Here he may have a dish no bigger than a saucer that shall cost him fifty shillings. The great people who frequent this place do not interrupt their polite amusements like the wretches at Garraway's with business any farther than to go down to Westminster one season to vote for a bill and the next to repeal it. Nor do they trouble themselves with literary debates as at Bedford's. Learning is beneath the notice of a man of quality. They employ themselves more fashionably at whist for the trifle of a thousand pounds the rubber or by making bets on the lie of the day. (For this contempt of learning at White's there is just cause. "Damn me, doctor," ejaculates an officer, "say what you will, the army is the only school for gentlemen. Do you think my Lord Marlborough beat the French with Greek and Latin? Damn me, a scholar, when he comes into good company, what is he but an ass?")

Among the original rules at White's is one to the effect that every member is to pay one guinea a year towards having a good cook, another that supper is to be on the table at ten o'clock and the bill at twelve, and a third that every member who is in the room after twelve o'clock and plays shall pay half a crown. It is no uncommon thing for the club to end by the members burning their wigs.

A typical night: Dinner at seven, play all night, one man unable to sit in his chair at three o'clock, a break up at six the next morning and the winner going away drunk with a thousand guineas.

It is quite true that Dick Steele in the early days dates or pretends to date many of his Tatlers from White's—"All accounts of gallantry and pleasure and entertainment shall be under the article of White's Chocolate House"—and the wise Addison knows the place:

> Long ere they find the necessary spark,
> They search the town and beat about the park,
> To all his most frequented haunts resort,
> Oft dog him in the ring and oft to Court

As love of pleasure or of place invites,
And sometimes find him taking snuff at White's.

But this is before White's becomes a Club. After that
date few literary men are admitted. Colly Cibber is an
exception, but Colly is a butt for the young fashionables.
He is "King Coll" to them, and they greet him with huzzas
when he enters. Perhaps it is Cibber's membership that
draws Pope's attention. He pictures King Coll,

Chair'd at White's amidst the Doctors sit,
Teach oaths to gamesters, and to nobles wit.

As Doctors are loaded dice, the innuendo is damaging. At
other times the poet is wrathful or caustic—

And now the British youth engaged no more
At Fig's or White's, with Felons or a Whore,
Pay their last Duty to the Court, and come,
All fresh and fragrant to the drawing Room.

But Pope, we must never forget, is a Tory, and White's has
a Whig flavor. Swift also is a Tory. "I have heard," says
he, "that the late Earl of Oxford, in the time of his ministry,
never passed by White's Chocolate House (the common
rendezvous of infamous sharpers and noble cullies) without bestowing a curse on that famous academy as the bane
of half the English aristocracy." Lord Lyttelton, mention-
ing his son in one of his letters, says he is afraid that if
the young man becomes a member of White's the rattling
of the dice box will shake down all the fine oaks of his
estates.

Had I whole counties I to White's would go,
And set lands, woods, and rivers at a throw.

To the straitlaced White's is a den of thieves. But to
the man of taste it is eminently respectable. McLean, the
fashionable highwayman, has a lodging in St. James's Street
over against White's, and he is as well known about St.
James's as any gentleman who lives in that quarter and who,
perhaps, goes upon the road too. When McLean is taken,
Lord Mountfort at the head of half White's goes the first

day to see him. His aunt is crying over him. As soon as they are withdrawn, she says to him—"My dear, what did the Lords say to you? Have you ever been concerned with any of them?"

William Hogarth contrives to drag White's into his Rake's Progress. In Plate IV we have a picture of St. James's Street. The Rake is being arrested to the horrid accompaniment of thunder and lightning. A tremendous flash of forked lightning issues from the heavens and points directly at a house near the Palace. At what house should it point but White's? And there is the sign painted plainly enough, for Hogarth never leaves anything to the imagination. In Plate VI we are taken inside White's (or a similar gaming house) and shown the gamblers at their cards. A highwayman with the pistols peeping out of his pockets waits by the fireside till the heaviest winner takes his departure. This as an indication of the kind of person you may expect to meet at the club.

George Selwyn, though not a highwayman, finds himself very much at home in White's. He is a member of the Young Club. The Old Club at White's has grown so quickly that it has become necessary to restrict the election of new members. A New or Young Club is therefore formed, under the same roof, of gentlemen who are waiting their turn for election to the charmed circle of the old society. Rank even the most exalted is not in itself sufficient to gain admittance to the Old Club. Selwyn has to wait nine years. He is very fortunate. Some members of the Young Club have to wait much longer and some, like the Earl of March and Ruglen, never get into the Old Club at all.

It is a rule of the Old Club that no more than one member is to be balloted for on the same night and that between the hours of eleven and twelve. Before being initiated it is necessary to be well with the ruling powers. A candidate is Mr. Richard Vernon, a very inoffensive good humored young fellow who lives on the strongest terms of intimacy with all the fashionable young men. When the night of the ballot comes, he is rejected by six black balls, although of twelve persons present, eight, his particular friends, promise him their votes. This makes a great noise. His friends find it necessary to clear up their faith to him. Ten of the twelve solemnly assure him upon their honor that they have given him white balls.

There is one young gentleman elected a member of White's at this time whose name you will not find in the list of members: we refer to Henry Esmond Warrington. He is frequently at the Club and meets George Selwyn there and Lord March and the Earl of Castlewood. They all three play at macco with him, and March wins some of his money fairly and Castlewood the rest, not fairly. "By George, Mr. Warrington," says Selwyn, waking up in a rare fit of enthusiasm, "you deserve to win! You treat your luck as a gentleman should, and as long as she remains with you, behave to her with the utmost politeness, *Si celeres quatit pennas*—you know the rest. No? Well, you are not much worse off—you will call her ladyship's coach and make her a bow at the step." . . .

White's keeps a large betting book for the express purpose of entering the numerous bets which the members are perpetually making and exchanging. The first bet in the book is for a hundred guineas that the Dowager Duchess of Marlborough outlives the Dowager Duchess of Cleveland. Some members have evidently great faith in the vitality of old Sarah. She has been ill two years before and has lain for hours without speaking, but when the physician says, "She must be blistered or she'll die," the old lady wakes up and replies, "I won't be blistered and I won't die." She does live until the latter part of 1744.

"Ld. Montfort wagers Sir Jno. Bland one hundred guineas that Mr. Nash outlives Mr. Cibber." *Note.* Both Lord M. and Sir Jno. Bland put an end to their lives before the bet is decided.

"Mr. Jno. Jeffreys betts Mr. Stephen Jansen fifty guineas that thirteen members of Parliament don't die from the first of Jan. 1744 to first of Jan. 1746, exclusive of what may be killed in battle.

"Mr. John Jeffries bets Mr. Dayrolle five guineas that Lady Kildare has a child alive before Lady Caroline Petersham. *N.B.* Miscarriages go for nothing.
pd."

"In consideration of 10 guineas received by me of Francis Salvador, Esq., I promise for myself, my heirs and executors, to pay unto the said Francis Salvador, Esq., his heirs or assigns, the sum of 100 guineas, that is to say, in case John Wilkes, now Alderman of London, shall be hanged. Tho. Roche."

"Ld. Leicester betts Lord Montfort one hundred guineas that six or more Peers of the British Parliament, including Catholics, Minors, Bishops, and Sixteen Scotch Lords, shall die between the 2 of December, 1744, and the first of December, 1745 inclusive."

"Ld. Darnley wages Mr. John Jeffreys one hundred guineas . . . one hundred pounds that. . . ."

"January the 14th, 1747/8. Mr. Fanshawe wagers Lord Dalkeith one guinea that his peruke is better than his Lordship's to be judged of by the majority of members the next time they both shall meet."

"Mr. Henry Pelham betts Lord Coke ten guineas that Lord Dartmouth outlives Siris the Dancing Master. July 28th 1746."

"Lord Montfort wagers Coll. Lyttleton two hundred guineas that the Custard Dun outlives the black breasted rosecomb, shittenwing red."
(# Bets entered here between Mr. Boone and Mr. Rigby have been *omitted*.)

One morning a man is suddenly observed to fall down just outside of White's. Instantly odds are laid and taken among the bystanders and spectators on the chances of his being alive. Somebody, however, proposes to bleed the poor fellow, whereupon loud protestations arise from a section of the betting men on the ground that the use of a lancet will affect the fairness of the betting.

Selwyn's name is not recorded in White's Betting Book. It is probable that he prefers to win or lose money at cards. It is more exciting and has the great merit of passing the time.

After 1755 White's moves to the "great house," 37 St. James's Street. One of its earliest occupants has been the Countess of Northumberland, who is one of the last to practise the unmaimed rights of the old peerage. When she goes out, footmen, bareheaded, walk on each side of her coach, and a second coach with her women attends her. And her grand daughter-in-law, the Duchess of Somerset, never sits down before her without her leave to do so.

The cuisine at White's is excellent, its service absolute, the table manners of its guests of the best ton—unlike the inns and taverns where every man helps himself from the dish with his own knife and fork. Sometimes in these places two or three knives or forks are engaged in the same dish together. Thus last Wednesday a gentleman meets with an odd accident in helping himself to some roast chicken. He finds that he has conveyed two joints of another gentleman's forefinger to his plate together with the wing which he has just taken off.

Selwyn spends more time at White's than at any other place in London, but occasionally he divides his allegiance. Perhaps he will drop in on the Golden Fleece Club, the members of which assume fancy names such as Sir Timothy Addlepate, Sir Nimmy Sneer, Sir Talkative Dolittle, Sir Skinny Fretwell, Sir Rumbus Rattle, Sir Boozy Prateall, Sir Nicholas Ninny Sip-all, Sir Gregory Growler, Sir Pay-little, and the like. The main object of the Club is a very free conviviality. Or the Everlasting which professes to go on forever, its doors being kept open day and night throughout the year, whilst the members are divided into watches like sailors at sea.

He is elected a member of the Dilettanti, composed of the most fashionable men of the day who would naturally sup with the Regent as he goes through Paris and find themselves at home in the carnival of Venice. The Dilettanti have two common objects: good taste and good cheer. Their rooms are a temple in which Bacchus and Apollo are sacrificed to in company. And so in a group painted by Sir Joshua, a gem and an Etruscan vase are being no less solemnly judged than a glass of wine and a magnum of port and apparently with equal gusto. The Dilettanti keep a painter. It is a rule that every member of the Society shall present his portrait in oil, done by the painter of the Society, or forfeit what is called "face money" every year till the neglect is repaired. The large room at the Thatched House Tavern where they meet is entirely hung with their portraits. Some of the members are pictured in Turkish or Roman dresses, or as gondoliers or cardinals. My Lord Le Despencer clasps a brimming goblet for his rosary and gazes up at the statue of Venus de Medici.

Any member calling this respectable society by the disrespectful name of club is fined a bumper. They drink to each other, the general toast proposed being *Viva la Virtu, Grecian Taste and Roman Spirit,* and *Absent Members.* To these are added *Esto praeclara, esto perpetua.* New members are proposed and seconded to the dinners and elected by ballot. The regulation is that no person can be proposed who cannot bring sufficient proof of his having been in Italy. And it is the opinion of the club that Avignon is in Italy, and that no other town in France is in Italy.

For a long time their Sunday dinners with their arch master of ceremonies in crimson taffeta robe, rich Hussar cap, and Toledo rapier are conspicuous. George Selwyn is a frequent diner and visitor. Here he can discuss good wine and pictures with Lord Mulgrave, bow to Topham Beauclerk's praises of his imported French waistcoat, raise his eyebrows at the news that Lord Holland is thinking of paying off Charles Fox's debts, and let fall the newest bon mot. Perhaps he will take part in the discussion of the dresses for the Henri Quatre and Charles II quadrilles at the next Almack's and drop off to sleep as Lord Spencer expatiates on the last Andrea Sacchi which he has bought for a Guido. It is a club where pleasure, good eating and drinking, and connoisseurship go hand in hand.

George is also a member of a society of a different sort— the rakehelly Medmenham Monks.

CHAPTER 5

HELL FIRE CLUB

MEDMENHAM ABBEY IS A VERY LARGE HOUSE on the banks of the Thames near Marlow. It was formerly a convent of Cistercian monks. The situation is remarkably fine. Beautiful hanging woods, soft meadows, a crystal stream, and a grove of venerable old elms near the house, with the retiredness of the mansion itself, make it as sweet a retreat as the most poetical imagination can create. Sir Francis Dashwood purchases the abbey and with George Selwyn and other gentlemen often retires there in the summer. Among other amusements they have, sometimes, a mock celebration of the mysterious midnight orgies of Pagan worship and of the rites of the Roman Catholic Church. Over the grand entrance is the famous inscription of Rabelais' Abbey of Thelème—*Fay ce que vouldras;* at the end of the passage over the door is *Aude, hospes, contemnere opes* (O Guest, dare to set riches at naught). At one end of the refectory is Harpocrates, Egyptian God of Silence; at the other the Goddess Angerona, that the same duty may be enjoined both sexes.

The garden, the grove, the orchard, the neighboring woods all speak the loves and frailties of the younger monks who sin naturally. There are no busts of Socrates, Epaminondas, or Hampden, but there is an indecent statue of an unnatural satyr. You see in one place, *Ici pâma de joie des mortels le plus heureux.* In another very imperfectly, *Mourut un amant sur le sein de sa dame.* In a third, *En cet endroit milles baisers de flamme furent donnés, et mille autres rendus.* Against a fine oak is

Hic satyrum naïas victorem victa subegit.
(Here the ravished nymph ravished the satyr who ravished her)

At the entrance of the cave is a naked statue of Venus stooping to pull a thorn out of her foot. The statue turns from you and just over the two nether hills of snow are these misapplied lines from Virgil—

Hic locus est, partes ubi se via findit in ambas
Hac iter Elyzium nobis: at laeva malorum
Exercet poenas et ad impia Tartara mittit.

(Here is the place where the road branches off in two directions. On this side is our way to the Elysian fields, but the left branch leads to evil Tartarus and exacts the penalties for wicked deeds.)

On the inside of the cave over a mossy couch is the following exhortation—

Ite, agite, O juvenes; pariter sudate medullis
Omnibus inter vos; non murmura vestra columbae
Brachia non-hederae, non vincant oscula conchae.

(Come on, get to work, you young fellows; let the sweat come from every part of your vitals; the doves would not drown your sighs, the ivy leaves not bind your arms, the drinking cups not stay your kisses.)

The favorite doctrine of the Abbey is certainly not penitence, for in the center of the orchard is the grotesque figure Priapus, and in his hand a reed stands flaming tipt with fire, to use Milton's expression, and you may trace out:

Peni tento
non
Peni tenti.

On the pedestal is a whimsical representation of Trophonius's cave, from whence all creatures are said to come out melancholy. Among that strange, dismal group you may, however, remark a crowing cock and a laughing Carmelite and the inscription—

Omne animal post coitum triste est, praeter gallum
Gallinaceum et facerdotem gratis fornicantem.

(Every animal is languid after coitus, except the rooster and the priest who fornicates gratuitously.)

Near the Abbey is a small, neat temple erected to the Goddess Cloacina (divinity of drains), inscribed: "This Chapel of Ease was founded in the year 1760." The entrance to the temple is the same narrow entrance by which we all come into the world and the narrow door (which cannot be more particularly described but whose symbolism is obvious) is what some idle wits call the door of life. Facing the entrance in the inside are the lines—

> Aeque pauperibus prodest, locupletibus aeque:
> Aeque neglectum pueris senibus nocebit,

which may perhaps be freely translated thus—

> Alike it benefits the poor, alike the rich,
> Alike when slighted, it will harm youths and old men.

The house contains nothing remarkable excepting that on the grand staircase there is a very moral painting of a maid stealing to her master's bed laying at the same time her fingers on her lips.

Sir Francis Dashwood, founder of the society and High Priest, has gained a European reputation for his pranks and adventures. In his youth he sets out on the Grand Tour and roams from court to court in search of notoriety. In Russia he masquerades as Charles XII of Sweden (dead for many years) and aspires to be the lover of or actually seduces the Tsarina Anne. (Horace Walpole comments tartly and jealously: "He has the staying power of a stallion and the impetuosity of a bull.") And at Rome he causes a riot and has to run for his life. It seems that on a Good Friday in the Holy City it is the custom for a devotee entering the Sistine Chapel to receive from the attendant at the door a small whip with which at a certain signal he is required to scourge himself. The chapel is lighted by three candles only, which are extinguished, one by one, at brief intervals of time, by the priest. On the blowing out of the first candle, the penitents divest themselves of their upper garments. A second candle is then extinguished on which a further disrobement takes place, and lastly on the blowing out of the third candle, which leaves the chapel in complete darkness, the several penitents commence flagellating themselves, giving vent at the same time to appropriate groans and lamentations. Sir Francis, who is present on one of these occasions, observes that the worshippers lay on the whip very lightly. Scandalised by this Papist lack of devotion, he provides himself with a horse whip, which he conceals beneath his coat, and on another day places himself demurely among the devotees. On the extinction of the third candle, he draws the riding whip from beneath his coat and lays about him right and left. The penitents, believing that the Evil One is amongst them, shriek out, "Il Diavolo! il diavolo!" In the confusion Sir Francis contrives to effect his escape. This experience suggests to him the idea of parodying the Roman Catholic ritual.

He has no difficulty in getting choice and daring spirits to join with him, and they form a society called the Franciscans or Medmenham Monks or Hell Fire Club or, as contemporaries refer to them, the Amorous Knights of Wycombe. Before their present abode they first met at the George and Vulture and at various other places, among them Twickenham. The number of members in the Inner Circle is restricted to twelve besides the Superior, but the total roster includes about fifty. It consists of Sir Francis Dashwood, the patriot and popular hero, John Wilkes (in scarlet waistcoat and breeches—tall, meagre, sallow, with an underhung, grinning jaw, and an awful squint), lumbering, huge Charles Churchill, Paul Whitehead (the Steward), Lord Sandwich (dubbed Jemmy Twitcher. The most abandoned man of his age. He has an awkward, shambling gait, and the half-hanged visage of one that has been cut down by mistake), Bubb-Dodington, George Selwyn, and others. They take over Medmenham Abbey and proceed to convert it into a luxurious retreat. The walls are covered with hangings, suitable furniture is installed, the cellars are filled with the choicest wines, and the larders groan with delicacies.

To intrude a confession. Sir Francis Dashwood is not

just dissolute and licentious, a mad cap prankster with a mania for the bizarre. He is honest, loves the classics, patronizes the arts and does an efficient job as administrator. True he is a lamentable choice as Chancellor of the Exchequer under Bute, but he himself records that he has had a profound aversion to mathematics all his life and is quite incapable of doing any sum which contains more than five figures. His first budget is received with hoots of laughter in the House of Commons. But he is a most competent Postmaster General under Pitt. Benjamin Franklin, who is a frequent and welcome guest at his house and considers him the best company in the world, attests him the man more than any other "who has reorganized the postal services of England and provided something like a national postal service." Besides, adds Franklin, he is a humane, liberal reformer in church affairs. Together, in 1773, the two men produce a revised Book of Common Prayer for the Church of England, the purpose of which is a humanitarian one, "to prevent the old and faithful from freezing to death through long ceremonies in cold churches, to make the services so short as to attract the young and lively, and relieve the well-disposed from the infliction of interminable prayers."

(These views are of the utmost importance in arriving at a true assessment of the character of the Squire of West Wycombe.)

The members of Dashwood's fraternity are divided into two orders—superior and inferior, the duties of the latter being to wait on their superiors during the celebration of the mysterious rites. The worship is addressed to the Goddess of Love, whom the monks call the Bona Dea, and the communion cup is curiously carved and shaped to remind the drinker of his ritual. No servants are permitted to enter the chapel for fear that they will make known the secrets of what happens. But woman, "fair and of sweet disposition," are—necessarily—present. Whether they are women of the town ("nuns" from the "abbeys" of such famous "abbesses" as Charlotte Hayes and Mother Stanhope) or women from the same class as the monks is uncertain. One entry in Mrs. Hayes's diary reads: "June 19, 1759. Twelve Vestals for the Abbey. Something discreet and Cyprian from the Friars." "Santa Carlotta always had a stock of virgins in store at King Street," declares Sandwich. "She supplies the Stock Exchange with real, immaculate maidenheads."

The nuns wear masks, and rules are carefully formulated to hide their identity, probably (we may conclude) because some are the wives of local squires or even the wives or sisters of the male members—some of Dashwood's half-sisters, for example. Anyway if a woman comes to Medmenham not undone, it is quite certain that she does not leave it in the same condition. Besides no women are present unless there are men and no men unless there are women. And every monk is religiously scrupulous not to infringe upon the "nuptial" alliance of any other brother. At other times the debauchees are in the habit of sleeping in cradles. (There is no evidence whatsoever that any member is a sodomite or a flagellant or that any form of unnatural vice is practised. The talk about necromancy and satanism is nonsense.)

Prior Sir Francis wears a red bonnet turned up with cony skin in contrast to the plain white hats of the lesser brothers. They wear white jackets and trousers, which remind Horace Walpole of waterman's outfits.

The brothers have a short meal, and when they have drunk their spirits up to a proper pitch, they retire to their respective cells to prepare for the solemnity they are going to celebrate. Clad in a milk white robe of finest linen that flows loosely about him, the member repairs at the tolling of a bell to the chapel, and knocking gently thrice at the door, it is opened to him to the sound of soft and solemn music. On his entrance he makes a profound obeisance and advances slowly towards a table that stands against the wall. As soon as he comes to the rails by which it is surrounded, he falls upon his knees and makes a profession of his principles—a mocking perversion of the articles of religion. When he has finished, another candidate advances in a like manner and makes his professions, and so on. In this manner the evening is wasted until supper, when they sit down in the chapel, vying with each other in loose and impious songs, &c.

The order continues to exist for several years, but politics no sooner infuses itself among the rosy anchorites than dissensions are kindled. Sandwich sacrifices the Friend of Liberty for party interest. "Wilkes," says Sandwich to him, "you will die of a pox or on the gallows." "That depends, my Lord," answers Wilkes, "on whether I embrace your principles or your mistress." Their enmity may be traced to this repartee. Besides the competition between Dashwood and Wilkes for High Priest ends in the latter's defeat. Wilkes arranges to have his revenge at the banquet which follows. He conceals a great baboon dressed as a devil in a box and by means of a string lets the baboon loose while Sir Francis is reciting a mock prayer. The terrified animal, glad to be delivered from his confinement, leaps upon the table and upon the shoulders of several of the members. Terrified out of their senses, they all roar out with one voice—"The Devil! the Devil!" and starting directly from their seats, make towards the door, tumbling over one another and upsetting everything. When the trick is discovered, Wilkes is under a shade: the tolerance and good fellowship of the members are greatly strained. But the affair becomes known in the neighborhood—the baboon is seen before he is caught—and the story is spread about that the end of these meetings is the worship of the Devil.

In time the order of the Medmenham monks is dissolved, and the buildings are converted into a pleasure house where Sir Francis entertains his friends. Besides he builds a church on the top of a hill (for the convenience and devotion of the town at the bottom of it), which serves the double purpose of convincing the populace of his regard for religion and of making a beautiful termination to a vista, which he has just cut through a wood, in his park. In the churchyard he places a sun dial with this inscription—

Keep thy TONGUE FROM EVIL—Speaking
Lying, and Slandering.

CHAPTER 6

RAKE'S PROGRESS

GEORGE IS AN INDOLENT PERSON, SO WE must not expect him to begin the day too early. He gets up at nine and plays with his dog Râton, then takes his great stick and walks out in his green frock with his hair in papers, and saunters about till ten.

Occasionally in the morning he will attend the levée of some fashionable lady. These same creatures in the simplicity of their nature will hold perfect levées in their chambers, nay even in bed, under the pretence of being indisposed and without any particular regard to the sex of their visitors. They put on their best looks and paint themselves for their reception. Their hair appears in a very nice disorder and their nightgowns are ruffled with great care. It is a very odd sight that a beautiful creature makes when she is talking politics with her tresses flowing about her shoulders and examining her face in the glass which does such execution upon all the rude standers-by.

George occupies himself in various ways. If there is an execution at Tower Hill, he goes eastwards to see it and on his return will stroll down St. James's Street looking in at Betty's the fruiterer's where the young men gather to gossip. He reaches White's about three or four in time for dinner. After dinner the serious business of the day begins. Gaming jackets are donned, and George and his friends sit down to play at macco or picquet or lansquenet. Meanwhile the wine circulates and bon mots are perpetrated with alarming frequency. Or they swear and tell naughty stories. Or they go to the public places of amusement—Vauxhall, Ranelagh, Marylebone (with its music, its wine, and its plum cake), and Cuper's Gardens.

St. James's Street is crowded with carriages of ladies and gentlemen who are walking in the Mall—the ladies with their heads in full dress and the gentlemen carrying their hats under their arms. The proprietors of Ranelagh and Vauxhall send decoy ducks among them, that is, persons attired in the height of fashion who every now and then exclaim in a very audible tone—"What charming weather for Ranelagh" or "for Vauxhall."

Vauxhall is more like a bear garden than a rational place of resort and most particularly on Sunday mornings. It is then crowded with gentry, girls of the town, apprentices, shop boys, etc. From four to six crowds of citizens are to be seen trudging home with their wives and children.

But of all the public places known, Ranelagh has most decidedly the preference. Lines of carriages extend from Tattersall's to Chelsea where the rotunda is built. (The fields between Chelsea and town are a notorious haunt of footpads and highwaymen, and patrols are regularly provided for the same conduct of visitors to Ranelagh.) The price of admission is two shillings and six pence. It is the custom for gentlemen to buy in the anteroom nosegays, myrtles, hyacinths, roses, etc., not only to wear themselves but also to present to the ladies. There are no cropped heads, trousers, or shoe strings seen here—such dresses are not admitted. Ranelagh is the élite of fashion. The gentlemen wear powder, frills, ruffles, and have gold-headed canes.

It is a very pleasing place of amusement. All is so orderly and still that you can hear the whisking sound of the ladies' trains as the immense assembly walks round and round the room. If you choose, you may have tea, which is served up in the neatest equipment possible. People generally go to Ranelagh between nine and ten o'clock.

Masquerades in the Venetian manner are often held here. They begin at three o'clock in the afternoon. The several loges are shops for toys, lemonades, glaces, and other refreshments. The next day come the fireworks at which hundreds of people certainly lose their lives or their limbs from the tumbling of scaffolds, the fall of rockets, and other accidents inseparate from such crowds. In order to repair this loss to society there is a subscription masquerade on the Wednesday following.

But Ranelagh pleasures are too tranquil and tame. George Selwyn and his friends doff their playing garments, snuff the candles, and go to Haymarket or drawing room to join in the revels—drums, festinos, ridottos, hurricanes, and Heidegger masquerades. The first is the highest object of female glory. The end thereof is to assemble as large a mob of quality as can possibly be contained in one house. For this purpose a woman of superior rank calculates how many people all the rooms in her house laid open can possibly hold, and then sends about two months before-hand among the people she knows to bespeak such a number she thinks will fill them—the more the better.

Private balls are sometimes called drums, and a drum on a large scale is a "squeezer." There are also drum-majors, routs, tempests, and hurricanes, differing only in degrees of multitude and uproar. At the fashionable routs where one hardly finds standing room on the staircase, one pushes and is pushed and is kept for hours in a hothouse temperature. A foreign visitor gets away to a rout at the Duke of Northumberland's, a small party of about a thousand persons. Music is performed in an immense picture gallery at thirty degrees of Réaumur. The crowd and bustle are, however, so great that one hears little of it. The atmosphere is like that of the Black Hole of Calcutta.

Every drawing room is different in its manners and its moods as it is in its company. One is celebrated for cards, another for wit, a third for beauties, a fourth for coxcombs, a fifth for old maids and scandal, a sixth for fashion, and a seventh for cotillons. Lady Townshend is always able to command a racquet, and her squeezers are celebrated.

Festinos are much more attractive scenes. Not only the whole house but the garden is illuminated. There are arches and pyramids of lights, diamond necklaces of lamps, spiral obelisks of candles, and dispersed over the lawn are little bands of kettledrums, clarionets, fifes, etc., and the lovely moon which comes out without a card. It is quite a fairy scene.

But all these forms of amusement pale their ineffectual fire before the prevailing mania for masquerades which first become fashionable under the famous Heidegger (mentioned by Pope in the *Dunciad*) who holds them during the season at the King's Theatre in the Haymarket. Tickets are issued to those only who subscribe to them at White's Chocolate House in St. James's Street, and no effort is spared to exclude the common herd. For the prevention of all disorders and indecencies Heidegger advertises that a sufficient guard will be appointed within and without the house and that strict orders will be issued not to deliver any bottles and glasses from the sideboards and to shut them up early. But in spite of these precautions masquerades are the source of an infinite amount of evil.

> The midnight orgy and the mazy dance,
> The smile of beauty and the flush of wine,
> For fops, fools, gamesters, knaves, and lords combine;
> Each to his humor—Comus all allows:
> Champagne, dice, music, or your neighbor's spouse.

The church inveighs against their vices and follies. Poets and essayists lash them. The grand jury of Middlesex prevents those that are to be held at the King's Theatre. Notwithstanding all this, masquerades remain the rage of the town, and the nobility continue to patronize Heidegger and later Mrs. Cornelys.

It is the fascination of the masquerade that alone induces George I to emerge from his habitual shyness and reserve. At the first masquerade given in his honor, after his arrival in England, a masked lady invites the monarch to accompany her to one of the buffets for the purpose of drinking a glass of wine. The damsel in blissful ignorance as to the identity of her partner, fills her bumper exclaiming, "Here, Mask, the health of the Pretender," and filling another glass hands it to his Majesty who graciously accepting it observes, "Madam, I drink with all my heart to the health of all unfortunate Princes."

At one of the subscription masquerades the beautiful Elizabeth Chudleigh comes attired in a close fitting costume of flesh colored silk. Her dress or rather undress is remarkable. She is Iphigenia ready for the sacrifice but so naked "the high priest may easily inspect the entrails of his victims." The maids of honor are so offended that they will not speak to her, and the Princess of Wales flings her own shawl over her. At the same ball Jenny Conway is killed by a draught of lemonade. Her death is commemorated—

> Poor Jenny Conway
> She drank lemonade
> at a masquerade
> So now she's dead and gone away.

What is a ridotto? When the popularity of masquerades begins to wane, Mr. Heidegger proves his true genius by rechristening them. They are no longer to be known as masquerades. Thenceforth they are ridottos. The hour it begins is nine; polite people do not come till eleven. The room is set out in the same manner as for the masquerade. It is the most entertaining sort of assembly because you are at liberty to wander about as much as you please, and there is dancing, tea, coffee, chocolate, and all sorts of sweetmeats. The ladies are sometimes in great distress for partners, for the greatest part of the clever men are gone to Newmarket. There is a prodigious crowd, and they dance till half past one.

This Heidegger, a native of Zurich in Switzerland, has come to England as a fortune hunter and begun in a small way at the Haymarket. His masquerades prosper, and he is much caressed by the Court and nobility. He gains a large income, much of which he expends in charity. He lives profusely and mixes with the highest society where his oddness and ugliness (he is nicknamed Count Ugly, the Swiss Count) make him sometimes the subject of practical jokes. On one occasion the Duke of Montagu invites him to a tavern where he is made drunk and falls asleep. In that situation a mould of his face is taken from which is made a mask, bearing the closest resemblance to the original. The Duke provides a man of the same stature to appear in a similar dress and thus to personate Heidegger on the night of the next masquerade when the King (who is apprized of the plot) is to be present. On his Majesty's entrance, Heidegger as is usual bids the music play, "God Save the King." But no sooner is his back turned than the impostor assuming his voice and manner orders them to play "Charley over the water." On this Heidegger rages, stamps, and swears, and commands them to recommence the loyal tune of "God Save the King." The instant he retires, the impostor returns and orders them to resume the seditious air. The musicians think their master is drunk but dare not disobey. The house is now thrown into an uproar. "Shame! shame!" resounds from all parts, and some officers of the guards who are in attendance upon the King insist upon kicking the musicians out, but the Duke of Cumberland (the King's son) who is also privy to the plot, restrains them. Heidegger now comes forward and offers to discharge his band, when the impostor advances and cries in a plaintive tone, "Sire, the whole fault lies with that devil in my likeness." This is too much. Poor Heidegger turns round, grows pale, but cannot speak. The Duke of Montagu seeing the joke take so serious a turn, orders the fellow to unmask. Heidegger retires in great wrath, seats himself in an armchair, furiously commands his attendants to extinguish the lights, and swears he will never again superintend the masquerades unless the mask is defaced and the mold broken in his presence.

With a hundred deep wrinkles on its front, his face looks like a map with a great many rivers upon it.

> "Hold, madam, pray what hideous figure
>   Advances?"—"Sir, that's Count H-d-g-r."
> "How could it come into his gizzard,
>   T'invent so horrible a vizzard?"
> "How could it, sir?" says she, "I'll tell ye:
>   It came into his mother's belly;

For you must know that horrid phiz is
   (Puris naturalibus) his visage."
"Monstrous! that human nature can
   Have form'd so strange burlesque a man?"

When play and masque and Heidegger begin to pall, Selwyn and his friends hail a coach and proceed to the three fairs dotting London—Bartholomew, Southwark, and May. Bartholomew Fair, which is held in Smithfield, is a haunt of pleasure pure and simple. It begins annually on St. Bartholomew's day, August 24, and lasts fourteen days, lovers of the marvelous like George Selwyn being enabled meanwhile to indulge their passion to the full at the innumerable booths, sheds, stalls, which are pitched in the neighborhood. The pick and flower of London and provincial society come in crowds to enjoy the broad laugh, the varieties of life, and to applaud the buds of genius who are to be found there. Giants and dwarfs, learned pigs, performing ponies, jugglers, tight rope dancers and acrobats have the entire place to themselves. Passages round are lined with tents, crammed with ginger bread, pastry, and all kinds and varieties of baubles. An occasional attraction is the firing of a gun by an elephant. There are wild beasts from all parts of the world roaring, puppets squeaking, sausages frying, kings and queens raving, pick-pockets diving their hands into everybody's pockets, merry-go-rounds twirling ("Come, who? Come, who rides, sir?"), hackney coaches and poor horses driving and all Smithfield alive 0.

Then there are about London, Punch and Judy shows and raree shows, cock fighting, prize fighting, boxing, bull and bear baiting, duck hunting and the like.

Advertisement: "At the New Red Lion Cockpit, near the London Spa, Clerkenwell, this present Monday, will be seen the royal sport of cock fighting for two guineas a battle. Tomorrow begins the match for four guineas a battle and twenty guineas the odd battle, and continues all week, beginning at four o'clock."

Two women fight for a new shift valued at half a guinea

in the Spa Fields near Islington. The battle is won by a woman called Bruising Peg, who beats her antagonist in a terrible manner.

Advertisement: "I, Elizabeth Wilkinson of Clerkenwell, having had some words with Hannah Highfield and requiring satisfaction do invite her to meet me on the stage and box with me for three guineas, each woman holding half a crown in each hand, and the first woman that drops her money to lose the battle."

Mrs. Highfield signifies her acceptance of this challenge in the following terms—"I, Hannah Highfield of Newgate Market, hearing of the resolution of Elizabeth, will not fail to give her more blows than words, desiring home blows and from her no favour."

And it is satisfactory to learn, on the unimpeachable testimony of the press, that these two Amazons maintain the battle with great valor for a long time.

The number of advertisements relating to Young Colossuses, Wonderful Giants, Irish Giants, and Tall Saxon Women, all fresh from the lands which gave them birth, is well nigh incalculable. A man dwarf, brought from Denmark, not quite three feet high, is presented to their Majesties. He stands under the Duke of Cumberland's arm, which feat mightily pleases his Highness. At another time

> A dwarf from France arriv'd in town
> Measuring but inches twenty-one,
> At court a wonder great was shown
> Where he, though aged forty-six,
> Performed twenty childish tricks.

Another phenomenon is the Reverend John Henley, better known as Orator Henley. Henley rents rooms in the neighborhood of Newport Market. Here every Sunday he preaches on theological questions and on Wednesday lectures on the sciences and other subjects. He strikes medals for admission tickets which bear the device of a rising star with the words *ad summum* (to the top) above, and *inveniam viam aut faciam* (I shall find a way or make one) below. He advertises on Saturday the subject of his next oration in mysterious terms to arouse curiosity and draw a crowd. Once it is merely "Something Alive;" at another time it is "A Merry Thought." Or they read: "The world toss at tennis, or a lesson for a King," "Whether man or woman be the finer creature," "À la mode de France, or the art of rising," "Over the hills and far away or Prince Eugene's march," "A Platonic chat on Box-hill, *de osculis et virginibus*," "The doctors ogling the ladies through their spectacles," "The Triumphs of Tag, Rag, and Bobtail—spic—span—new!"

On one occasion a large audience of shoemakers assembles enticed by the promise that he will show them a new and speedy method of making shoes. This, he explains, in the course of his oration, is by cutting the tops off boots. On another occasion he delivers "a butcher's lecture," lauding the trade extravagantly.

He claims to be the restorer of eloquence to the church. His manner is theatrical. His pulpit blazes in velvet and gold, and his language usually varies from oratory to familiar buffoonery and irreverent wit. Bishop Warburton says—"Sometimes he breaks jests and sometimes that bread which he calls the Primitive Eucharist." In his service book he prints his creed and doxologies in red letters.

Selwyn and his gay friends often heckle Henley and once create a minor disturbance. Henley offers to admit of a disputation and promises that he will impartially determine the merits of the contest. But he is overmatched, for Selwyn and his friends, supported by a strong party, enter the list, the one to defend the ignorance, the other the impudence of the restorer of eloquence himself. As there is a door behind the rostrum which leads to his house, the Orator silently drops out, postponing the award to some happier day. Henley fills a few niches in the *Dunciad*—

> Oh, Great Restorer of the good old Stage,
> Preacher at once, and Zany of thy age.

Our young fashionable goes to hear a concert of Handel or—after refreshing his body with three dishes of bohea and purging his brain with two pinches of snuff—draws his chair to the fire and forms one of a cozy circle of gossip and scandal—

George II is the unloved head of an unsympathetic family and his children are the best humored asses that ever were born. A doggerel verse maker endeavors to convey this at the death of Frederick, Prince of Wales.

Here lies Fred
Who was alive and is dead;
Had it been his father,
I had much rather,
Had it been his sister,
Noone would have missed her;
Had it been his brother,
'Twould have been better than any other.

The King feels a stronger inclination for Mary Bellenden than he ever entertains for the Queen. Miss Bellenden by no means feels a reciprocal passion, and his avarice disgusts her. One evening sitting by her he takes out his purse and counts his money. He repeats the enumeration a second time. The giddy Bellenden loses her patience and cries out, "Sir, I cannot bear it! If you count your money any more, I will go out of the room." The clink of the gold does not tempt her more than the person of his Royal Highness. In fact her heart is engaged, and the King suspects it. George makes Mrs. Howard the confidante of his passion for Miss Bellenden, and Mrs. Howard has the sense to engage the King's affections to herself.

She prefers the advantages of her situation to "the ostentatious éclat of it," but many obstacles stand in the way of total concealment, nor has love any share in the sacrifice she makes of her virtue. She has felt poverty and is far from disliking power. And Mr. Howard is as little agreeable to her as he is worthless. The King, though very amorous, is less attracted by a love of variety than by a silly idea he entertains of gallantry being becoming. And he adds the more egregious folly of fancying that his inconstancy proves he is not governed, but so awkwardly does he manage that artifice that it but demonstrates more clearly the influence of the Queen. With such a disposition secrecy will by no means answer his Majesty's view. Yet publicity of the intrigue is especially owing to Mr. Howard, who far from ceding his wife quietly, goes one night into the quadrangle of St. James's, and before the Guards loudly demands her to be restored to him. Being thrust out, he sends a letter to her by the Archbishop of Canterbury reclaiming her, and the Archbishop by his instructions consigns the summons to the Queen, who has the malicious pleasure of delivering the letter to her rival. The Queen has an obscure window at St. James's that looks into a dark passage, lighted only by a single lamp at night, which looks upon Mrs. Howard's apartment.

Mrs. Howard is of medium height, well made, extremely fair, with the finest light brown hair and is remarkably genteel. She has no bad qualities and is constant to her connection. She preserves uncommon respect to the end of her life and is always treated as if her virtue has never been questioned. Her friends even affect to suppose that her connection with the King is confined to pure friendship. Unfortunately his Majesty's passions are too indelicate to be confined to Platonic love.

Her credit is extremely limited by the Queen's superior influence. Except a Barony, a red ribband, and a good place for her brother, she can succeed only in very subordinate recommendations. No established mistress of a Sovereign ever enjoys less of the brilliancy of her situation than does Mrs. Howard. She is elegant, her lover the reverse and most unentertaining and void of confidence in her. His motions too are measured by etiquette and the clock. He visits her every evening at nine, but with such dull punctuality that he frequently walks about his chamber for ten minutes with his watch in his hand, if the stated minute is not arrived. But from the Queen she takes more positive vexations. Till she becomes Lady Suffolk, she constantly dresses the Queen's head who delights in subjecting her to such servile offices, though always apologizing to her *good* Howard. Often her Majesty has a more complete triumph. It happens more than once that the King, coming into the room while the Queen is dressing, snatches off her handkerchief and turning rudely to Mrs. Howard cries, "'Because you have an ugly neck yourself, you hide the Queen's." ("Oh! that you saw that royal neck!" suddenly exclaims Horace Walpole to the little circle. "Since the days of Homer who admired the cow-like eyes of Juno, never, I believe, were seen such Dugs that would assort so well with the delineation of that quadruped.")

Lady Bristol, whose apartment is separated from Mrs. Howard's only by a thin wainscot, often hears the King talking there in the morning in an angry and impatient tone. Mrs. Howard, who always speaks in a low voice, talks a long while together, and the King every now and then interrupts her by saying over and over again—"That is none of your business, madam. You have nothing to do with that."

The King always goes to bed on his return from Hanover as soon as he comes out of the drawing room, as he does every day after dinner. Her Majesty, who values herself on her art, affects to act philosophically and indifferently to the King's amours and pretends to think it mighty reasonable that as she is growing old, the King should have a mistress. But the cunning woman never supposes that anybody else has penetration. She is one day exerting that flimsy disguise to Robert Walpole and on his smiling, says, "Why, don't I know that he goes every evening at nine to Lady Suffolk and do I complain?" "But after dinner! Madam!" say Walpole. "May I tell your Majesty a story of an elderly gentleman in Norfolk who made love to his wife's chambermaid and gave her a letter with an assignation. The girl showed the letter to her mistress who said—'Let me alone. I will break him of these tricks.' After dinner the wife drew the husband into a civility and then threw the letter to him, saying, 'There, you old fool, you! Go and do your worst!"

Queen Caroline is said to have been very handsome at her marriage, soon after which she has the smallpox, but she is little marked by it and retains a most pleasing countenance. It is full of majesty or mildness as she pleases. Her voice too is captivating and her hands beautifully small, graceful, plump.

A serious scandal arises at Court. One day at the royal table an insect of an odious kind (which it is scarcely polite to name) is found in his Majesty's plate. This disgusting occurrence is laid to the habits of the cooks who are at once ordered, under pain of dismissal, to submit to having their heads shaved and to wear wigs like their betters. The cooks make a spirited resistance and indeed send up remonstrances couched in anything but respectful tones. The master cook, Mr. Dixon, who possesses little remains of his youthful tresses, is not a whit less strenuous than the youngest beau of the kitchen. But after many parleys they yield. One young man, however, named Bear, refuses and is dismissed. His case is represented as one of hardship and is greatly taken up in radical circles. It is this incident which prompts the coarse muse of Dr. Wolcot to issue cantos of what he calls "The Lousiad," which is eagerly bought.

THE PETITION OF THE COOKS

Your Majesty's firm friends and faithful cooks,
　　Who in your palace merry live as grigs,
Have heard with heavy hearts and downcast looks,
　　That we must all be shaved and put on wigs:
You, sire, who with such honour wear your crown,
　　Should never bring on ours disgraces down.
Oh! tell us, sir, in loyalty so true,
　　What dire, designing ragamuffin said,
That we, your cooks, are such a nasty crew,
　　Great sir, as to have crawlers in the head?
My liege, you cannot find through all our house,
　　Not if you give a guinea for't, a *louse*.

Two other remarkable events intrigue our gentleman of fashion. The Thames freezes over. It is a solid block of ice, and booths for the sale of brandy, wine, ale, and other exhilarating liquors are fixed there for some time. Thousands of people cross it and with wonder view the mountainous heaps of water congealed into ice. On Thursday a great cook's shop is erected there, and George Selwyn and his intimates meet as frequently to dine as at White's or an ordinary. Numbers of coaches, wagons, and carts are driven over the ice. And one enthusiastic preacher sees fit to improve the occasion and harangues most eloquently a motley congregation which assemble together on the Thames. (The zeal with which the Reverend sir discourses is fiery enough to thaw himself through the ice.)

Then one day in February, 1750, the inhabitants of London are alarmed by a rumbling noise and a shock which shakes all houses with such violence that house bells ring and furniture and utensils are moved from their places. On the same day next month a second shock is felt between five and six in the morning and causes greater consternation because it awakens people from their sleep. It is preceded by a succession of thick, low flashes of lightning and a rumbling noise like that of a heavy carriage rolling over a hollow pavement. The shock consists of repeated vibrations which last some seconds and violently shake every house from top to bottom. George Selwyn feels his bolster lift up his head and thinks somebody is getting from under his bed, but he soon remembers that it is an earthquake. His servant comes in almost frightened out of his senses. In an instant he hears all the windows in the neighborhood flung up. He gets up and finds people running into the streets but sees no mischief done and returns to bed. However, there is some—two old houses toppled down, several chimneys, and much chinaware. The only visible effect is on the ridotto at which the following night there are about four hundred people. A parson coming into White's the morning of the quake and hearing bets laid on whether it is an earthquake or the blowing up of powder mills, goes away exceedingly scandalized and says—"I protest they are such an impious set of people that I believe if the last trumpet was to sound they would bet puppet-show against Judgment."

But the alarm occasioned is seized upon by religious enthusiasts as an opportunity for admonishing their fellow countrymen against the immorality and profaneness of the times. A shower of sermons, essays, poems, exhortations appears. These earthquakes, according to one Bishop, are sent to punish bawdy prints, bawdy books, gaming, drinking, and all other sins, natural or not. Books on earthquakes and their effects are eagerly bought up and with equal rapidity issued from the press, and people begin to look forward with apprehension to the third shock. These apprehensions gain ground towards the end of March when a soldier of the life guards, driven mad by the preaching enthusiasts, runs about town crying out that on the same day four weeks after the last shock, Thursday, the fifth of April, another earthquake will swallow up the whole metropolis and destroy its inhabitants as a punishment of their sins and that Westminster Abbey will be buried in the ruins and disappear forever. The prophet is arrested and placed in a madhouse, but this does not calm the fears of the multitude which increase as the fatal day approaches.

It is remarkable how good the people are grown. Nobody makes a suit of clothes now but of sackcloth and ashes. A fast day is kept so devoutly that Dick Edgecumbe, finding a very lean hazard at White's, says with a sigh—"Lord, how the times are degenerated! Formerly a fast would have brought everybody hither; now it keeps everybody away." And a few nights before, as two men are walking up the Strand, one says to the other, "Look how red the sky is. Well, thank God! There is to be no masquerade." Rigby and a friend who sup and stay late at Bedford House the other night, knock at several doors and in a watchman's voice cry—"Pa—a—st four o'clock and a dreadful earthquake."

Popular credulity is so great that on the first of April some hundreds of people go through the heavy rain to Edmonton upon the report that a hen has laid an egg there the day before on which is inscribed in large capital letters the words *Beware of the third shock.* During the following days many people who possess the means of absenting themselves leave London under different excuses and repair to various parts of the kingdom. All the roads leading from London to the country are thronged. And in the course of Wednesday afternoon, April 4, whole families lock up their houses and go into the open fields outside the metropolis which are filled with an incredible number of people, assembled in chairs and carriages as well as on foot, who wait in trembling suspense. The women wear earthquake gowns—that is, warm gowns to sit out of doors all night. Some of the religious citizens put on their double-channeled pumps and trudge to St. James's Street in expectation of seeing judgment executed on White's—angels with flaming swords and devils flying away with dice boxes.

One woman, most heroic, comes to town on purpose. She says all her friends are in London, and she will not survive them. But my Lady Pelham, my Lady Arundel, and Lord and Lady Galway go this Wednesday evening to an inn ten miles out of town where they play at brag till five in the morning and then come back to look for the bones of their husbands and families under the rubbish.

Turner, a great china man, has a jar cracked by the shock. He originally asks ten guineas for the pair. He now asks twenty, because, he says, "it is the only jar in Europe that has been cracked by an earthquake."

But George Montagu says of the last earthquake—"It was so tame you might have stroked it."

George II dies and at his interment the burlesque Duke of Newcastle falls into a fit of crying the moment he comes into the chapel, and flings himself back in a stall, the Archbishop hovering over him with a smelling bottle. But in two minutes his curiosity gets the better of his hypocrisy, and he runs about the chapel with his glass to spy who is or who is not there, spying with one hand and mopping his eyes with the other. Then returns the fear of catching cold, and the Duke of Cumberland, who is sinking with the heat, feels himself weighed down, and turning round finds it is the Duke of Newcastle standing upon his train to avoid the chill of the marble. . . .

CHAPTER 7

NELLIES

GEORGE IS A COMPLETE BEAU, THE MOULD of form and the glass of fashion. It is true that he fails to make open love to the orange wenches in Covent Garden; it is true, too (and 'tis a pity, perhaps), that he fails to make open or even secret love to ladies of higher station, but he is a complete beau nevertheless. He fails to fit snugly or loosely in the categories listed below. Perhaps he is a gentleman of fashion or beau with a difference.

The beaux of the period are roughly divisible into three classes. There is one class familiarly known as the Bloods, apt with the gloves and mighty in the use of broadsword, who act the parts severally of fine gentlemen at balls and assemblies, sharpers in the gambling hells, and bullies at places of public resort. They are distantly allied to the Bold Bucks who deny the Supreme Being and attempt females of their own species promiscuously, grandmothers and mothers as well as daughters. Even their own sisters fear their violence and fly their privacies. Blind and Bold love is their motto.

A second class of beaux passes under the name of Frolics, gentlemen who display their powers to great advantage in crippling or maiming the watchmen, in running tavern drawers through the body, and making bonfires of their cloaks. The Frolics manifest their regard for the fair sex in a strange way. At an entertainment where a celebrated lady of pleasure is one of the party, her shoe is pulled off by a young man who fills it with champagne and drinks it off to her health. To this delicious draught he is immediately pledged by the rest, and then to carry the compliment still farther, he orders the shoe itself to be dressed and served up for supper. The cook sets himself seriously to work upon it. He pulls the upper part of it (which is damask) into fine shreds and tosses it up in a ragout, minces the sole, cuts the wooden heel into very thin slices, fries them in butter and places them round the dish for garnish. The company testifies their affection for the lady by eating very heartily of this exquisite impromptu.

The Pretty Fellows or Beaux proper constitute a third class. They are heavily scented with orange flower water, civet-violet, or musk, and they carry dragon or Jamree canes curiously clouded or amber-headed. Knocking the cane upon the shoe, leaning one leg upon it, or whistling with it in the mouth are such reliefs to them in conversation that they do not know how to be good company without it. They are such pretty fellows that they call each other at White's or St. James's by the names of Betty, Nelly, and so forth.

When Lady Holland wants to get rid of one of them, she says, "I beg your pardon, but I wish you would sit a little farther off. There is something on your handkerchief which I don't quite like."

The creatures form a Beau's Club (a stinking society or Lady's Lap Dog Club) which meets at a certain tavern near Covent Garden. Every afternoon the fantastical idols, assemble themselves in a body to compare dresses, invent new fashions, talk luscious bawdy, and drink healths to their mistresses. At the upper end of their Club room there stands a side table which is constantly furnished with a dozen flannel muckenders decently folded up for rubbing the dust off their upper leathers or an unfortunate speck off the scabbards of their swords, that their Spanish pumps and their hogs-skin sheaths may be kept as spot free as a Dutch housewife does the outside of her kettle. Upon the same table, which is every day covered with a fresh damask cloth, there lie two or three dozen Seville oranges and lemons, and by the side of the table a white glazed basin.

Thus if any Beau has been contaminating his fingers by any exercise, he may rinse off the savory remains with the acid juice of the fruit and mundify the defiled member that has been tickling the honor of some over frigid lady into an amorous uproar. Next to these stands an olive box full of the best perfumed powder crowned with three or four mighty combs. Round the edges of the table lie strewn, by way of garnish, scissors, toothpicks, tweezers, patches, essences, and pomatums, points, pastes, and washes—all the useful implements that pride and folly can invent to turn men into monkeys. When the modish creatures have drunk enough of sham wine instead of champagne at 7 1/2d. a flask, to elevate their spirits and put their tongues in tune to attack the masked ladies who hang about the theatre, they pay their reckoning, and walk bareheaded to the play-house. They commonly arrive about the third act by which time the ladies who care not much to appear by daylight sneak into the pit and eighteen penny gallery without tickets at the courtesy of the doorkeepers. They tattle away the playtime, then according to custom divide themselves between drinking, whoring, gaming till the next morning.

> To be a modish fop, a Beau compleat,
> Is to pretend to, but be void of Wit:
> 'Tis to be squeamish, critical, and nice
> In all things, and fantastic to a Vice;
> 'Tis to seem knowing, tho' he nothing knows,
> And vainly lew'd to please his brother Beaus;
> 'Tis in his Dress to be profusely gay,
> And to affect, whore-like, a wanton way,
> 'Tis to be charm'd with each new fashion'd Whim,
> And to be modish to a vain Extream,
> 'Tis to attack the ladies with a Grace,
> And still transfer his love to each new Face,
> Flutter about her charms, till, like a Fly,
> Burnt by the Flame, he's scorch'd amidst his Joy;
> Then cursing of the B——ch, is forc'd to cool
> The pocky heat, by running oft to Stool;
> Till with repeated Purges, by degrees,
> The pricking Pains and Inflammations cease.

Then pleas'd to find that he so sound is made,
Resolves in vain to grow a cautious Blade;
So wives in travail vow to kiss no more,
But soon forget the Torment when it's o'er.

Thus eas'd by Powders, Bolus, and by Pill,
He damns the Whore, and pays the Surgeon's Bill;
But soon, forgetting the venereal Smart
That teaz'd and bridl'd the unruly Part,
Renews his Courage, still pursues the Game,
Makes Lust his Leader, Maidenheads his aim,
Till caught a second time by some lascivious Dame.

Cursing and swearing habitually are considered accomplishments as indispensable to the beau as the above-mentioned virtues and the minuet. George is sitting down to an early dinner at a country inn on the road to Matson when his ears are saluted by a genteel whistle and the noise of a pair of slippers descending the staircase. He soon beholds a very beauish gentleman with a huge laced hat on, a wig somewhat disheveled, and a face which at once gives you a perfect idea of emptiness, assurance, and intemperance.* His eyes, which are scarce open, fix on George with a stare which testifies surprise, and his coat is immediately thrown open to display a very handsome second hand gold laced waistcoat. In one hand he has a pair of saddlebags and in the other a hanger of mighty size both of which, with a graceful *God damn you,* he places upon a chair. Then advancing towards the landlord, he says, "By God, Landlord, your wine is damnable strong."

When the landlord protests that he has it from London and from a considerable merchant, a Richard Kirby, the beau acknowledges that he has cracked a bottle with him and knows his brother too, a partner.

"I believe, sir," says the landlord, "you are out, sir, for that gentleman has no brother."

"Damn your nonsense with you and your outs," says the

---

* For this episode see Henry Fielding's *Covent Garden Journal.*

Buck, "as if I should not know better than your country puts, I who have lived in London all my lifetime."

"I ask a thousand pardons," says the landlord. "I hope no offence, sir."

"No, no," cries the other. "We gentlemen know how to make allowances for your country breeding." Then stepping to the kitchen door, with an audible voice, he calls the ostler and in a very graceful accent, says, "Damn your blood, you cock-eyed son of a bitch, bring me my boots. Did you not hear me call?"

The ostler produces the boots, which the gentleman takes in his hand. Then placing himself in a chair, he looks the landlord full in the face and asks him if he has ever been at Drury Lane Playhouse which he answers in the negative. "What," says he, "you never heard talk of Mr. Garrick?"

"No, sir," says the landlord.

"By God," says the gentleman, "he is the cleverest fellow in England." He then spouts a speech out of King Richard which begins with, "Give me a horse. There," says he, "that is just like Mr. Garrick." Vastly pleased with his performance, he shakes the landlord by the hand and says, "By God, you seem to be an honest fellow and good blood. If you'll come and see me in London, I'll give you your skin full of wine and treat you with a play and a whore every night you stay. I'll show you how it is to live, my boy. But here, bring me some paper, my girl. Come let's have one of your love letters to air my boots."

Upon which the landlord presents him with a piece of an old newspaper. "Damn you," says the gentleman, "this is not half enough. Have you never a Bible or Common Prayer Book in the house? Half a dozen chapters of Genesis with a few prayers make an excellent fire in a pair of boots."

"Oh, Lord forgive you," says the landlord. "Sure you would not burn such books as those."

"No," cries the spark, "where was you born? Go into a shop in London and buy some butter or a quartern of tea, and then you'll see what use is made of these books."

Here a country fellow who has been standing up in

one corner of the room eating cold bacon and beans, and who trembles at every oath the spark swears, takes his dish and pot and marches out of the room fearing that the house will fall down about his ears, for, he is sure, he says that the man in the gold laced hat is the Devil.

The young spark, having now displayed all his wit and humor and exerted his talents to the utmost, thinks he has sufficiently recommended himself to Selwyn's favor. So with an air he drinks a dram, observes that a man should not cool too fast, pays 6d. more than his reckoning, calls for his horse, gives the ostler a shilling, and gallops out of the inn thoroughly satisfied that all agree with him in thinking him a clever fellow and a man of great importance.

The landlord smiling takes up his money and says that he is a comical gentleman but that it is a thousand pities he swears so much, for he is a very good customer and as generous as a prince, for the night before he treated everybody in the house. Selwyn then asks him if he knows the comical gentleman, as he calls him.

"No, really, sir," says the landlord, "though a gentleman was saying last night that he was a sort of rider or rideout to a linen draper at London." . . .

The inn room is warm and cozy, with a glowing fire in the hearth, the floor of sanded brick, samplers and ballads adorning the walls. George returns to the meal he has started. It is a sumptuous country dinner—mutton, ham, chicken, duck, tarts and cheese with such embellishments as capers, gherkins, and mushrooms. Washed down by Oxford ale or Dorset beer. After the cloth is drawn, port. Then George lights his pipe, stretches his legs, and begins to read the latest batch of newspapers and journals with which the landlord provides him. (A man who attempts to read all the items must do as a flea does—skip).

WANTED

A Genteel Black or Negroe GIRL, very handsome, with a soft Skin, good Teeth, sweet Breath, at least five feet three inches high and not above Eighteen. Whoever has such a Girl to dispose of, may hear of a Gentleman who will give

Fifty Guineas for her, by applying at the Bar of the Shakespeare's Head Tavern, Covent Garden.

Note. At the same Place any genteel *White* GIRL may hear of something to her advantage.

LOST

In the dark wall at Vauxhall on Tuesday, the 24th instant, two female reputations: one of them had a small spot occasioned by some dirt thrown upon it last week in the road to Ranelagh; the other never soiled. Whoever will bring them back to the owners, shall receive five thousand pounds, with thanks.

MUST BE SOLD

The owner being a bankrupt, a vote for a member of ——, for the borough of ——, at the next general election. To prevent trouble, the price is four score pounds.

A BON MOT

On a lady's wedding being on the twenty first of December.

> Return'd from the op'ra, as lately I sat,
> Indiff'rently chatting of this thing and that,
> My Chloë I ask'd how it enter'd her head,
> To fix on St. Thomas, of all days to wed.
> To which she replied, with reason the strongest,
> Though shortest the day is—the night, Sir, is longest.

ADVERTISEMENT

Lodgings for genteel young men, who are taken in and done for.

FRENCH CHARADE

> Mon premier est un tyran, mon seconde est effroyable,
> Mon tout est, pour un garçon pire que le diable.
> Reader, do you give it up?—It is Mari—age.

IN A SHOEMAKER'S SHOP WINDOW:

Wanted here a respectable woman's man.

NOTE.

On Monday last four Malefactors were executed at Tyburn. As one was a *woman*, they weren't all of them Male-factors.

EXTEMPORE

On the death of General Wolfe.

All conq'ring cruel death, more hard than rocks,
Thou shouldst have spar'd the Wolfe and took the *Fox*.

INTELLIGENCE EXTRAORDINARY

Ship News

July 1. For some time past the wind has been generally at North but is now come about to the South East and blows fresh.

August 25. We hear that his Majesty's ship Newcastle will soon have a new figure head, the old one being almost worn out.

'Tis reported from good authority that all the petty officers who have served on board the Cumberland—

(But this again is politics and is quite boring—Selwyn turns the page.)

NOTE

WHEREAS a person who styles himself Esquire Ketch has falsely and scandalously aspersed the characters of several gentlemen, members of the Black-leg Club, it is unanimously agreed at a meeting of the Black-leg Club held this day at the Pillory and Tumbrel Tavern, Tyburn, that the said Ketch be expelled the old hazard-room called Hell, at Newmarket, a society instituted purposely to exclude all persons, except those whose *conduct* and *characters* entitle them to be received into the company of gentlemen.

Mat o' the Mint	John Blueskin
Nimming Ned	Tricking Tom
Jack Bagshot	Thomas Dupe
Jemmy Twitcher	Crook-finger Jack

GENTLEMAN OF WIT AND FASHION

Timothy Shuffle
Cogging Jack
Anthony Sweepstakes
Timothy Diver
John Filch
Will o' the Turf
Anthony Win-all
Pious George

John Peachum
Henry MacHeath
Knowing Will
Timothy Skull
John Thieftaker
Blaspheming Ned
George Slug
Will Desperate—

(Selwyn hurriedly skips over the remaining names and leaves the room for a few moments. He returns to his seat and lights his pipe again.)

ANECDOTE

A Bishop of Exeter, having established a poor house for twenty-five old women, one day, being in conversation with Lord Mansfield, asks his Lordship for an inscription to place in front of the building. Upon which his lordship takes out his pencil and writes on a slip of paper the following:

Under this roof
The Lord Bishop of Exeter
Keeps
Twenty-five Women.

————

Me literulas stulti docuere parentes
                    Mart.
My father was a fool
When he sent me to school.

————

A MODERN GLOSSARY

Angel. The name of Woman, commonly of a very bad one.
Author. A Laughing Stock. It means likewise a poor Fellow and in general an Object of Contempt.
Beauty. The qualification with which women generally go into keeping.
Brute. A word implying Plain Dealing and Sincerity, but more especially applied to a philosopher.

[78]

Fool. A complex Idea compounded of Poverty, Honesty, Piety, and Simplicity.

Gallantry. Fornication and Adultery.

Honor. Duelling.

Humor. Scandalous Lies, Tumbling, and Dancing on the Rope.

Knowledge. In general, means Knowledge of the Town, as this is indeed the only kind of Knowledge ever spoken of in the Polite World.

Nobody. All the People in Great Britain, except about 1200.

Opportunity. The Season of Cuckoldom.

Patriot. A Candidate for a Place at Court.

Politics. The Art of getting such a Place.

Promise. Nothing.

Religion. A Word of no Meaning, but which serves as a bugbear to frighten children with.

Shocking. An Epithet which fine Ladies apply to almost everything. It is indeed an Interjection (if I may so call it) of Delicacy.

Teasing. Advice, chiefly that of a Husband.

Virtue
Vice } Subjects of Discourse.

Wit. Prophaneness, Indecency, Immorality, Scurrility, Mimicry, Buffoonery, Abuse of all good men, and especially of the clergy.

Worth. Power. Rank. Wealth.

Wisdom. The Art of Acquiring all Three.

World. Your own Acquaintance.

Selwyn now adopts an improvement in reading the papers which is practised in the country with great success. That is, after reading the paper in the old trite, vulgar way, i.e., each column by itself downwards, he next reads two columns together onwards and by this new method finds more entertainment than in the common way of reading.

1. This morning the Right Honorable the Speaker—
was convicted of keeping a disorderly House.

2. This day his Majesty will go in state to—
   sixteen notorious common prostitutes.

3. A certain Commoner will be created a peer.—
   †‡† No greater reward will be offered.

4. Last night the Princess Royal was baptised—
   Mary, alias Moll Hacket, alias Black Moll.

5. Yesterday the new Lord Mayor was sworn in,—
   and afterwards toss'd and gor'd several persons.

6. At a very full meeting of the Common Council—
   the greatest show of horned cattle this season.

7. He was examined before the fitting Aldermen—
   and no questions asked.

8. Any lady desirous of lying in privately—
   will be delivered at any part of the town.

9. Wanted an housekeeper to an elderly gentleman,—
   warranted found, wind and limb, free from blemish.

10. Notice is hereby given,—
    and no notice taken.

11. The Turk's Head Bagnio is now opened.—
    where may be had, price 5s. in sheets.

12. Notwithstanding the present exhorbitant price of
    candles—
    some dark transactions will soon be brought to light.

13. Yesterday the Queen was safely delivered.—
    to be continued annually.

14. He was buried in the same vault with his spouse.—
    At present below par; but it is thought they will be
    up again.

15. A young woman, genteely educated, is willing—
    A Captain of the Irish Establishment would be glad to—

16. Last night a desperate gang broke into a house in
    Pall Mall—
    and they all had the honour to kiss his Majesty's hand.

17. And we hear that several eminent patriots—
    ☞ Beware of such for they are counterfeits.

18. 'Tis whispered that a noble L— has married his
    mistress,—
    In pursuance of a late Act for inclosing Commons.

19. Soho. A new Hotel is opened—
    —Very best Drabs at One Guinea.

LONDON TOWN

A Poem

Houses, churches, mixt together,
Streets unpleasant in all weather,
Prisons, palaces contiguous,
Gates, a bridge, the Thames irriguous,
Gaudy things enough to tempt ye,
Showy outsides, insides empty,
Bubbles, trades, mechanic arts,
Coaches, wheelbarrows, and carts.

Warrants, bailiffs, bills unpaid,
Lords of laundresses afraid,
Rogues that nightly rob and shoot men,
Hangmen, aldermen, and footmen,
Lawyers, poets, priests, physicians,
Noble, simple, all conditions,
Worth, beneath a threadbare cover,
Villainy, bedaub'd all over.
Women, black, red, fair, and grey,
Prudes, and such as never pray,
Handsome, ugly, noisy still,
Some that will not—more that will,
Many a beau without a shilling,
Many a widow not unwilling,
Many a bargain, if you strike it,
This is LONDON!—HOW D'YE LIKE IT?

CHAPTER 8

FIRST SELWYN CIRCLE:
GILLY, DICK AND OLD Q.

SELWYN GOES DOWN TO ST. JAMES'S AND talks to the King and makes his bow to the Queen. The King says he doesn't believe George will ever leave off play as long as he lives and George smiles and hopes his Majesty is not prophet as well as King. Chatham is a gouty old man who takes the waters at Bath for his health; the Duke of Grafton comes into Almack's and gets a cool nod from Selwyn who is writing letters there. Mr. Fox is merely Charles, an aspiring patriot who has a faculty for involving himself in an extraordinary number of debts. Or if you are interested in beauty, Lady Sarah Bunbury will meet Selwyn to hear the latest news of her idolater Lord Carlisle, who is absent on the Grand Tour, and Elizabeth Gunning will complain that "Mr. Selwyn and Mr. Williams promised to send me a constant account of my sister, Lady Coventry, but they never wrote me one line."

This is George Selwyn's world. He moves in it easily and naturally, nodding to this one and chatting to that, and turning his back on the other. He is a universal friend: Everybody speaks of him as the "Great George"; he is equally at home with politicians, dilettanti, children. He is a man of such sound sense and unfailing good nature that everyone likes to be in his company. But he frequently complains that hardly anybody really cares for him. "I do not agree with you," writes Gilly Williams to him once, "in your constant declarations that except three or four people the rest are indifferent to you." He certainly has three or four intimates, but the rest are by no means indifferent to him. On the contrary, no man of his time has more people who are genuinely attached to him.

Amid political bitterness he pursues the tranquil tenor of his way. A quick wit and a kind heart, sincerity and love of society, a capacity to enjoy the world in every stage. But this has its strict limitations. George, for example, is essentially a man's man. He numbers many women among his friends, but they are mostly clever, witty women who talk well at dinner, chat divertingly in the drawing room— and they are only friends. We never hear of a love affair in his life. He has a certain aversion to the other sex. He himself professes (an exaggeration and to keep in character, of course) to have had connection with a woman but seven times and the last time with a maid at the inn at Andover when he was twenty-nine. This gives a great deal of amusement to his male acquaintances. Lord Holland, for example, writes to him: "My Lady Mary goes to a masquerade dressed like Zara, and I wish you to attend her dressed like a black eunuch." And in another letter Gilly Williams makes an unmentionable reference to Selwyn and Horace Walpole based on the aversion to women of both these gentlemen.

Women have simply no attraction for him. March is fond of his Zamperinis and his Renas. Well, that is all right, but give Selwyn a fine dress, a good dinner, a bottle of wine, and the "rigour of the game," and he is perfectly happy. He loves children, but he does not love women. It is extraordinary.

And yet he is a most intimate friend of the elder of those goddesses the Gunnings—Elizabeth, soft blue eyes and golden hair, and Maria, the elder, dark and laughing. Their story is interesting. They are two Irish girls of no fortune who are declared the handsomest women alive. They cannot walk in the park or go to Vauxhall, but such crowds follow them that they are generally driven away. They go the other day to see Hampton Court. As they are entering the beauty room, another company arrives, and the housekeeper says, "This way, ladies. Here are the beauties." The Gunnings fly into a passion and ask her what she means.

They come to see the palace, not to be shown as a sight themselves. When, in 1752, two murderesses, Mrs. Jeffries and Mrs. Blandy are hanged at Newgate, Sir Joshua remarks, "The general attention is divided between the two young ladies who were married and the two young ladies who were hanged."

But the event which makes most noise is the extempore wedding of the younger of the two Gunnings, Elizabeth. Lord Coventry, a grave young Lord, has long dangled after Maria, virtuously with regard to her honor, not very honorably with regard to her credit. Then the Duke of Hamilton, the very reverse of the earl, hot, debauched, extravagant, and equally damaged in his fortune and person, falls in love with Elizabeth at the masquerade and determines to marry her in the spring. However, two nights afterwards, being left alone with her while her mother and sister are at Bedford House, he finds himself so impatient that he sends for a parson. The doctor refuses to perform the ceremony without a license or ring. The Duke swears he will send for the Archbishop. At last they are married with a ring of the bed curtain at half an hour after midnight at Mayfair Chapel. The Scotch are enraged, the women mad that so much beauty has had its effects. And what is more silly, my Lord Coventry declares that now he will marry the other sister. In less than three weeks Maria Gunning follows Elizabeth to the altar.

When the Duchess of Hamilton is presented at court, the crowd is so great that even the nobles in the drawing room clamber upon chairs and tables to look at her. There are mobs at the door to see the sisters get into their chairs and people go early to get places at the theatre when it is known they will be there. A shoemaker at Worcester gets two guineas and a half by showing at a penny a head a shoe he is making for the Countess.

A few months after her marriage Maria travels Parisward. Her genius is not equal to her beauty; every day she utters some new howler. She becomes so fond of her husband that when Lord Downe meets them at Calais and offers her a tent bed, for fear of bugs in the inn, "Oh," says she, "I had rather be bit to death than lie one night from my dear Cov." (But when her dear Cov proposes to carry the chambermaid in the same vehicle with them by placing a stool for her in the fore part, "No, my Lord," says the Countess in broad Irish, "then you will put your legs between her thighs as you used to do between mine.")

The French will not conceive that Lady Coventry is beautiful. But poor Maria is under piteous disadvantages, for besides being very silly, ignorant of the world, and of breeding, speaking no French, and suffered to wear neither powder nor rouge, she has that perpetual drawback upon her beauty—her lord, who is sillier, as ignorant and ill bred, and speaking very little French himself—just enough to show how ill bred he is. He is jealous, petulant, scrupulous. He uses Lady C very brutally and makes her cry more than once in public. On one occasion at a dinner, he chases his wife round the table with a napkin to wipe off the rouge that she will persist in daubing on her face.

Lady C, though lovable in herself, does not meet much affection from her husband. He soon wearies of her, and she consoles herself with numerous flirtations and by the amusements of the card table. Quadrille is her favorite game. She plays it for four hours a day and often loses from twenty to thirty pounds at a sitting. She also flirts considerably. People never tire of running after her, and one Sunday evening she is mobbed in Hyde Park. The King orders that to prevent this for the future she shall have a guard. And on the next Sunday she makes herself ridiculous by walking in the Park from eight till ten P.M. with two sergeants of the guard in front with their halberds and twelve soldiers following.

Certainly Lady C lacks tact. George II at the close of his long life is conversing with her on the dullness of the town and regretting for her sake that there have been no masquerades during the year. "As for sights," says the beauty, "she is quite satisfied with them; there is only one which she is eager to see and that is a coronation."

It is said that Lady C dies from immoderate use of cosmetics in which there is a large quantity of white lead, but consumption is the real cause of her death. After she takes to bed she will have no light in her room except the lamp of a tea kettle and will never allow the curtains of her bed to be undrawn. She keeps a pocket mirror under her pillow which she looks at from time to time so as to note the ravages made by the disease in her once lovely features. She dies at the early age of twenty-seven, leaving a son and two daughters. Public interest in her continues even after her death, for ten thousand people go to see the outside of her coffin.

Among Selwyn's host of other friends, two men claim the first place in his regard. One is "Gilly" Williams; the other the Earl of March and Ruglen. These two are even a little jealous upon the point. "Thank you, my dear George," writes Gilly Williams once, "for including me in your pacquet of friends. Not even March himself is worthier of that appellation, for noone can esteem and love you better." And again: "March says he intends to write to you this post and as I love you as much as he does, I am determined for this time to be a better correspondent." However, there is little doubt as to who should be placed first, and it is not Gilly Williams. March is the nearest, the most trusted, and the most constant of Selwyn's friends. Gilly Williams comes next at a not very long interval. But Williams is so sprightly and so amusing that we cannot keep him waiting, even for such a man as the Earl of March and Ruglen.

Nothing very much is known about George James ("Gilly") Williams. He is the son of William Peere Williams. William Peere is a successful lawyer; his son is only a successful man about town. He is born in the same year as Selwyn, lives in the same street in London, is a member of the same club, has the same friends, and very much the same virtues and vices. He is one of the partie quarrée (out-of-town party) which meets at Strawberry Hill, the other members being Selwyn, Dick Edgecumbe, and the master of Strawberry himself. Gilly is a placeman also, appointed no doubt by his nephew Lord North. He marries a natural daughter of Lady Coventry. The rest is silence.

He is an amusing companion and a warm hearted friend. He adopts as his motto a sentiment from Sir William Temple—"Old wood to burn, old friends to converse with, and old books to read." His reputation for wit a little alarms him. "I have desired Lord Robert Bertie to propose me at White's," he observes. "Don't let any member shake his head at me for a wit, for God knows he may as well reject me for being a giant." (Gilly is a man of huge stature.)

George Selwyn is always dining with Gilly or playing pharo with him or seeing him in the house of some mutual acquaintance. In his last published letter to Selwyn, he says—"I always found myself treated in that set (Mme. du Deffand's) as a jeune garçon, qui n'avait point encore l'habitude du monde. Faith! there may have been some ground for it." There is indeed some ground for it. Gilly is always a jeune garçon, boyish, irresponsible, gay. He never quite grows up, which is perhaps why Selwyn likes him.

My Lord March has not one but several devils. He loves cards, he loves horse racing, he loves betting, he loves drinking, he loves eating, he loves wenching. And he does not care a damn for anybody; he is a law unto himself.

He is a little sharp looking man, very irritable, and swears like ten thousand troopers. He is certainly not handsome, but he is the grand seigneur.

He pursues racing with increasing ardor for well over half a century. It is not indeed until he is eighty that his colors cease to be seen at Newmarket. But then he is too decrepit to leave London and can do little more than eat, drink, and watch the ladies. As a jockey he is the best amateur of his day. Besides acquiring by purchase and careful breeding an unsurpassed stud of racehorses, he bestows special attention on his stablemen and jockeys whom he dresses in scarlet jackets, velvet cap, and buckskin breeches. On the turf he is considered very straight, and he expects his jockeys to be straight too. On one occasion one of them comes to him and tells him that an attempt has been made to bribe him to sell a race. March determines to give a lesson to those who try to tamper with his stable. He goes to the saddling paddock in a long coat, looks at his horse, and declares its appearance so good that he will ride it himself. Taking off his overcoat, he reveals himself in his well known scarlet and black colors, rides the horse, and wins.

He is always willing to bet on horses. To bet with him is dangerous, for he is a careful student of events, and there is little or nothing that he does not know about horses. But it is to be noted that he does not bet with those who cannot pay. There is nothing on which he will not bet. He sets the fashion of laying absurd and ludicrous wagers, such as on maggot races, cricket matches of twelve wooden-legged against twelve one-armed men, etc. He bets that he will have a letter carried fifty miles in an hour and this he accomplishes by putting the letter in a cricket ball which is then thrown around from hand to hand by twenty cricketers standing at intervals in a wide circle.

When Mr. Warrington is urged by letter to go to Tunbridge Wells and orders a chaise to carry him there, March immediately lays wagers on the journey. "Bet you, you don't do it within an hour. Bet you, don't do it within five quarters of an hour! Bet you four to one—or I'll take your bet which you please—that you're not robbed on Blackheath! Bet you, you are not at Tunbridge Wells before midnight!" cries Lord March. "Done," says Mr. Warrington. And my Lord carefully notes down the terms of the three wagers in his pocket book.

At a dinner at Newmarket a Mr. Pigot and a Mr. Codrington bet to "run their fathers" without, it may be presumed, previously consulting the gentlemen. The elder Pigot is over seventy, the elder Codrington but fifty years old. Lord Ossory, being consulted as to the handicap, computes it as 500 to 1600 guineas. Mr. Codrington, not approving, Lord March takes the bet. Now it so happens that on the very morning on which the wager is laid, Mr. Pigot senior dies suddenly from gout in the head, a fact, of course, unknown to either party to the bet. Lord March thereupon claims payment of the five hundred guineas. But Mr. Pigot objects, basing his contention on the recognised turf condition that if a horse dies before the race he is entered for, the bets on it are called off. Lord March will not recognise the analogy and after much discussion brings an action in the King's Bench against Mr. Pigot for the amount. The case is tried before Lord Mansfield, and after the hearing of a great number of witnesses a verdict is returned for the plaintiff. Lord March is accommodated with a seat on the bench during the proceedings and sits calm and unruffled awaiting the result. During this year he is blackballed at Boodle's and Almack's.

On the whole he does very well on the turf, especially in 1771, when he pockets £3000 in stakes alone.

Lord March loves horses and he loves betting. After horses he loves women, and is faithful to them in his fashion. But in a licentious age he is noted for his licence and changes his mistresses far more often than he changes his sky. There is an explanation for this. In early life he falls in love with Miss Frances Pelham. It is her misfortune that with good and noble qualities and the power of being extremely agreeable, she has strong passions, a warm temper, and no self control. Mr. Pelham, aware of March's libertine character, refuses his consent, and his daughter submits to her father's decision.

She cannot recover from her passion for about ten years. She goes to bathe in the sea to wash away the remains of her complaints but there is one which salt water seems to have no effect on, and that is, her inclination for Lord March. (Formerly a leap into the sea used to be a cure for love, but, we suppose, it has lost its efficacy.)

Ever afterwards she retains a sort of interest about the object of her first love which manifests itself in a jealous fidgeting anxiety. This is so teasing to him that in revenge he takes a pleasure in flirting before her face with the youngest and prettiest girls he can find and playing all the tricks of a male coquet. Sometimes she cries, sometimes she cannot restrain her anger. On one occasion she flies out and tells him he need not try to make conquests with that old wizened face. He replies that his face must be pretty old since he remembers hers so long. At another time, at Ranelagh, she puts herself in a fury and strikes him a blow in the side because Selwyn presents the Rena (March's newest mistress) with a rose he has from her. Once again at a large gathering, after supper, March sings catches which enrages Miss Pelham so much that notwithstanding the utmost efforts of those at her table to keep her quiet, she calls to him, and bestows a volley of curses upon him, the rest making what noise they can to keep her from being heard. After the tables are removed, she flies at him and swears she will tear his eyes out, but the rest of the ladies hold her whilst the gentlemen persuade March to make off.

Poor Miss Pelham has always been fond of play. As she grows older all other passions merge into that of gambling. She ruins herself and nearly ruins her sister. Poor, poor Miss Pelham! She is a person one cannot help pitying with all her faults. One who does not love her applies to her these lines of Pope—

> Strange flights and stranger graces still she had,
> Was just not ugly and was just not mad.

Mary Coke sees her at that villainous faro table putting the guineas she has borrowed on a card with the tears streaming down her face—the wreck of what has been highminded and generous.

March becomes more wicked than ever. He flirts with everybody, is flirted with by one of the Misses Bladen and pays court to Lady Hester Stanhope. He does not parade his conquests, but he does not hide them. When there is a rumor of his marriage, the following lines appear—

> Say, Jockey Lord, adventurous Macaroni,
> So spruce, so old, so dapper, stiff and starch,
> Why quit the amble of thy pacing pony?
> Why on a filly risk the name of March?

His noted affairs are mostly with ladies of the opera whom he greatly loves. If they are French or Italian he loves them more. Thus it is that he comes to be regarded as the outstanding patron of foreign and vocal talent. He is himself musical, can hum operatic airs, can sing passably, and can accompany himself on the harpsichord. Into his life comes a succession of stars—the Rena, the Tondino, the Zamperini, and so on, all beautiful and all kind. March loves them all, and not only one at a time. He meets the Countess Rena at a ridotto in the Haymarket and finds favor with the Countess by asking her to walk a minuet with him. This ceremony both accomplish so gracefully that it is considered the best performance of the minuet ever witnessed in these rooms. The result of this meeting is the establishment of relations lasting at least a dozen years, during which time he is devoted also to the Tondino and the Zamperini. The last named, who is only fifteen when he meets her, he treats with a great deal of respect, driving her to Newmarket in his chaise while her family follows them in a landau. "The Zamperini," he tells Selwyn, "has a father, mother, and sisters, but they all like their own dirt better than anything else, so that we dine very little together. They sometimes dine here, but not often."

"I like this little girl," he writes when he finally takes up with the Zamperini, "but how long this thing will last, I cannot tell. It may increase or be quite at an end before you arrive." Again: "Nous avons boudé un peu pour deux jours, but we shall make it up. This is an unlucky passion. I wish I had never seen her." As for the Rena: "I have intended a thousand times to have wrote; something or other, however, has always prevented me, but I certainly will write by this post . . . I would not for the world give her any mortification, for I really love her very much, and it is for that reason that I wish her not to come here just now. Pray, say something to her for me for not writing. Contrive anything rather than she should appear to be neglected."

Indeed he has the greatest difficulty in keeping his various loves in good humor and believes women are "all so exceedingly wrongheaded." They will not see that when the unlucky passion abates, it is time to go. Certainly March shows them the door very gracefully; he even weeps at parting from them. One Wednesday morning: "I am just preparing to conduct the poor little Tondino to Dover. My heart is so full that I can neither think, speak, nor write. How shall I be able to part with her, or bear to come back to this house, I do not know. The sound of her voice fills my eyes with fresh tears. My dear George, j'ai le coeur si serré que je ne suis bon à present qu'a pleurer. . . . Take all the care you can of her. Je la recommande à vous, my best and only real friend." Yes, it is very sad, but somehow we get over these things. "Our attachment as lovers has long been at an end"—but this is concerning the Rena— "and when people live at as great a distance as we have done for some time past, it is ridiculous to think of it, but I have really the greatest friendship . . ." So the Rena gives place to the Tondino and the Tondino to the Zamperini, and the Zamperini to somebody else.

March's collection of shells is said to be the best in England. He never acquires a taste for reading. He asks his friend Wraxall, "What advantage or solid benefit have you ever derived from the study of books?" Nor does he care for scenery. "What is there to make so much of the Thames. There it goes, flow, flow, flow, always the same."

He has no taste for affairs of honor. He loves his life too well. Once at a public "hell" in St. James's Street, he has a very uncomfortable experience. He has a dispute with a big, violent Irishman, Roche, nicknamed "Savage." Roche seizes him by the ears and lifts him out of his chair, calling out to the room—"See, gentlemen, how I treat this little cock sparrow! As a man he is too much beneath me or I would treat him as a gentleman." March takes no steps to wipe out the insult.

He is accustomed to say—"Beware of popularity," adding his usual oath, for March, though not un héro, continually verifies Voltaire's verse which says—

> Tout héros anglais
> jure G— d—

"I have been twice in Scotland (since I have been Duke of Queensberry). The first time I was popular, and the people of the country took the horses from my carriage and drew me home. Some years afterwards, when I returned again,

I was pelted with stones, mud, and execration, and God damn me, I liked the last, by God, better than the first reception, damn my blood."

The Duke's habit of swearing appears very extraordinary, for in all other respects he is a perfectly well-bred man. The Dowager Lady Essex, who lives in his neighborhood and is an old acquaintance of his, writes a note to him to say she will come and dine with him some day. He however declines receiving her in a civil answer, excusing himself on account of ill health, but he says to a friend, "By God, she shan't dine with me, nor any woman I can't kick out as soon as I am tired of her." (We hear of no ladies who dine with him this summer but Mme. Vandreuil, Mrs. Horsley, and the Grassini.)

At his house in Richmond, after drinking a glass of some champagne, he says—"This is the best champagne in England, God damn me, and he who says it is not, by God he lies." After ringing his bell, the servant comes into the room, stands some time without March speaking or looking at him, and then asks if his lordship wants anything, whereupon March says to him—"God damn you, am I obliged to tell you what I want?"

The finest thing in the life of Lord March is his close friendship with George Selwyn. It begins in their very early days in London and continues without a break until Selwyn's death. These two men have not so very much in common. March loves women and horses; Selwyn is indifferent to both. Selwyn dabbles in politics and is a House of Commons man for over thirty years. March looks on politics with a cold, contemptuous eye and wonders how any sensible man can engage in them when there are so many other interesting things to do. But both love play, clubs, Paris, the easy life of the man of pleasure and of fashion.

Their fondness for each other has all the extravagance and blindness of passion. It is called a sort of sentimental sodomy. March's attachment is like that of a younger to an elder brother in whose judgment and good sense he reposes the most unwavering confidence. "How can you think, my dear George," he writes, "and I hope you do not think, that anybody or anything can make a tracasserie between you and me? I take it ill that you even talk of it, which you do in the letter I had. I must be the poorest creature upon earth after having known you so long and always as the best and sincerest friend that anyone ever had—if anyone alive can make any impression upon me, where you are concerned. I told you in a letter I wrote some time ago that I depended more upon the continuance of our friendship than anything else in the world, which I certainly do, because I have so many reasons to know you, and I am sure I know myself."

And again: "There is now one thing that I depend upon in this world, which is that you and I shall always love one another as long as we remain in it."

Their love is so genuine that they draw freely upon each other's banking accounts, which is a severe test of friendship. "I shall be obliged," says March, "to take a thousand of yours to go down (to Newmarket), but it will be replaced in a few days." On another occasion:

MY DEAR GEORGE,—I have lost my watch and am quite broke. I cannot tell you how much. I am obliged to you for thinking of my difficulties and providing for them in the midst of your own. Let me hear soon. Yours very affectionately,

M & R.

It is the same when Selwyn loses. "So you have lost a thousand pounds," March to Selwyn, "which you have done twenty times in your lifetime and won it again as often, and why should not the same thing happen again? As to your banker, make yourself easy about that, for I have three thousand pounds now at Coutts'. There will be no bankruptcy without which we are both ruined at the same time."

Legends gather thick about the head of Lord March when he is no longer Lord March but "Old Q," the fourth Duke of Queensberry. Like Wilmot, Earl of Rochester, he pursues pleasure under every shape and with as much ardor at four-score as he has done at twenty. He owns a villa at

Richmond where he is in the habit of holding orgies assisted by his friends of the corps de ballet. Three of the most beautiful females to be found in London present themselves before him precisely as the divinities of Homer are supposed to have appeared to Paris on Mount Ida. While he, habited like the Dardan shepherd holding a gilded apple in his hand, confers the prize on her whom he deems the fairest. In the metropolis there is almost a universal prejudice against drinking milk, for it is supposed that this common necessary of life may be retailed from the daily lavations of Old Q. It is also said that he applies raw cutlets to his cheeks to improve his complexion.

When he becomes very infirm, he always has within call his French medical attendant, the Père Elisée, formerly physician to Louis XV, to whom he allows a large sum for every day that he lives and nothing more after his death. In the morning he sits in a cane chair on a balcony ogling every pretty girl that passes by. There is a groom on horseback ready to pursue the girl at a nod from his master. In the afternoon he totters down a little iron staircase to his vis-a-vis, a dark green vehicle with long-tailed black horses. During winter he carries a muff, two servants sit in the rumble, while the indispensable Jack Radford rides behind to execute his commissions.

Once he meets with an accident, his chair being run into by a hackney coach and upset, and he himself being slightly injured. The mishap is quite enough for the scribes of the day to suppose his death, and there appears an elegy preceded by a quotation from Horace:—"Longa Tythonum minuit senectus."

> And what is all this grand to do
> That runs each street and alley through?
> 'Tis the departure of Old Q,
> The Star of Piccadilly.
>
> The King, God bless him! gave a whew!
> "Two Dukes just dead—a third gone too,
> What! what! could nothing save Old Q,
> The Star of Piccadilly."

"Thank Heaven! Thank Heaven!" exclaims Miss Prue,
"My mother and grandmother too
Can now walk safe from that vile Q,
The Star of Piccadilly."

The jockey boys, Newmarket's crew,
Who know "a little thing—or two,"
Cry out, "He's done! We've done Old Q,
The Star of Piccadilly!"

The Monsieurs and Signoras too,
Like cats in love set up their mew,
"Ah morto, morto, pov'ro Q!"
The Star of Piccadilly.

Old Nick he whisked his tail so blue,
And grinn'd and leer'd and look'd askew—
"Oho," says he, "I've got my Q,
The Star of Piccadilly."

But the Devil does not get his Q until four years later. When he lies dying his bed is covered with billets and letters to the number of at least seventy, mostly addressed to him by women of every rank and description, from duchesses down to whores. Unable to open or peruse them, he orders them as they arrive to be laid on his bed, where they remain, the seals unbroken, till he expires. He dies unmarried at the age of eighty-six. He would have lived longer but for his imprudent indulgence in eating fruit.

"—met Dick Edgecumbe," writes Horace Walpole, "and asked him with great importance if he knew whether Mr. Pitt was out. Edgecumbe, who thinks nothing important that is not to be decided by dice and who consequently had never once thought of Pitt's political state, replied, 'Yes,'— 'Ay! How do you know?'—'Why, I called at his door just now and his porter told me so.'"

Richard Edgecumbe is the next name on the list of Selwyn's friends. A most extraordinary mixture of art and absurdity, parts, folly, business, idleness and dissipation of every sort. He is one of the choicest spirits of the time but throws his life away at the gaming table. When he is a young man, he so completely ruins himself by play that his father smuggles him on board ship and sends him to Constantinople where he leaves him under the care of the Ambassador to the Porte. On the passage he engages the captain in play and they lose and win to each other during the voyage £22,000. He is one of those who are assembled by Horace Walpole to hear the poet Gray read in manuscript his "Ode to Lyric Poetry." The others are, besides Gray and Walpole himself, Mason, Gilly Williams, and George Selwyn, and from the motto, they call themselves the συνετοι. When Gray gets to the second stanza, Dickie Edgecumbe leans towards Williams who sits near him and says— "What is this? It seems to be English, but by God I don't understand a single word of it." (When the author first publishes this poem and the following Ode, "The Bard," he is advised even by his friends to subjoin some explanatory notes, but he has too much respect for the understanding of his readers to take that liberty.)

Edgecumbe is a little chubby man, so little indeed that he is less than George II, a fact which pleases the other little man immensely.

> When Edgecumbe spoke, the Prince in sport
> Laughed at the merry elf,
> Rejoiced to see within his Court
> One shorter than himself.
> "I'm glad," cried out the quibbling squire,
> "My lowness makes your Highness higher."

Edgecumbe has a mistress, Mrs. Ann Franks, alias Day, of whom he is very jealous. Once he is shut up with the itch. The ungenerous world ascribe it to Mrs. Day, but he denies it, owning, however, that he is very well contented to have it, as nobody will venture on her. He writes an amazing letter to Walpole: "Pray, dear Horry, do not refuse me an account of what you know concerning her since I left London, as who appears at Ranelagh, if any except the tailor. Who knows but I am now applying for intelligence to a happy rival? I am sure, if her word goes for anything, it may be so. And to tell you the truth, as I know she must and will do bawdy with somebody, I should be as little vexed to hear she had with you as anybody. This is an amour that in its nature cannot admit of much delicacy, and my chief jealousy is for the possession of my part of a whole which neither I, nor any other, will be able to keep entire."

When the handsome Irish Major Johnson is chosen at White's, Sir Charles Williams presents Dick Edgecumbe to him and says (half in jest, half in earnest), "I have three favors to beg of you for Mr. Edgecumbe. The first is that you will not lie with Mrs. Day; the second that you will not poison his cards; the third that you will not kill him." The fool answers gravely, "Indeed, I will not."

Edgecumbe is something of a connoisseur, is a member, for example, of the Dilettanti Society, and he himself dabbles both in paint and in poetry. He paints a portrait of the convict Mary Squires and is among the first to recognise the genius of Sir Joshua. Poor Edgecumbe has a short but merry career. He dies unmarried at the early age of forty-five. He leaves four illegitimate children, however, by his mistress Ann Franks, for whom he appoints Horace Walpole trustee. History does not record what Walpole thinks of his trusteeship.

Outside the inner circle of Selwyn's friends we find many less intimate acquaintances. There is Richard Rigby, for example, Paymaster of his Majesty's Forces, a bon vivant of the first order and a statesman of the second. The only virtue he possesses is that he drinks fair. He is excessively corpulent with a jolly rubicund face: invariably in purple, without lace, close buttoned with his sword thrust through his pocket. All the comforts of the pay office are eloquently depicted in his countenance. At his death he leaves near half a million of public money. He never marries, but like most gentlemen he has a natural daughter.

Then there are Lord Buckingham with whom Selwyn lodges for a time, "up two pair of stairs in a room at half a guinea a week," George, afterwards first Marquis Townshend, and his brother Charles, and a host of others. Then

Sir Charles Hanbury Williams, Selwyn's first cousin, whose father, John Hanbury, has married a sister of Colonel John Selwyn. Charles Hanbury has a godfather named Williams who has fled from England upon killing a person in a duel and amassed a fortune in Russia. He leaves young Hanbury a legacy of £70,000 on condition that he take his god-father's name, which he accordingly does.

Sir Charles is rich and handsome, has a pretty turn for light verse, and is a model of fashion for all the young bucks of St. James's Street. He is a wit and a conversationalist; he flashes like a meteor across the fields of literature, poli-tics, and diplomacy. At Eton he is the friend of Henry Field-ing. Fielding depends on him for a guinea whenever he needs one and regularly submits to him his plays. After Eton he makes the Grand Tour. And in 1734 he is elected to Parliament. Diplomacy calls him, or rather he calls to it, and he goes abroad as envoy extraordinary at Berlin. His extreme acuteness in scenting out bribes displeases Fred-erick the Great and, as he says, "it were vain to contend with so mighty a Prince." The King of Prussia demands his recall with some acerbity, and Sir Charles is ordered to Dresden, then to Vienna, and finally to St. Petersburg. Here he at first carries all before him. He is a brilliant diplomatist, if writing brilliant despatches entitle him to that adjective, and as it happens his brilliancy is his undoing. So rapid is his success that within seven weeks of his arrival a treaty is signed with Russia, in which Austria is to join, providing for 55,000 Russian troops to enter English pay. Unfortu-nately in the interval, Frederick, thoroughly alarmed, secretly offers terms to the English, and at the last moment Maria Theresa withdraws, the British government with-draws, and Sir Charles receives from home not praise but a cold letter of censure. This is distinctly unjust, for the government and even the King himself have pressed on the treaty by every means in their power. But governments and kings are like that, and if Williams instead of being brilliant were humdrum; if instead of forcing the peace in the "honeymoon" of his ambassadorship, to use his own phrase, allowed things to drift in the ordinary diplomatic

manner, all would have been well. The result of this mis-
carriage is very sad. Sir Charles's mind is unhinged. He
comes home by slow stages to England, and dies, it is said,
by his own hand—a victim of brilliancy, an awful example
of the value of humdrum in politics.

He is only fifty-one when he dies. He is undoubtedly a
man of distinguished parts. Burke alludes to him as "the
polished courtier, the votary of wit and pleasure." Walpole
regards him as a model for the gilded youth of his day. But
Johnson speaks contemptuously of "our lively and elegant
though too licentious lyrick bard, Hanbury Williams," and
says he has no fame but from the boys who drink with him.

He is a great hand at badinage and an effective squib
writer. Sir Charles's pen is dipped in gall. Observe how he
torments William Pulteney, first Earl of Bath, with his "Ode
to the Earl of Bath," "New Ode to the Earl of Bath," "A
Newer Ode than the Last" (to the Earl of Bath), "Ballad"
(to the Earl of Bath), "Lines" (to the Earl of Bath),—all
of which the nobleman never reads but hears about from
his dear friends. No wonder Sir Charles is offered so many
positions of less freedom and greater responsibility on the
Continent. Horace Walpole defends Sir Charles against unfair charges of peculation while admitting that Williams
"had innumerable enemies: all the women, for he had poxed
his wife; all the Tories, for he was a steady Whig; all fools,
for he was a bitter satirist; and many sensible people, for
he was immoderately vain."

Sir Charles has no reputation as a writer of prose, perhaps because he writes so little.

He has full cheeks, heavy chin, blue eyes, and warm
coloring.

George Selwyn never remembers a time when his cousin
Charles is not also his friend. But the difference between
them of eleven years makes the relationship rather one of
patron and pupil than of equals. At intervals they meet in
London at the house in Cleveland Court and at White's.
Williams is the gayest of the gay and keeps the table in a
roar as he relates entirely apocryphal stories of his cousin
George. Once he is telling a large company a story about

Selwyn "with many strokes of rich humor" when a gentle-man who is sitting next to Selwyn, says to him in a low voice, "It is strange, George, so intimate as we are, that I should never have heard of this story before." "Not all all strange," he replies in the same voice, "for Sir Charles has just invented it, and knows that I will not by contradiction spoil the pleasure of the company he is so highly entertain-ing." No one is more responsible for George Selwyn's bent towards the life of pleasure and of fashion than Sir Charles Hanbury Williams.

At the close of Sir Charles's published letter to Selwyn, he says: "Mr. Walpole sits by me while I write. Always think of him with affection for he delights in you." Horace Walpole is by far the most distinguished of Selwyn's circle and as yet he has been left entirely out of the picture. But Horace deserves a chapter or two to himself.

CHAPTER 9

STRAWBERRY HILL

A LONG SLENDER FIGURE WITH REMARKABLY
bright eyes enters a study in Arlington Street, London. Lav-
ender suit, waistcoat embroidered with silver, partridge silk
stockings, gold buckles, and lace ruffles and frills. His wig
combed straight and queued behind showing a forehead
very pale and smooth. He enters the room with a style of
affected delicacy—chapeau bras between his hands as if he
wishes to compress it, knees bent and feet on tiptoe as if
afraid of a wet floor. He comes to spend the morning in
London . . .

He knows everybody and goes everywhere. He is at
home in the social world in which he is born. Its sayings
and doings, its passions, its scandals, its diversions, its laughter delight and interest him.

He is a dilettante in everything. He is a dilettante statesman. His father's influence and position take him into Parliament. He attends regularly for a good many years and sometimes speaks. "I go to balls and to the House of Commons—to look on; and you will believe me when I tell you
that I really think the former the more serious occupation
of the two."

His tastes are literary, but he has a morbid dread of
being taken for a literary man. When his friends congratu-
late him on one or other of his literary productions, he
makes haste to deny the soft impeachment. He snubs one
fellow who presumes to defend him against the *Critical
Review* calling him a puppy for so doing. He loves to be
esteemed an idle gentleman. Grub Street and its associa-
tions are hateful to him. "Pray, my dear child," he writes to

Sir Horace Mann, "don't compliment me any more upon my learning; there is nobody so superficial. Except a little history, a little poetry, a little painting, and some divinity, I know nothing. How should I? I who have always lived in the big busy world, who lie abed all the morning, calling it morning as long as you please, who sup in company, who have played at pharaoh half my life, and now at loo till two or three in the morning, who always loved pleasure, haunted auctions—in short who don't know so much astronomy as would carry me to Knightsbridge, nor more physic than a physician, nor in short anything that is called science. If it were not that I lay up a little provision in summer, like the ant, I should be as ignorant as all the people I live with. How I have laughed when some of the magazines have called me *the learned gentleman!* Pray don't be like the magazines."

He has by nature a propensity and by constitution a plea for being captious and querulous, for he is a martyr to the gout. He writes prose and publishes it; he composes verses and circulates them, and is an author who seems to play at hide and seek with the public. His conversation has great marks of preparation and study.

When he succeeds his nephew as fourth Earl of Orford, the accession of this dignity seems rather to annoy him than otherwise. He never takes his seat in the House of Lords, and his unwillingness to adopt his title is shown in his endeavors to avoid making use of it in his signature. He seldom if ever signs himself Orford. There is in this a tinge of affectation. Bishop Warburton styles him as "insufferable coxcomb," Nothing, indeed, but that coxcombry can induce him to sign himself in his social letters, "The Uncle of the late Earl of Orford." These are, however, but trifling failings and ought to detract but little from his many good qualities.

He is a charming letter writer. Lively, sarcastic, brilliant, acute, malevolent, scoffing, full of the pleasantest gossip and the grossest scandals. Nothing is too great or too small to appear in one of his letters. The fate of Kings and empires, battles and christenings, parties, murders, marriages, the new poem and the thickness of the paint on my lady's face are discussed side by side and with the same richness of detail.

He is never dull or stupid. He at least is independent. Why should a gentleman praise a poem or a picture because he is told to? These things are made for him, not he for them. If they please him, well and good, if not, who cares what they are? Thus if Virgil bores him, he says so, and his comment on Dante is refreshing—Dante was extravagant, absurd, disgusting—in short, "a Methodist parson in Bedlam."

He is a warm friend, hates tyranny and intolerance, and craves the affection of those for whom he really cares. The real kindness of his heart is shown in his love for children and animals. In a letter to Lady Ossory he describes a picture of a little girl "who looks so smiling and good-humored that one longs to catch her up in one's arms and kiss her till she is in a sweat and squalls." We hear also of a party of two or three children and two or three and forty dogs. "I generally prefer both," he remarks, "to what the Common people call Christians."

In the summer of 1760 the dread of mad dogs rages like an epidemic, and Walpole loudly denounces their ruthless extermination which it provokes. He writes: "In London there is a more cruel campaign than that waged by the Russians. The streets are a very picture of the murder of the innocents—one drives over nothing but poor dead dogs! The dear, good-natured, sensible creatures! Christ! how can anybody hurt them? Nobody could but those Cherokees the English, who desire no better than to be hallo'd to blood: one day Admiral Byng, the next Lord George Sackville, and today the poor dogs!"

When Lunardi the aëronaut makes an ascent taking a cat and some other animals in the balloon with him, Walpole writes: "So far from respecting him as a Jason, I was very angry with him. He has full right to venture his own neck but none to risk the poor cat's." And nothing shocks him so much as when he hears that in the excitement of the famous election which breaks up the Fox-North coalition of 1784 a mob at Dover "roasted a poor fox alive by the most diabolical allegory!—a savage meanness that an Iroquois would not have committed. Base, cowardly wretches! How much nobler to have hurried to London and torn Mr. Fox himself piecemeal! I detest a country inhabited by such stupid barbarians. I will write no more tonight; I am in a passion."

At Cambridge he is looked down upon as a milksop because he drinks tea for his breakfast when all the rest of the University drinks beer. He shrinks nervously from the great eaters and drinkers among the country gentlemen and ladies and vows he fears they will fall upon and carve one another. He does not look like a man of strong passions, but then neither does Lord Hervey, brother to the man whom many hold to be Horace Walpole's true father. Yet Queen Caroline, a very plain spoken lady, is continually rallying Lord Hervey about his visits to London to his nasty guenipes. Nobody brings any such charge against Horry. If they accuse him of anything, it is of an absurd partiality for the society of old ladies. He loves the company of beautiful women, but he never wants to establish any one of them permanently at his hearthside.

Horry is much acquainted with Lady Brown, and when neither of them is any longer young, he writes these lines upon her—

> When I was young and debonair,
> The brownest nymph to me was fair,
> But now I'm old and wiser grown,
> The fairest nymph to me is Brown.

(This jeu de mots is also a jeu d'esprit. He must be a very squeamish critic who will not allow its merit. Though it is not so good as Lord Erskine's on Lady Payne. He is suffering with the toothache and Lady Payne expresses her pity for him.

> I own I am ill,
> But I do not complain,
> He never knew pleasure
> Who never knew pain.)

Shenstone calls Horace Walpole a water gruel bard.

Walpole occupies a unique position in the circle of

George Selwyn's friends. He is the Boswell of the party with a quick and nimble curiosity. Selwyn is a sayer of good things; he utters just that kind of light and airy speech which may sparkle afterwards in a chatty letter to a friend. Walpole notes down the words as they come, jots them down on the back of an envelope and elaborates them at leisure in a letter to General Conway or Mr. George Montagu.

Their friendship begins when both are young men upon the town. The references to Selwyn in Walpole's correspondence begin very early and continue until very late. One of the earliest occurs in 1746 when we are told that "The Prince of Hesse had a most ridiculous tumble t'other night at the opera. They had not pegged up his box tight after the ridotto and down he came on all four. George Selwyn says he carried it off with an unembarrassed countenance."

Many a night these two spend at White's though Walpole has no real interest in the gaming table. No doubt he looks on at the play and perhaps takes a hand at picquet as a gentleman should, and then comes home to his house in Arlington Street quite sober and at a respectable hour. Once he finds a housebreaker awaiting him. "Last Sunday night," says Walpole in a letter to George Montagu, "being as wet a night as you shall see in a summer's day, about half an hour after twelve, I was just come home from White's, and undressing to step into bed, I heard Harry, who you know lies forwards, roar out 'Stop thief!' and run downstairs. I ran after him. Don't be frightened; I have not lost one enamel, nor bronze, nor have been shot through the head again. A gentlewoman, who lives at governor Pitt's next door but one to me, was going to bed too, and heard people breaking into Mr. Freeman's house, who, like some acquaintance of mine in Albemarle Street, goes out of town, locks up his doors, and leaves the community to watch his furniture. (N.B. It was broken open two years ago, and I and all the chairmen vow they shall steal his house away another time, before we will trouble our heads about it.) Well, madam called out 'Watch!'; two men, who were sentinels, ran away and Harry's voice after them. Dawn came, and with a posse of chairmen and watchmen found the third fellow in the area of Mr. Freeman's house. Mayhap you have seen all this in the papers, little thinking who commanded the detachment. Harry fetched a blunderbuss to invite the thief up. One of the chairmen who was drunk cried, '*Give me the blunderbuss. I'll shoot him!*' But as the General's head was a little cooler, he prevented military execution, and took the prisoner without bloodshed, intending to make his triumphal entry into the metropolis of Twickenham with his captive tied to the wheels of his postchaise. I find my style rises so much with the recollection of my victory, that I don't know how to descend, so tell you that the enemy was a carpenter and had a leather apron on. The next step was to share my glory with my friends. I despatched a courier to White's for George Selwyn, who, you know, loves nothing upon earth so much as a criminal, except the execution of him. It happened very luckily that the drawer, who received my message, has very lately been robbed himself, and had the wound fresh in his memory. He stalked up to the Clubroom, stopped short, and with a hollow trembling voice said, '*Mr. Selwyn! Mr. Walpole's compliments to you, and he has got a housebreaker for you!*' A squadron immediately came to reinforce me, and having summoned Mereland with the keys of the fortress, we marched into the house to search for more of the gang. Colonel Seabright with his sword drawn went first, and then I, exactly the picture of Robinson Crusoe, with a candle and lanthorn in my hand, a carbine upon my shoulder, my hair wet and about my ears, and in a linen night gown and slippers. We found the kitchen shutters forced, but not finished; and in the area a tremendous bag of tools, a hammer large enough for the hand of a Jael, and six chisels! All which *opima spolia* as there was no temple of Jupiter Capitolinus in the neighborhood, I was reduced to offer on the altar of Sir Thomas Clarges.". . .

But it is when Walpole establishes himself at Strawberry Hill that he and Selwyn pass most time in each other's company.

"You perceive by my date," Walpole writes to his cousin Conway, in June, 1747, "that I am got into a new camp and have left my tub at Windsor. It is a little plaything house that I got out of Mrs. Chenevix's shop, and is the prettiest bauble you ever saw. It is set in enamelled meadows with filigree hedges. Two delightful, dusty roads supply me continually with coaches and chaises: barges as solemn as the barons of the Exchequer move under my window . . . Dowagers as plenty as flounders inhabit all around and Pope's ghost is just now skimming under my window by a most poetical moonlight."

It is so small that he is inclined to wrap it up and send it to his friend Mann in a letter. The prospect is as delightful as possible, commanding the river, the town, and Richmond Park, and being situated on a hill (almost a misnomer), descends to the Thames through two or three little meadows where he has some Turkish sheep and two cows all studied in their color for becoming the view. (The desire of fashionable people to have a country box to escape to from the noise and smells of London has already set a fashion. The preference of George II for Kensington and of George III for Richmond stimulates it. White's Club even takes a house at Richmond to come to every Saturday and Sunday to play at whist. It is so established a custom to go out of town at the end of the week that people do go, though it be only to another town.)

The house is built by a coachman of the first Earl of Bradford. It is called Chopped Straw Hall, for the villagers suppose that by feeding his lord's horses with chopped straw, the coachman saved enough money to build it. Walpole pays for it £1356, 10s. to Mrs. Chenevix, the famous toy woman and present owner, and alters its name to Strawberry Hill. By fresh purchases he extends his territory to fourteen acres which he assiduously plants and cultivates. Then he begins to improve and enlarge the structure itself. "I am going to build a little Gothic Castle at Strawberry Hill," he says in January, 1750. Accordingly he constructs a grand parlor or refectory with a library above it, and to these he soon adds a picture gallery and cloister, a round tower and a cabinet or tribune. (It is so much in the Italian taste for shade and coolness that half of his family are dying of violent colds.) There are, besides, a Breakfast Room (with blue paper and blue and white linen), a Blue Bedchamber, a Yellow Bedchamber or Beauty Room (with grey spotted paper, bed and chairs of yellow silk), a Red Bedchamber (hung with crimson paper and with crimson damask chairs), Mr. Walpole's Bedchamber, up two pairs of stairs, the Star Chamber (painted green with golden stars in mosaic), a Green Closet, China Room, Cottage in the Flower Garden, etc.

The gem of his library collection is a manuscript copy of the Psalms on Vellum, finely bound with silver gilt clasps and corners and is preserved in a satinwood case ornamented with lapis lazuli and agates. Another of his treasures is the traveling library of Sir Julius Caesar, Chancellor of the Exchequer under James I—forty-four little white vellum volumes enclosed in an oakcase which is morocco covered and tooled to resemble a large folio. The collection is quite innocent of order. Floyer on *Cold Bathing* is sandwiched between Cheyne's *Christian Religion* and *A Relation of the Earthquake at Luna*. The books, generally, are in a sombre condition and in want of new or mended covers.

Walpole now Gothecizes his place to his heart's content with painted glass ("lean windows fattened with rich saints"), battlements, and arches. (For his battlements there is, indeed, some authority in the text in Deuteronomy which reads: "When thou buildest a new house, then shalt thou make a battlement for thy roof, that thou bring not blood upon thy house if any man fall from thence.") Why Gothic? He thinks Englishmen should be proud of their native Gothic. He grows still more patriotic on his travels when he finds Frenchmen and Italians condescending to Englishmen as untutored Northerners deficient in the arts and "the graces! the graces!" "Gothic" among the cognoscenti is a word of contempt, an underdog attraction to him. Besides the irregularity of Gothic suits the hidden "wildness" in himself.

John Chute and Richard Bentley encourage him in his

Gothicism. The three of them make up what Walpole calls "The Committee." They are not moved by fashionable boredom. "One must have taste to be sensible of the beauties of Grecian architecture," Walpole says. "One only wants passion to feel Gothic." The Committee pore over prints, especially those of tombs, and pick and choose and adapt.

But it is all a kind of gingerbread Gothic. Strawberry Hill displays examples of Gothic details in ways which would make the original architects stare. Walpole and his friends have no idea how Gothic buildings were constructed, nor do they care. What they are after is atmosphere. The fabric of Strawberry Hill is lath and plaster. Gilly Williams says, long before its master dies, that Mr. Walpole has already outlived three sets of his battlements.

The abundance of stained glass and the lowness of many of the rooms make the house a little gloomy. But "I did not mean," Walpole writes, "to make my house so Gothic as to exclude convenience and modern refinements in luxury." Bentley designs Gothic furniture, but Walpole also has "a thousand plump chairs, couches, and luxurious settees covered with linen of blue and white stripes adorned with festoons." When Mann assumes that the garden will be Gothic as well as the house, Walpole puts him straight at once: "Gothic is merely architecture. . . . One's garden, on the contrary, is to be nothing but *riant* and the gaiety of nature."

However, having adorned his "little plaything," he next proceeds to cram it with all the objects most dear to the connoisseur and virtuoso, knicknacks of all sorts which give it the aspect partly of a museum and partly of a curiosity shop (where the goods are not for sale). Finally in 1774 he prints a quarto "Description of the Villa of Horace Walpole . . . at Strawberry Hill, near Twickenham, with an Inventory of the Furniture, Pictures, Curiosities, &c." Even a partial list is informative and revealing:

Saxon tray with squirrels, 19 small heads of the court of Charles II in oil, a toilette worked by Mrs. Clive, Hogarth prints, a rich enamel hunting horn over a table of Sicilian jasper, antelopes holding shields, a missal attributed to Raphael.

A Conversation by Reynolds, 2 ice pails of Sèvres China.

A bronze Caligula with silver eyes and a white snuff box (a gift from Mme. de Sevigné, Walpole claims, but really sent by Mme. Du Deffand.)

Jar of Roman faience, Chinese lanthorns of scraped oyster shells, white Dutch tiles with borders of blue. A silver bell carved with masks and insects with which Pope Clement VII cursed the caterpillars (designed by Benvenuto Cellini), the clock which Henry VIII gave to Ann Boleyn.

Emperor Vespasian in basalt and the incomparable Greek Eagle from the baths of Caracalla and portraits of his three nieces. Green glass tumblers with golden edges, card table of rosewood.

A firescreen of admirable needlework representing a vase of flowers, mounted in mahogany, carved and inlaid with ivory.

A speculum of cannel coal, the red hat of his Eminence, Cardinal Wolsey, the very spurs worn by King William III at the ever glorious Battle of the Boyne.

The Identical *Iliad* and *Odyssey* from which Pope made his Popsian translation. Carpets with blue tulips and yellow foliage.

Van Tromp's pipe case.

A landscape in needlework, a landscape in India ink. A lady's head, an infant's head, a boy's head in red and black chalk, an old head in a laced night cap and ruff. A girl's head—very lively. Cleopatra in water colors—not a head. A friar and a lady at her toilette, a woman hiding her lover from her blind husband, a woman fainting in a man's arms, a lady with Italian mottoes in a round, two kittens in marble, a gentleman's head, Mr. Pope in water colors, the Farnese Hercules in wax, two landscapes in soot water, noblemen and boors, orange flowers and roses, Magdalens and sons of the Old Pretender, views and views, carnations.

Enamels by Petitot and Zincke, miniatures by Cooper and the Olivers.

China from Venice, Japan, Worcester, Portugal, Sèvres, Vienna, St. Cloud, Chantilly, Chelsea, Saxony, Caen, Staffordshire, Berlin.

Water cups, chocolate cups, standing cups, white China cups with Cupids (painted in Europe), caudle cups, custard cups, coffee cups, tea cups, egg shell cups—black and white, red and white, blue and white, white, white with green festoons, white with gold festoons, lilac and gold, a cup and saucer (all over strawberries); red clouded, red glazed, white within, without japanned black and mother of pearl, green with landscapes.

White saucers, red saucers, white and blue saucers, blue and gold, brown with flowers, green and gold, blue and gold in zigzags and garlands on white (very beautiful).

A crucifix of ivory, a moonlight on copper, the Four Seasons, Macbeth in the witches' cave, gypsies, Mr. Pope himself, a herb and fish market, the Virgin and child and two Angels holding tapers, a masquerade at Vauxhall in bister, top of a warming pan that belonged to Charles II with his arms and his motto—"Sarve God and live forever," (As it is dated 1660 it was probably used for his Majesty and his mistress, the Duchess of Cleveland), and swords, quivers, lances, bows, Persian shields, Indian scimitars, maces, hatchets, halberds, battle axes, and a bandelier. Illuminated missals.

A girl with a cat, a boy with a flute, a greyhound in bronze (to keep down papers).

Cameo of an Egyptian duck, ditto of a sleeping Hermaphrodite, the Queen of Bohemia, a square snuff box of lapis lazuli, a round snuff box ditto, a crystal sceptre, a broken patera engraved, ewers, tea kettles, needlecases, antique rings, silver seals, cornelian seals, a toothpick case of Egyptian pebble, a smelling bottle of agate, a toothpick case of gold, a green and white snuff box, an egg shaped snuff box, an amber jewel box.

A young gladiator in bronze, Diana in Serpentine stone, a bronze bull, a sphinx, a dog drinking, a woman carrying a pig to be sacrificed, the circumcision on copper, Mme. de Sevigné, the Virgin and Child, Ulysses, the Duchesses of Cleveland and Portsmouth, a bagpiper in bronze, a sacrificing priest ditto, Ninon L'Enclos, the education of Jupiter, Jacob traveling from Laban and a piece of rocks.

And dishes, bowls, plates, jars, medallions, filigree, cut paper, enamels, gems, coins, bas reliefs, Venetian glass, porcelain, basins, candlesticks, Tuscan vases, earthenware pots, chests, sea pieces, bureaus, commodes, black and red earthenware vases, lacrymatories, prints, drawings, tea pots, urns, tea canisters, Indian bronzes, squalling parrots, Chinese josses, shells, piping shepherds, cupids, tables, chairs, damask chairs, chintz chairs, chairs of yellow silk, chairs of patchwork, chairs of ebony, chairs of oak, chairs covered with purple lined with white satin, bottles, salvers, baskets, pitchers, mugs, flower tubs, flower pots, looking glasses—

"Lord God Jesus!" my lively Lady Townshend cries out as she rustles up the staircase, sweeping aside many an ornament with her ample silk petticoats. "What a house! It's just such a house as the parson's where the children all be at the foot of the bed."

George Selwyn describes Strawberry Hill as a catacomb or at best a museum rather than a habitation and the master of it one of the most carefully finished miniatures and best preserved mummies in the whole collection.

We pass from the Castle and garden to Horace Walpole's private printing press, the Officina Arbuteana, as he christens it, next the neighboring farmyard. Here he issues his own and others' works. He affects to ridicule his latest passion—paraphrasing Pope.

> Some have at first for wits, then poets passed;
> Turned printers next and proved plain fools at last.

He flutters around the printer while the slow process of composition proceeds. Future edition mongers, he hopes, will say of those of Strawberry Hill that they have all the beautiful negligence of a gentleman.

He does not seek the famous; most of his authors are rather obscure. More than once the Officina Arbuteana is used for the aid of some struggling person. In one case it is for a poor reading tailor" of Buckingham, who, in spite of poverty, has learned Latin, Greek, and Hebrew, and has been living for many days on water and tobacco. The press is never employed in politics or satire.

Every visitor is shown through the printing office. It is an unusual and delightful spectacle. One day Lady Rochford, Lady Townshend, and a Miss Bland dine with Walpole. They must needs be taken to the little cottage in which Mr. William Robinson, an Irishman, is at work. (Of this first printer, Garrick says—"I would give any money for four actors with such eyes.") After the merry party looks about, Robinson is directed to take an impression, and in a moment Walploe has the pleasure of handing her ladyship Townshend, a piping hot "pull" as a souvenir of her call at the Officina Arbuteana.

As he expects the ladies wish to see the printer compose, he gives him therefore four lines from *The Fair Penitent*, which Robinson sets. But as Walpole diverts the attention of the visitors, the printer whips away what he has just set, and to their great surprise, when they expect to see "Were ye fair," he presents to Lady Rochford, who has been Miss Young, these printed lines—

> The press speaks:
> In vain from your properest name have you flown,
> And exchanged lovely Cupid's for Hymen's dull throne;
> By my art shall your beauties be constantly sung,
> And in spite of yourself you shall ever be Young.

"You may imagine," says Walpole afterwards, "whatever the poetry was, that the gallantry of it succeeded."

The press comes to a standstill. William Robinson, whom Walpole thinks has the most sensible look in the world, proves to be only "a foolish Irishman who takes himself to be a genius," and who grows angry when Walpole thinks him extremely the former and not the least of the latter. The first printer at Strawberry Hill leaves the amarinthine shades that delight him, and Walpole has difficulty in finding a successor. For two years the office remains unoccupied, and Walpole gloomily predicts that in the future he shall not print anything more important than Mrs. Clive's benefit tickets. But in 1765 he hires Thomas Kirgate, the printer, who remains with Walpole until his death.

Strawberry Hill becomes one of the show places of England. Walpole shudders when the bell of his gate rings. It is as bad as keeping an inn, he complains, and he is often tempted to deny sightseers admission. In self defence he makes the regulation that only four visitors shall be admitted on any one day. It becomes necessary for Mr. Kirgate to print cards of admission, labels for the various collections, and rules for the curious callers at Strawberry Hill. The regulations are very quaint and courteous and begin thus—"Mr. Walpole is very ready to oblige any curious person with the sight of his house and collections, but as it is situated so near London and in so populous a neighborhood, it is but reasonable that such persons as send for tickets should comply with the rules he has been obliged to lay down for showing it:

"No ticket will serve but on the day for which it is given. If more than four persons come with a ticket, the Housekeeper has positive orders to admit none of them.

"Persons desiring a ticket may apply either to Strawberry Hill or to Mr. Walpole in Berkeley Square, London. If any person does not make use of the ticket, Mr. Walpole hopes he shall have notice; otherwise he is prevented from obliging others on that day, and thence is put to great inconvenience.

"They who have tickets are desired not to bring children."

Visitors from all countries come to inspect Strawberry Hill. Horry loves to entertain and show the treasures of his house. He greets his French guests once in the cravat of Gibbon's carving and a pair of gloves embroidered up to the elbows that belonged to James I. The French servants stare and firmly believe this is the dress of an English gentleman. They go to see Pope's grotto and garden and return to a magnificent dinner in the refectory. During dinner there are French horns and clarionets in the cloister, and after coffee he treats them with a new collation or syllabub milked under the cows that are brought to the brow of the terrace. On another occasion they walk, have tea, coffee, or lemonade in the gallery, which is illuminated with a thousand or thirty candles (we forget which) and play whisk and loo till midnight. Then there is a cold supper and at one the company returns to town, saluted by a chorus of fifty nightingales who, as tenants of the manor, come to do honor to their lord.

Strawberry Hill is grown a perfect Paphos. It is a land of beauties. Lady Coventry, the Duchesses of Hamilton and Richmond, and Lady Ailesbury dine there. The two latter stay all night. He enthrones the Archbishop of Canterbury in a purple chair from the Holbein Room.

He has to dinner M. and Mme. de Guerchy, Mlle. de Nangis, the Prince of Masserano, etc. Indeed everything succeeds to a hair. A violent shower in the morning lays the dust, brightens the green, refreshes the roses, pinks, orange-flowers, and blossoms. A storm of thunder and lightning leaves a rich coloring to the sky and the sun appears.

Madame de Juliac comes from the Pyrenees, very handsome, not a girl, and General Schuwalof, the favorite of the late Czarina—absolute favorite for a dozen years, without making an enemy. Then Madame Dusson, who is Dutch built, and Mme. de Boufflers, a passionate admirer *de nous autre Anglois*, and Chevalier D'Eon who dresses in petticoats and whose sex is doubtful, and others. Walpole gives an assembly to show his Gallery and it is glorious. But happening to pitch upon the feast of the Tabernacles, none of his Jewish friends can come, though Mrs. Clive, the actress, proposes to them to change their religion. So he is forced to exhibit once more. His next assembly is entertaining: there are five countesses, two bishops, fourteen Jews, five Papists, a doctor of Physic, and an actress (Mrs. Clive), not to mention Scotch, Irish, East and West Indians.

The Abbot of Strawberry is very much offended if not taken at his own evaluation. When the Duc de Nivernais visits him, he says, "I cannot say he flattered me much or was much struck." And he is indignant when Nivernais removes his hat on entering the Gothic room thinking it is a chapel. (Perceiving his error, the Duke says, "Ce n'est pas une chapelle pourtant," and seems a little displeased.)

The Swiss footman does not think there is so great a prince in the world as he. One day as he comes to breakfast, he tells Walpole coolly that the Duke of Wirtemburg called at eight o'clock and wanted a ticket for Strawberry Hill. "Bless me," says Horry, "and what did you say?"—"I told his Grace you was not awake, and bade him come again at ten."—"Good God!" says Horry, "tell him to call again! Don't you know he is a Sovereign Prince?"—"No, I did think he was only a common Duke!" Walpole cannot help laughing though he is shocked. In short the Duke calls again, and is again sent away, nor can David yet conceive that Walpole is to be waked. Walpole is forced to write a thousand lies and excuses and swear he is bedridden with the gout and cannot pay his duty to his Serene Highness. Upon the whole, though, he is very glad for being reduced to plead gout.

Friday morning. Walpole is very tranquilly writing. He hears the bell at the gate ring and calls out as usual, "Not at home." But Harry who thinks it will be treason to tell a lie, when he sees the red liveries, owns Mr. Walpole is, and comes running up—"Sir, the Prince of Wales is at the door and says he is come on purpose to make you a visit!" There is Horry in the utmost confusion, undressed, in his slippers, and with his hair about his ears. There is no help— "*insanum vatem aspecet*" and down he goes to receive him. *Him* is the Duke of York. Behold Walpole's breeding of the old court. At the foot of the stairs, he kneels down and kisses the Duke's hand. The Duke is, as he always is, extremely good humored, and Walpole, as he is not always, extremely respectful. He stays two hours, nobody with him but Morrison. Walpole shows him all his castle.

At Strawberry Hill Walpole generally rises at about nine o'clock and appears at breakfast in the bow-windowed room on the first floor, his favorite Blue Room, looking pleasantly on the Thames. His approach is proclaimed and attended by Patapan, his favorite little dog. A tea kettle, stand, and heater are brought in, and he drinks two or three cups out of the most rare and precious ancient porcelain of Japan. The dog has a liberal share of breakfast, and as soon as the meal is over, Walpole mixes a bowl of bread and milk and tosses it out of the window to the troops of squirrels who presently come down from the high trees round the lawn. Dinner is served in the small parlor or large dining room, in winter generally in the former. He eats most moderately of chicken, pheasant, or any light food. Pastry he dislikes as it is difficult to digest though he will taste a morsel of venison pie. Only once does he drink two glasses of white wine—he never tastes any liquor except ice water. If the guests like wine, they must call for it during dinner, for almost instantly after he rings the bell to order coffee upstairs. (At the close of dinner, the smell is removed by a censor or a pot of frankincense.) Thither he passes about five o'clock and generally resuming his place on the sofa will sit until late in the evening in chitchat, full of singular anecdotes, wit, and acute observations, occasionally sending for books or curiosities or passing to the library as any reference happens to arise in the conversation. After his coffee he tastes nothing, but his snuffbox is not forgotten. (When the gout is very bad, he is carried from room to room by two footmen who deposit him on a sofa or in a chair with his prints and books and newspapers. Around his neck is a whistle that he works up to his lips when he wants something, and he then blows with vigor.)

Such is the private rainy day of Horace Walpole. Sometimes he goes out into his garden and all over the wet grass in a light silk waistcoat and thin slippers to feed his poultry of all sorts. And he never wears a hat. On his first visit to Paris he is ashamed of his effeminancy when he sees every little meagre Frenchman, whom even he can throw down with a breath, walking without a hat which he cannot do, without a certainty of that disease termed by the nation, *le catch-cold*. The first trial costs him a slight fever, but he gets over it and never catches cold again. Draughts of air, damp rooms, windows open at his back, all situations are alike to him in this respect. He will even show some little offence at any solicitude shown by his guests on such an occasion and will say with a half smile—"My back is the same with my face and my neck is like my nose."

After an evening of scandal at Marble Hill with the Countess of Suffolk or taking a card at little Strawberry Hill, he will return to his Gothic castle and in the Library or Blue Room write letters of news (sometimes he hears a jest of Selwyn's—it floats through the window—and down it goes), acknowledge cards of invitation from peers and peeresses, give life to the antiquarian notes of Vertue the engraver, paste Faithornes and Hollars into his volumes of English heads, annotate a favorite author, and retire to rest about two in the morning.

The next day he will rise late, saunter about his villa, play with his dog Patapan, and give directions to the workmen employed in repairing battlements, repainting walls, or gilding his favorite gallery. At twelve his light bodied chariot will appear at the door with his English coachman and Swiss valet, and Walpole will take his favorite drive from his villa at Strawberry Hill to his town house in Arlington Street, Piccadilly, London.

During nearly fifty years he takes that drive many, many times a year. What more natural than that he should desire pleasant companionship in his chariot to beguile the journey? Walpole knows where and how to pick his men. White's is the place; there are no dull dogs at White's. And where can you find three more cheerful fellows than George Selwyn, Gilly Williams, and Dick Edgecumbe? Remember Horace's requirements. He will have no mere crack-pated man of fashion. What he wants is agreeable company—people who talk well and brightly—who know something about life and (perhaps) literature, and (certainly) art. Now all three, Selwyn, Williams, and Edgecumbe, fulfil these requirements. They are witty, they move in Walpole's circle, Edgecumbe is a draughtsman of some ability, and Gilly Williams decidedly knows good literature and good art from bad. These four form the out-of-town party. They often drive out together from St. James's Street to Twickenham and dine there in bachelor state. Sometimes they return the same night, sometimes they spend a few days at Strawberry Hill. They are held at Easter and Christmas certainly. Many, many days Selwyn receives a note like this—

DEAR GEORGE,

If you and Mr. Williams are disposed to charity, you will find me any time this evening with a gouty foot on cushions.

Yours,

H. Walpole

The members of the out of town party amuse themselves in various ways. One wet afternoon is spent in designing a coat of arms for the Club at White's, and Edgecumbe paints it. Or they play whist for small stakes. More often they chat, tell anecdotes and stories, gossip, and talk scandal.

This evening they are sitting around a table in the Grand Gallery. Selwyn and Dick Edgecumbe each has a bottle of port and a green tumbler before him. Gilly Williams in a scarlet frock coat with gold button holes is smoking. Under the table is a pail of ice in which stands a decanter of water with which Walpole refreshes himself from time to time. Six or seven candles flickering in the sockets dimly light a part of the gallery and throw weird shadows on the fine vases and cisterns of majolica, busts, bronzes, pictures. Occasionally Walpole glances at one or other of his treasures. His eyes light with pleasure, and a slight smile hovers about his lips.

Gilly Williams begins the conversation. He tells a story of some acquaintance of his who killed himself and left a note in one of his pockets explaining that he was "tired of buttoning and unbuttoning."

He tells the tale of the beautiful, mad Duchess of Queensberry, Prior's Kitty. She was going along the Strand in a chariot with her mother when they were stopped by the crossing of a cart which, turning down the street, passed their carriage before it began again to move. The carman was sitting in the cart with a pipe which he had been smoking. As he passed he looked into the carriage, full in the face of Lady Kitty, and after a moment said, "My dear, my pipe is gone out, pray lend me those eyes of yours to light it again."

Horace Walpole says he once drank to her and by way of a toast remarked, "I wish you may live to grow ugly." She answered, "I hope, then, you will keep your taste for antiquities."

Selwyn relates an incident that occurred at one of her balls. The gallery where the guests were dancing was very cold. Lord Lorn, Walpole, and himself retired to a little room and sat comfortably by the fire. The Duchess looked in, said nothing, and sent a smith to take the hinges of the door off. The three understood the hint and left the room and so did the smith with the door.

Walpole turns the conversation to her cousin, the mad Earl of Clarendon. He was a clever man. His great insanity was dressing himself as a woman. When Governor in America, he opened the assembly dressed in that fashion. When some of those about him remonstrated, his reply was, "You are very stupid not to see the propriety of it. In this place and particularly on this occasion, I represent a woman (Queen Anne) and ought in all respects to represent her as faithfully as I can."

Gilly Williams says his father did business with him when he was dressed in women's clothes. He used to sit at the open window so dressed to the great amusement of the neighbors. He employed always the most fashionable milliner, shoemaker, staymaker, etc. Gilly saw a picture of him in Worcestershire in a gown, stays, tucker, long ruffles, etc.

Williams tells some curious circumstances of the Duke of Marlborough's imbecility. He says the Duke always wore his hat in and out of doors and even at dinner, but whenever any great man was mentioned, as Prince Eugene, etc., or any great battle or action, he pulled it off and so repeatedly as often as they were mentioned.

Gilly is bubbling over this evening with stories and anecdotes. He relates one of Charles, Earl of Halifax, the outstanding financier of his time and a patron of literature. It seems Pope (like other wits and poets) had been advised to read his works to him for his approbation or correction. He accordingly went one day, accompanied by the physician and poet, Dr. Garth (author of *The Dispensary*) and read to him some hundred lines he had lately finished of his Iliad. While he was reading, Lord Halifax at intervals would stop him and say—"Mr. Pope, I beg your pardon, you are certainly a much better judge than me, but I do not quite understand such a line. Read it again. This was done. "Well, I protest I do not quite understand it. Surely it is very obscure. I submit to you whether you had not better recast that passage." He did this in several instances.

When the two authors went away, Pope said, "I really do not feel the obscurity which struck Lord Halifax and cannot tell how to mend the lines objected to." "Lord!" said Garth, "you do not seem to know these people. Do not alter your lines but return in about a fortnight with the verses as they are, but tell Lord Halifax, you have corrected them according to his lordship's generous criticism and advice and then read them to him. You will find he will be delighted with your deference to his taste, and will not discover that the lines are as they were." Pope acted accordingly, and the event was exactly as Garth foretold.

Lord Halifax was the great patron of Sir Isaac Newton. But Gilly finds that Sir Isaac's niece was Lord Halifax's mistress. Sir Isaac had a niece unmarried by the name of Mrs. Barton, a good-looking person of talent and reading. Sir Isaac lived with her in Leicester Fields, and at her house there used to be a meeting in the evenings of men of learning and science. But it was a fixed rule that the meeting broke up at nine, and at that hour exactly Lord Halifax's chariot used to stop at the door. The nature of the relations between Halifax and the gay and witty Catherine Barton remains a mystery. Three views have been maintained, says Gilly: 1.) that they were platonic, 2.) that they were not, 3.) that there was a secret marriage.

Selwyn tells them some anecdotes of George I and George II. The former when he came from Hanover in 1714, understanding very imperfectly the English language, found himself so weary while assisting at the service in the Chapel Royal, that he frequently entered into conversation in French or German with the persons behind him. Charles II who could not plead the same excuse used to fall asleep, and the Earl of Arlington usually woke his Majesty towards the conclusion of the sermon.

Horry gives the party the history of John Law's duel, not as gospel, but merely as the current story of the time, a story the more to be questioned, he says, because one similar to it is told of Sir William Temple's father and the Grand Duchess of Tuscany. The story of Law's duel is this:

A remarkably handsome young man of those days was seen asleep under a tree in Kensington Gardens. That evening he received a message telling him that if he followed the guide sent to him, he would meet with an adventure, probably agreeable, and much to his advantage. He did, and through secret ways and passages was brought in the dusk into a bedchamber in which he passed the night with a lady who paid him very liberally and made an early new appointment. The intercourse continued, perhaps agreeably to both, certainly profitable to him as it enabled him to live at great expense. But he was told from the first that though the lady would perhaps often see him in company (which she did), he must not attempt to find her out. That the instant he should come to know who she was he would certainly be put to death. He had found that the lady wore a particular ring on her finger even in the night, which he knew very well by the touch. One day at play, he sat near a lady on whose finger he perceived the very ring, and had the indiscretion, at their next meeting, to let her know that he had discovered her. The day after, on some pretext, he received a challenge from Law, then a gambler and adventurer about London, and was killed. Law fled the country and retired to France. . . .

The candles are guttering in the sockets. Dick Edgecumbe is fast asleep and Gilly Williams looks drowsy. Selwyn finishes the remains of his port, gives Edgecumbe a rousing shake, and with his friends starts to leave. A coach rolls up to the door, they bid adieu to the Abbot of Strawberry, and through the dark night drive to London, waking the echoes of Hammersmith and Kensington with the sound of their chariot wheels.

CHAPTER 10

MR. SELWYN, THE WIT

SELWYN'S FULL CURLING LIPS SEEM MADE
for saying witty things, and the Princess Marie Liechten-
stein will have it that his slightly retroussé nose proclaims
his power of repartee. But there are dangers in the reading
of physiognomy. The Princess, for example, sees in George's
face the love of corpses combined with the facility for
jokes for which, according to tradition, he is famous. Now
most people looking at the various portraits of Selwyn will
entirely fail to perceive this extraordinary combination in
his face. Mr. Pitt likes a particular kind of pork pie and Mr.
Fox has a passion for buff waistcoats. Yet no female biographer of these distinguished men has ever confirmed such
predilections from their published portraits. But still the
Princess may be right.

For George is Lord of the Manor of Bon Mot to whom
the right of all waifs and strays belong. He is regarded as
supreme and unapproachable. His witticisms are collected
and repeated with extraordinary zest. They are enjoyed by
members of Parliament at Westminster and by fashionable
ladies in the drawing rooms of St. James'.

He has the manner of the born wit. He says trite things
gracefully. And he knows also the value of contrast. He has
a dark face, with a demeanor solemn and serious; he is "the
weary King Ecclesiast." When he drops a bon mot, the
effect is heightened by the unexpectedness of the thing. It
is said with a grave voice and an expressionless countenance, and he has a habit of turning up the whites of his
eyes. Again he is a very somnolent person. According to

his friends, he is continually falling asleep. He sleeps in the House of Commons (he snores in unison with the first minister, Lord North), he sleeps at the card table. The only place perhaps where he does not sleep is in bed. The effect of his jests when falling from his lips is greatly augmented by the listless and drowsy manner in which he utters them. "I don't know a single bon mot that is new," says Horace Walpole. "George Selwyn has not waked yet for the winter. You will believe that when I tell you that t'other night having lost £800 at hazard, he fell asleep upon a table with near half as much before him, and slept for three hours with everybody stamping the box close at his ear. He will say prodigiously good things when he does wake." (Yet the sparkle of these "good things" has died out; the laughter and fun are gone. We are acutely conscious of a sense of disappointment. We have not the manner of the speaker, the look in his eyes, the tones of his voice, his trick of gesture. Even his best things miss fire. But perhaps we must remember that Helen's face was never so fair as to those who actually launched the thousand ships.)

Here is Selwyn's adventure with the eccentric Ethelreda, Lady Townshend—Ethelreda who is remarkable for saying as many good things and doing as many improper ones as any lady in England. They say she is the original of Lady Bellaston in *Tom Jones*, but this is distinctly a libel. One Sunday George is strolling home to dinner at half an hour after four. He sees my Lady Townshend's coach stop at the Catholic Caracioli's Chapel. He watches, sees her go in; her footman laughs; George follows. She goes up to the altar; a woman brings her a cushion; she kneels, crosses herself, and prays. He steals up and kneels by her. Conceive her face, if you can, when she turns and finds him close to her. In his demure voice he says, "Pray, madam, how long has your Ladyship left the pale of our Church?" She looks furies and makes no answer. Next day he goes to her, and she turns it off as curiosity, but, as Walpole says, is anything more natural?

When a namesake of Charles Fox is hanged at Tyburn, "Did you attend the execution, George?" asks Fox. "No,

Charles," drawls Selwyn, "I make a point of never attending rehearsals."

Horace Walpole happening to observe that there existed the same indecision, irresolution, and want of system in the politics of Queen Anne as now distinguish those of the reign of George III, adds, "But there is nothing new under the sun." "No," says Selwyn, "nor under the grandson."

One of the waiters at Arthur's Club being committed to prison for a felony, "What a horrid idea," says Selwyn, "he will give of us to the people of Newgate."

George II for some reason or other does not like Selwyn and calls him "that rascal George." "Rascal?" murmurs Selwyn when he hears it, "that's an hereditary title of the Georges, isn't it?"

The open court at Sion is turned into a circle and finely illuminated. Lord Huntingdon on entering it cries out, "I have never seen this apartment before." "If your lordship," says Selwyn, "will look up, perhaps you may recollect the ceiling."

When there is gossip that Charles Fox is languishing at the feet of Perdita Robinson (cast off of Prince Florizel), George Selwyn says, "Well, whom should the Man of the People live with but the Woman of the People?"

When the same statesman has ruined himself by excessive gambling, and a subscription is being raised for him, someone remarks that it will require some delicacy in breaking the matter to him, and adds, "I wonder how Fox will take it?" "Take it?" interrupts Selwyn, "why, quarterly, to be sure."

At the sale of Mr. Pelham's effects, Selwyn who is present observes thoughtfully, as he points to a silver dinner service, "Lord! How many toads have been eaten off these plates!"

He is on one occasion a passenger in a stage coach when one of his fellow travelers imagining from his appearance that he is suffering from illness keeps wearying him with good natured but constant inquiries as to the state of his health. At length to the repeated question of "How are you now, sir?" Selwyn replies, "Very well, I thank you, and I mean to continue so for the rest of the journey."

Soon after the marriage of Francis, Lord North, to his third wife, Miss Furnese, somebody remarking that it is very hot weather in which to marry so fat a bride, "Oh," replies Selwyn, "she was kept in ice for three days before the wedding."

At the glittering coronation of George III, Lady Harrington, covered with all the diamonds she can borrow, hire, or seize, and with the air of Roxana, is the finest figure at a distance. She complains to Selwyn that she is to walk with Lady Portsmouth who will have a wig and a stick. "Pho!" says George, "You will only look as if you were taken up by the constable." (She tells this everywhere thinking the reflection is on Lady Portsmouth.)

"How did you like the farce?" queries Horace Walpole in a letter. "George Selwyn says he wants to see High Life below Stairs as he is weary of Low Life above Stairs."

Hearing much talk of a sea war or a continent, Selwyn observes, "I am for a sea war and a continent *admiral*."

A young gentleman, Mr. Thomas Foley, having fled to the continent from his creditors, " 'Tis a pass-over," remarks Selwyn, "that will not be much relished by the Jews." When the same gentleman later applies to Parliament to have his father's will set aside in order that he may be able to pay his debts to the moneylenders, Selwyn adds, "The New Testament will now be more favorable to the Jews than the Old."

At the trial of the rebel lords (Kilmarnock and Balmerino), observing a Mrs. Bethel's hatchet face looking wistfully at them, "What a shame it is," remarks Selwyn, "to turn her face to the prisoners till they are condemned."

Walking once with Lord Pembroke, Selwyn is besieged by a number of young chimney sweeps, who keep asking him for money. "I have often," says he, with a bow, "heard of the sovereignty of the people. I presume your Highnesses are in court mourning?"

He dines one day in a large party when Bruce, the

celebrated Abyssinian traveler, is one of the company. In the course of the evening, Bruce entertains the party with some of the strange stories of novelty and adventure which at the time are thought little worthy of credit. When one of the company asks him what musical instruments are used in Abyssinia, Bruce hesitates for a moment and at length says— "I think I saw one lyre there." "Yes," whispers Selwyn to his next neighbor, "and there is one less since he left the country."

Selwyn makes one good and one bad House of Commons joke. Here is the good one. When his friend George Grenville, to whom Parliamentary business is of the utmost enjoyment, faints in the House, and there are loud calls from the members for ammonia and cold water, Selwyn is heard exclaiming, "Why don't you give him the Journals to smell to?"

And here is the bad one: Observing Mr. Ponsonby, Speaker of the Irish House of Commons, tossing about bank bills at a hazard table, "Look," he says, "how easily the Speaker passes the money bills."

Once, too, a certain M.P. meets Selwyn leaving the House of Commons. "What?" says he, "Is the House up?" "No," replies Selwyn sadly, "but Burke is."

He calls Fox and Pitt the Idle and the Industrious Apprentices.

On the fall of the Bedford ministry, more than one discomfited member of that government ascribes the downfall of their party mainly to the enmity which exists between the Princess Dowager and the Duchess of Bedford. "These gentlemen," says Selwyn, "put me in mind of thieves, who on their way to execution always assign their ruin to lewd women."

When Lord North goes out of office, someone asks where Keene and Williams, his confidants, are. "Sitting up with the corpse, I suppose," replies Selwyn.

One day observing Wilkes (who would undoubtedly have lost his ears had he lived in the days of the Star Chamber) listening to the reading of the King's speech, previous to its delivery from the throne, Selwyn exclaims in the words of the *Dunciad*, "May Heaven preserve the ears you lend."

Mad Lord George Gordon (who leads the riots against the Catholics and afterwards in repentance turns Jew and is circumcised) asks Selwyn whether he will return him again for the pocket borough of Ludgershall and Selwyn replies, "My constituents will not." "Oh, yes, if you recommend me they would choose me if I came from the coast of Africa," returns Gordon. "That is according to what part of the coast you came from," says Selwyn. "They certainly would if you came from the Guinea coast."

Here are some indifferent ones. Selwyn one evening at White's sees the Post Master General Sir Everard Fawkener losing a large sum of money at Picquet. Pointing to the successful player, he remarks, "See how he is robbing the mail."

When the public journals are daily containing an account of some fresh town which has conferred the freedom of its corporation in a gold box on Mr. Pitt, Selwyn proposes to the Old and New Club at Arthur's that he shall be deputed to present to Pitt the freedom of each club in a dice box.

Lady Coventry is one day exhibiting a new dress to Selwyn. It is blue, with spots of silver of the size of a shilling, and a silver trimming, and costs, says Walpole, "my lord will know what." She asks George how he likes it, and he replies, "Why, you will be change for a guinea."

Lord Pembroke is greatly interested in the Westminster Bridge in the course of construction. When one of the piers settles some sixteen inches, George sends to him to know how the bridge rested.

The cry in Ireland is against Lord Hilsborough supposing him to mediate a union between the two islands. Selwyn seeing him sit the other night between my Lady Harrington and Lord Barrington (who have a fancy for each other), remarks, "Who can say that my Lord Hilsborough is not an enemy to an union?"

King George III the year after he has been at Selwyn's house at Matson (famous for the escape of Charles I) goes mad. Selwyn upon this observes, "It is odd enough that the only two kings that visited Matson have both lost their heads."

When a Mrs. St. Jack declares that if her husband goes to America she will accompany him, Selwyn says she will make an excellent breastwork.

The Royal Duke's horses and dogs are so much to his taste that he not only has them on his buttons but also their copulations and at a dinner given to him points out the particular representations to Lady Duncannon. Selwyn says "that buttoning is worse than unbuttoning as there may be some reason for the one, but there can be none for the other."

When there is a malicious report that the eldest Tufton is to marry Dr. William Duncan, one of the King's physicians, Selwyn remarks, "How often will she repeat that line of Shakespeare—

'Wake Duncan with thy knocking: would thou couldst.'"

Sir John Day before leaving England marries Miss Ramus whose father is an old favorite of His Majesty's, upon which occasion, going to pay his compliments at St. James's, he receives the honor of knighthood. Selwyn exclaims, "By God, this is outheroding Herod. I have long heard of the extraordinary power his Majesty exercised, but until this moment could not have believed that he could turn Day into Knight and make a Lady Day at Michaelmas." (This circumstance occasions a witticism in the newspapers from its having occurred in the ninth month, September.)

Fox and his friend Richard Fitzpatrick once lodge together at Mackie's, an oilman in Piccadilly. Someone mentions this at Brooks's and says it will be the ruin of poor Mackie. "On the contrary," replies Selwyn, "so far from ruining him, they will make Mackie's fortune, for he will have the credit of having the finest pickles in his house of any man in London."

When Fox loses office, Selwyn says, "Charles, for the future, I will eat salt fish on the day you was turned out. You shall be my Charles the Martyr now [referring to Charles I], for I am tired of your great grandfather, the old one. His head can never be sewed on again, but as yours can be, I will stick to you."

And on Sir Joshua's candidature for Plympton. "He is not to be laughed at. He may very well succeed in being elected, for Sir Joshua is the ablest man I know on a canvass."

Fox is once boasting at Brooks's of the advantageous peace he has ratified with France, adding that he has at length prevailed upon the Court of Versailles to relinquish all pretensions to the gum trade in favor of Great Britain. Selwyn, who is present but apparently asleep in his chair, exclaims, "That, Charles, I am not at all surprised at, for having permitted the French to draw your teeth they would indeed, be damned fools to quarrel with you about your gums."

When Pitt's carriage is drawn in triumph past the windows of Brooks's, a sudden and furious onslaught is made upon it by a body of ruffians armed with bludgeons and the broken poles of sedan chairs. (It is rumored that more than one member of the Club quit the faro table for the purpose of taking part in the dastardly attack.) The door of the carriage is forced, and several blows are aimed at Pitt. Indeed, for some seconds the life of the minister is in considerable danger, nor is it till after a severe contest that Pitt and his relatives are enabled to effect their escape into White's. Fox is suspected as bearing a part in the assault. When a friend taxes him with it, he not only emphatically denies the truth of the charge but pleads in proof of his entire innocence that he was in bed at the time with his mistress, Mrs. Armistead, who is prepared to substantiate the fact upon oath. "Fox's vindication of himself," says Selwyn, "reminds me of the favorite defence of the rogues at the bar of the Old Bailey, who first of all plead an alibi, and then produce their concubines as their witnesses."

It is at Earl Gower's dinner table that Charles Townshend and George Selwyn once have a combat of wit, the honors at the end remaining even. After the party breaks up, Charles carries George in his chariot to the door of White's. "Good night," cries Charles as they part. "Good night," replies Selwyn, "and 'member this (hic) is the first (hic) set down you have given me tonight."

As time passes Walpole records fewer and fewer of Selwyn's witticisms for the very good reason that Selwyn grows wiser and graver and sadder even as he grows older. He has little inclination to laugh and joke and cut capers. His mode passes too, and why record the bon mots of a demoded person even if he be your dearest friend. But amongst Selwyn's letters in later years, we find a wintry gleam of humor here and there. The sun comes out and shines uncertainly for a moment, and then the clouds roll up again and there is nothing but gloom.

He recommends his butcher to Lord Carlisle with the remark—"So much for that, and more it is not meat for me to say."

Something better is his description of a certain engraving which he sees in a shop in St. James's Street. "His design is ingenious; it is the story of Pharaoh's daughter finding Moses in the bulrushes . . . I would have a pendant to it, and that should be of Pharaoh's sons where might be introduced a good many of our friends and acquaintances from the other side of the street."

Selwyn is an inveterate punster, but his wit is not like Chesterfield's, "all puns." Feeble as it is at times, it is not so feeble as that. There is humor in his reference to a certain invitation to dinner. "It was to meet Mr. Pitt and to eat a turtle: *quelle chère!* The turtle I should have liked, but how Mr. Pitt is to be dressed I cannot tell . . . You will not believe it perhaps, but a minister of any description, although served up in his great shell of power, and all his green fat about him, is to me a dish by no means relishing, and I never knew but one in my life I could pass an hour with pleasantly, which was Lord Holland."

Besides George has good common sense. "The endeavor to prove too much has made more atheists than any book wrote on purpose to establish Infidelity . . . I wish a man to satisfy me about his morals, without which his talking of his honour is a jest. When his morals are unimpeached, I will take his Religion as I find it." Again, speaking of young Frederick Howard, Earl of Carlisle, he says: "I hope he will, besides being a very moral and honorable man, be a good Christian, but not a solemn one, qui rendrait sa piété suspecte."

"His (God's) ways," writes Selwyn, "are inscrutable, and yet there is not one, from his grace of Canterbury to the lowest fish woman in St. James's Market who is not constantly accounting for everything He does."

George scourges folly and pretension. One morning when he is at the home of Old Q, a newly appointed Commissioner of Taxes makes his appearance. This man is in a tumult of joy at his preferment. But though it is to the Duke he is primarily indebted for his good fortune, he hardly thanks him and assumes several consequential airs, thinking he is now as great a man as the Duke himself.

"So, Mr. Commissioner," says Selwyn, "you will excuse me, sir, I forget your name—you are at length installed, I find." (The word "installed" conveys an awkward idea, for the new Commissioner's grandfather was a stable boy.)

"Why, sir," replies the other. "If you mean to say that I am at length appointed, I have the pleasure to inform you that the business is settled. Yes, I am appointed and though our noble friend, the Duke here, did oblige me with letters to the Minister, yet these letters were of no use, and I was positively promoted to the office without knowing a syllable about the matter, or even taking a single step in it."

"What, not a single step?" cries George.

"No, not one, upon my honor," replies the new fledged placeman. "Egad, sir, I did not walk a foot out of my way for it."

"And egad, sir!" retorts Selwyn, "you never before uttered half so much truth in so few words. Reptiles, sir, can neither walk nor take steps—nature ordains they should creep."

But George has all the snobbish ways of an English gentleman of his set. Happening to be at Bath when it is nearly empty, he is induced, for the mere purpose of killing time, to cultivate the acquaintance of an elderly gentleman he is in the habit of meeting in the Rooms. In the height of the following season he encounters his old associate in St. James's Street. He endeavors to pass unnoticed but in vain. "What! do you not recollect me?" exclaims the indignant provincial. "I recollect you perfectly," replies Selwyn, "and when I next go to Bath, I shall be most happy to become acquainted with you again."

Probably Selwyn's last recorded bon mot is that which he scribbles upon a letter to his niece Mary Townshend. "I am sorry to put you to this expence," he writes, "but I hope at the Resurrection to repay you in franks."

CHAPTER 11

THE AMATEUR

GEORGE SELWYN HAS A MOST EXTRAORDI-
nary passion for coffins and corpses and executions. Not
only is he a constant frequenter of Tyburn Tree and the
dead house, but the details of crime, the private history of
the criminal, his demeanor at his trial, in the dungeon,
and on the scaffold, and the state of his feelings in the hour
of death are to him matters of the deepest interest.

"You know," writes Horace Walpole to Montagu,
"George never thinks but à la tête tranchée; he came to
town t'other day to have a tooth drawn and told the man
that he would drop his handkerchief for the signal."

Lord Holland is always poking fun at George on this
subject. "You saw Mr. Delmé the night before he shot himself," he writes, "and I suppose you took care to see him
the night after." Shortly before his lordship's death, when
he is told that Selwyn has called to inquire after his health,
"The next time Mr. Selwyn calls," he says, "show him up.
If I am alive, I shall be delighted to see him, and if I am
dead, he will be glad to see me."

Once when walking in Westminster Abbey with Lord
Abergavenny, he meets the man who shows the tombs. "Oh,
your servant, Mr. Selwyn, I expected to have seen you here
the other day when the old Duke of Richmond's body was
taken up."

He says to Walpole, "Arthur Moore has his coffin
chained to his whore's." "Lord!" says Horry, "how do you
know?" "Why, I saw them the other day in a vault at St.
Giles's."

Thus Gilly Williams: "Almost forgot to tell you that the day I left you I rode near ten miles on my way home with the Ordinary of Gloucester and have several anecdotes of the late burnings and hangings which I have reserved for your private ear. I do not know whether he was sensible you had a partiality for his profession, but he expressed the greatest regard for you, and I am sure you may command his service."

And the first Marquis Townshend writes: "To my well-beloved friend and companion, George Selwyn, from my cell at Dundee . . . I know you will not dislike this style which gives my epistle the air of a malefactor's confession."

On one occasion at court when the King is about to knight an ambitious squire, Selwyn withdraws and goes away. The King afterwards in his closet expresses his astonishment to the Groom-in-waiting that Mr. Selwyn should not have wished to stay to see the ceremony of his making the new knight, observing, "It looked so like an execution that I took it for granted Mr. Selwyn would stay to see it."

According to Walpole, Selwyn has a great hand in bringing a footman of Lord Dacre to confess that he murdered the butler. The young fellow is cool. As he is writing his confession, "I murd—," he stops and asks, "How do you spell murdered?"

Here is a story characteristic of Selwyn, though probably apocryphal. The execution of Damiens, the celebrated assassin (he is not exactly an assassin: he only gives his Majesty, King Louis XV, a slight wound with a pen knife) so excites Selwyn's curiosity that he goes over to Paris a month before that event to purchase in time a convenient place to behold so novel a spectacle. When the day arrives, every window and balcony in the Place de Grève is filled with eager spectators and elegantly dressed ladies of the Court who play cards to while away the moments of waiting. (During the Renaissance, this very Place de Grève saw coiners of false money boiled alive at pigmarket, robbers and assassins broken on the wheel and left to linger in slow agony, Lutherans treated like vermin.) The horrid ceremony begins. Witness, messieurs the patricians of France, the last moments of Damiens who expires under the most acute tortures. They lacerate his flesh with red hot pincers and pour boiling oil and boiling lead into the wounds. After this preliminary pleasantry they tie his limbs separately to four horses and the horses tear him to pieces. The remains are then burned and the ashes scattered to the winds. One of the fine tender ladies present at the execution, has her sensibilities aroused by the difficulty which the horses have in tearing Damiens to pieces. "Oh, the poor horses!" says she, "how sorry I am for them!"

George has taken his stand, dressed in a plain brown bob wig and a plain suit of broadcloth, an attire which at that time of the day evidently points him out as a person in the humbler walks of life. When the ceremony commences, Selwyn, from his dress and the deep interest and sympathy which he shows upon this occasion, so attracts the notice of a French nobleman that coming round to him on the scaffold, and slapping him on the shoulder, he exclaims: "Eh, bien, monsieur, êtes vous arrivé pour voir ce spectacle?" "Oui, monsieur," replies Selwyn. "Vous êtes bourreau?" (a hangman?). "Non, non, monsieur, je n'ai cette honneur; je ne suis qu'un amateur."

CHAPTER 12

TYBURN TREE

LONDON IS A CITY OF GALLOWS. PASS UP the Thames, there are gibbets along its banks. Land at Execution Dock, and a gallows is being erected for the punishment of some offender. Enter from the West by Oxford Street, and there is the gallows tree at Tyburn. Cross any of the heaths, commons, or forests near London, and you will be startled by the creaking and clanking of chains from which some gibbeted highwayman or footpad is dropping piecemeal. Nay, the gallows is set up before your own door in every part of the town.

There are more than two hundred crimes punishable with death. If a man breaks down a fish pond where fish may be lost, or cuts down trees in an avenue or garden, he is hanged. If he falsely swears, pretends to be a Greenwich pensioner, he is hanged. If he steals 5s. from a shop, or picks pockets above 1s., or robs a dwelling house of 40s., he is hanged. Juries are more merciful than the law. Thus when Jane Adams is indicted for stealing a Crape Gown and Petticoat, value 40s., a Camblet Cloak, value 20s., a Crimson Poplin Cloak, value 20s., and other things (in a dwelling house), the Jury in a very gentlemanly way finds her guilty to the value of 39s. only, and so she is transported and not hanged, and Catherine Delavan who steals 9 guineas and 11s. is found guilty to the value of 4s., 10d.

Hanging days are festive occasions. At an early hour in the morning thousands of mechanics and others who on the previous night have agreed upon their making "a day of it," meet at their proposed stations. It is common throughout the whole metropolis for master coachmakers, framemakers,

[138]

tailors, shoemakers, etc., who engage to complete orders within a given time, to bear in mind to observe to their customers, "That will be a hanging day, madam, and my men will not be at work."

Young bucks give execution breakfasts to their friends and adjourn afterwards to the vicinity of the Marble Arch and watch the last scene in the life of some wretched criminal. Parties are formed at the coffee houses and taverns among the fine gentlemen who frequent them. Foote, the comedian, speaking of this class or coterie, designates them "The Hanging Committee."

A much respected nobleman attends at the Tower disguised as a barber to perform the operation of shaving one of the Scottish rebel lords during their confinement a few days previous to their being beheaded on Tower Hill. Another nobleman, a great patron of the arts, is present by favor at most of the private examinations in Bow Street and frequently goes to Newgate in disguise to see the extraordinary characters under sentence of death. It is said of this nobleman from his attending the condemned sermons at Newgate that though he is not remarkable for his attendance at church, yet he is a constant chapel-goer.

A mob early in the morning surrounds the felon's gate at Newgate to see the malefactors brought forth. Other crowds appear at various stations. The throng is occasionally so great as entirely to fill Oxford Street from house to house on both sides of the way. Some are at the windows, some upon wagons, thousands standing and jostling one another in the surrounding fields, shouting, "Well done, little coiner. What a brave fellow he is!" etc. When the cart passes, tens of thousands of hats forming a black mass are taken off simultaneously. Friends await the malefactor's coming in different places, some holding a pot of beer in their hands, others a measure of gin to give him, for which purpose the cart halts. Others throw oranges and apples to him. A number of constables walk beside the cart or ride after it. The journey lasts half an hour.

There are stands where ale is dispensed, stalls for gingerbread, pies, nuts, and apples. Ballad mongers bawl the latest song of the criminal, boys cry the last dying speech and confession. (Many a doomed man going to Tyburn purchases a penny biography of himself and reads what he has said at the last moment before his last moment is reached.) They all use the same words and the same tone in chanting them. "Here's all the right and true last dying speech and confession, birth, parentage, and education, life, character, and behavior of the three or six or ten unfortunate malefactors who were executed this morning at Tyburn—also a copy of the letter which the noted——sent to his sweetheart or wife the night before his execution." Some blow horns during the morning and indeed till the middle of the afternoon. The stories are the same according to the Ordinaries—"Departing from the early paths of Virtue and Integrity, where the Flowers of Innocency may be pluckt, he stray'd among the Profligate and the Abandon'd and became a High-way Man." Or "he became a Flash Cull and set up half a dozen Doxies of his own, who empty'd his Pockets as soon as he filled 'em."

Around the gallows at Tyburn there are placed a number of boxes (Mother Proctor's pews), a temporary erection of seats in tiers which are raised upon a plot of ground belonging to this widow of a cowkeeper who lets them out to spectators at so many shillings per head, according to the position of the applicant and the notoriety of the criminal. At the execution of Earl Ferrers in 1766 the woman receives for her sittings a sum amounting to more than five hundred pounds.

Such enormous crowds press to see the famous highwayman Jack Shepherd in jail before he pays the extreme penalty that the turnkeys make £200 for showing him while Dr. Dodd is exhibited at two shillings a head for two hours before being taken to the gallows.

Sometimes the spectators themselves are the actors as in the case of Mrs. Brownrigg when the mob calls out to the Ordinary to "pray for her damnation as such a fiend ought not to be saved." And of Williamson, who is hanged at Moorfields for starving his wife to death and who seems apprehensive of being torn to pieces and hastens the executioner to perform his office.

When the appetite of the mob is disappointed, they are positively furious. A mariner is condemned for the murder of his wife, but on the night preceding his execution he finds the means to poison himself in his cell whereupon the people are so incensed at his hardened wickedness that they dig up his body after it has been buried in a cross road, drag his viscera about the highway, pick his eyes out and break almost all his bones, after which his body is taken and buried in a very deep grave near the gallows. Again, when having paid their money to see Dr. Henesey hanged, he is not hanged but reprieved instead, enraged at this shameful breach of faith, they wreck the seats and depart in a by no means appeased ill humor.

Fashionable men will sooner lose their night's rest than miss seeing the criminals turned off. And if there are no more than six or seven of them, they will come grumbling and disappointed home to breakfast, complaining that there were hardly any fellows hanged this morning.

"How can you live in such a dull spot?" asks a friend of one who has recently moved out of town to the rival solitude of Westbourne Grove. "Dull?" cries the fair lady. "Dull? Why we have hangings every week at Tyburn just across the fields." (But the lady exaggerates. Executions take place every six weeks.)

The prisoner is perfectly at liberty to order anything that he happens to fancy or desire for his last supper, and the Ordinary of the prison is generally expected to be present and to partake of the repast by way of keeping up his spirits until he has shuffled off the mortal coil. Once a runner calls to another and orders a chicken boiled for Rice's supper. "But," says he to the cook, "you need not be curious about the sauce, for he is to be hanged tomorrow." "That is true," says the other, "but the Ordinary sups with him, and you know he is a devil of a fellow for butter."

On the eve of an execution it is the custom for the watchman to proceed under the walls of Newgate and as midnight sounds slowly from the belfry of St. Sepulchre to repeat the following verses—

> All you that in the condemned hold do lie,
> Prepare you, for tomorrow you shall die,
> Watch all, and pray, the hour is drawing near,
> When you before the Almighty must appear.
> Examine well yourselves, in time repent,
> That you may not to eternal flames be sent;
> Forswear your sins, trust in Christ's merit,
> That Heavenly Grace you may inherit;
> And when St. Sepulchre's bell tomorrow tolls,
> The Lord have mercy on your souls.

"Pa—a—st twelve—and a sho—o—wery morning."

It is to be feared the hardened criminals do not altogether relish being awakened from their sleep. Of another sort is Sarah Malcolm who dies for the murder of her mistress. "D'ye hear, Mr. Bellman?" she shouts out from her window. "Call for a pint of wine, and I'll throw you a shilling to pay for it."

It is the fashion to die merrily. The day appointed by law for the thief's shame is a day of glory in his own opinion. His procession to Tyburn and his last moments there are all triumphant. He is arrayed in fine and gaudy apparel, wears white gloves and often carries a huge nosegay of flowers given by his friends or relatives. Thus John Matthews, convicted for high treason, wears a rich Persian silk and "everything as befits a gentleman" and Charles Ratcliffe, who suffers decapitation on Tower Hill, is attired in scarlet, faced with black velvet, trimmed with gold. When John Ran (Sixteen fingered Jack), coachman to Lord Sandwich, convicted of robbing the chaplain to the Princess Amelia of 18d. in money and his watch in Gunnersbury Lane, proceeds to his execution at Tyburn, he wears a bright pea green coat with an immense nosegay, and his nankeen small clothes are tied with sixteen strings at each knee. John Docke Rouvelett, alias Romney, is dressed in a blue coat with metal buttons, striped trousers, green slippers, and a fur cap, while Joseph Wall wears a mixed col-

[142]

ored loose coat, with a black collar, swan down waistcoat, blue pantaloons, and white silk stockings. Sometimes the girls dress in white with great silk scarfs, and carry baskets full of flowers and oranges, scattering these favors all the way they go.

Criminals consider it a mark of reproach to die with their shoes on. They kick them off to the spectators repeating the common saying: "Our parents often said we should die on a fish day, and with our shoes on, but though the former part of their prediction is true, yet we will make them all liars in the latter part of it."

When the cavalcade reaches Holborn, it halts at a tavern, the Bowl, where the malefactor is allowed to drink a parting cup. All the good plucked ones are not only expected to take their ale but to make a joke about coming back to pay for it. Some surly ruffian may be moved, once in a while, to draw the bowl, fling it empty at the landlord, and bid him "wait for payment till he meets him in Hell." But that is ungentlemanly and the assignation not certain of fulfillment.

On his arrival at Tyburn the executioner stops the cart under one of the cross beams of the gibbet and fastens to that ill favored beam one end of the rope, while the other is round the wretch's neck. This done he gives the horse a lash with his whip, away goes the cart, and there swings my gentleman kicking in the air. Friends make haste to hang on by his legs so as to bring his sufferings to a speedy end.

> As clever Tom Clinch while the rabble was bawling,
> Rode stately through Holborn to die at his calling,
> His waistcoat and stockings and breeches were white,
> His cap had a new cherry ribbon to tie't.
> The maids to the doors and the balconies ran,
> And said, 'Lackaday, he's a proper young man!'
> And as from the windows the ladies he spied,
> Like a beau in a box, he bowed low on each side.
> And when his last speech the loud hawkers did cry,
> He swore from the cart, 'It's all a damn'd lie!'
> The hangman for pardon fell down on his knee;
> Tom gave him a kick in the guts for his fee:

Then said, 'I must speak to the people a little,
But I'll see you all damn'd before I will whittle!
My honest friend Wild (may he long hold his place)
He lengthen'd my life with a whole year of grace.
Take courage, dear comrades, and be not afraid,
Nor slip this occasion to follow your trade;
My conscience is clear, and my spirits are calm,
And thus I go off, without prayer book or psalm;
Then follow the practice of clever Tom Clinch,
Who hung like a hero and never would flinch.'

When one Dick Hughes, a housebreaker, is going to execution, his wife meets him at St. Giles's Pound where the cart stopping, she steps up to him and whispers in his ear—"My dear, who must find the rope that's to hang you, we or the Sheriff?" Her husband replies, "The Sheriff, honey, for who's obliged to find him tools to do his work?" "Ah," replies his wife, "I wish I had known so much before, 'twould have saved me two pence, for I have been and bought one already." "Well, well," says Dick again, "perhaps it mayn't be lost, for it may serve a second husband." "Yes," quoth his wife, "if I've any luck in good husbands, so it may."

Tom Rowland, highwayman, whilst he lies under sentence of death, is very refractory and so abominably wicked that the very morning on which he dies, a common woman coming to visit him in the Press Yard, he has the unparalleled audaciousness to act carnally with her and glories in the sin as he is going to his execution.

Roderick Audrey departs to the tune of a penitential psalm, being no more than sixteen years of age. He goes very decently to the gallows, being in a white waistcoat, clean napkin, white gloves, and having an orange in one hand.

As Will Ogden and Tom Reynolds, housebreakers and highwaymen, are riding to the place of execution, Ogden flings a handful of money out of the cart to the people saying, "Gentlemen, here is poor Will's farewell." And when he is being turned off, he gives two extraordinary jerks with his legs, which is much admired by all the spectators.

Zachary Clare, instead of preparing for his end, does nothing but sing, swear, play at cards, and get drunk from morning till night.

Thomas Reeves, footpad, behaves in a most hardened manner, affects to despise death, and says he believes he may go to Heaven from the gallows as safely as from his bed.

James Farr, William Sparry, and William Biddle, forgers, all behave penitently and with resolution but with resignation. Farr fixes the knot of the halter under his left ear and then exclaims, "I have but a few moments to stay in this world. I have found it a wicked world—a very wicked world indeed!" The other two malefactors decline to address the populace and are immediately launched into eternity.

The notorious Captain Kidd the pirate goes to his death drunk which as the Ordinary of Newgate observes, "so decomposed his mind that now it was in a very bad frame." The rope breaks and he falls to the ground, which somewhat sobers him, and before he is finally strangled, he listens to the chaplain's ministrations.

A previous chaplain is roughly treated by one Tom Cox, a highwayman, for before he is turned off, Mr. Smith, the Ordinary, desiring him to join with the rest of his fellow sufferers in prayers, he swears a great oath to the contrary and kicks him and the hangman off the cart.

Of those executed there are Henry Berthand, Elizabeth Burrell, Martha Crowten, Charlotte Goodall, Thomas Cludenboul, John Lafee. They all behave very penitent.

But the Reverend Thomas Hunter does not. He closes his life with the following shocking declaration. "There is no God—I do not believe there is any, or if there is, I hold him in defiance."

On the road to the gallows, William Alcock sings part of the old song of Robin Hood, adding to each verse the chorus of derry down, etc. At intervals he swears, kicks, and spurns at any person who touches the cart. On being told by a person in the cart with him, who wishes thus late to reclaim him, that he had much better read and repent than so vilely swear and sing, he strikes the book out of the man's hands, damns the spectators, and calls for wine. During the singing of psalms and the reading of prayers, he is employed in talking and nodding to his acquaintances, kicks his shoes off, and with his last words inveighs against the injustice of his cause.

Jonathan Wild, a whimsical fellow to the last, picks the pocket of the Ordinary on the way. The article stolen is a corkscrew, and Wild dies with the eloquent trophy in his hand.

"Monday: Five condemned malefactors executed at Tyburn, viz., Kiffe and Wilson for footpadding, in the first cart; Macdonald and Lartin, alias Pup's Nose, for horse stealing, in the second cart, and Morpeth for footpadding in a coach." The two in the second cart behave very audaciously, calling out to the populace and laughing aloud several times, though it cannot be said they are in liquor, the order of the Lord Mayor and Alderman having been strictly observed by the Keepers.

"Several malefactors executed at Tyburn, namely William Lewis, Patrick Gaffney, Edward Togwell, Peter Matthews, Isaac Dennis, and William Phillips, alias Clark." They all behave decently and with seeming penitence, except Lewis, who tosses up his shoes among the populace as soon as he gets into the cart and uses several idle expressions.

Richard Haywood is the most hardened sinner of all. Before he departs from Newgate he calls in a loud voice to the prisoners who are looking through the upper windows at him, "Farewell, my lads, I am just going off. God bless you." "We are sorry for you," reply the prisoners. "I want none of your pity," rejoins Haywood. "Keep your snivelling till it be your own turn." Immediately upon his arrival at Tyburn he runs up the scaffold with great agility, and in a loud laugh, gives the mob three cheers, introducing each with a Hip, ho! While the cord is being prepared, he continues hallooing to the mob, "How are you? Well, here goes," and kicks off his shoes among the spectators, many of whom are deeply affected by the obduracy of his conduct.

There is William Maw, hardened criminal also, who in the evening of his life is at last committed to Newgate and indicted for extracting from a house eight pewter plates with other goods, from another house, twenty-four pairs of leather clogs, robbing a gentleman upon the highway of a watch, five gold rings, some money and goods, robbing upon the highway a woman of three shillings and six pence and a gentleman of some money and goods. For these different crimes he is sentenced to suffer death.

A person who thinks Maw already dead and buried (he was convicted but not punished years before), seeing him in the cart, is struck with amazement, and calls thus out to him, "Oh, dear Mr. Maw, I really thought you had been dead and buried five years ago." "Why, so I was," replies Maw, "but don't you know that we must all rise again at the day of *judgment*." "Yes," replies his acquaintance, "but the day of *judgment* is not come yet." "Ay, but it is," says Maw, "and passed too, twelve days ago at the Old Bailey, where, I am sure, 'twas the judgment of the Court to send me to be hanged now." So his friend wishing him a good journey and a safe return, they part.

Arthur Bailey shows the greatest firmness on his way to the fatal tree. When under the gallows he joins fervently in prayer and addresses the spectators audibly—"I hope you will all take warning," and holding a prayer book in his hand, "I beg you to look often into this book, and you will not come to shame. Be sure to be honest, and not covet money, cursed money, and particularly money that is not your own." He is then "deprived of his mortal state of existence, dying without a struggle."

Thomas Simpson declares on the scaffold that while he continued to rob on the highway, he prayed at the same time that God would forgive it, and that "it eas'd his mind something." And it is added that though he had wounded several persons, yet he affirmed he never murdered any, which, to be sure, was very forbearing and obliging of him.

Thomas Turlis, hangman, engages in a terrific scuffle with an Amazonian Irishwoman, Hannah Dagoe, who is one of his clientele at Tyburn. When the cart is drawn beneath the gallows, she tears off the rope that binds her arms and throws her gloves, bonnet, and cardinal—which are the hangman's perquisites—to a friend in the crowd. Tom promptly pinions her again, but once more she gets loose from her cords and struggles fiercely when he makes another effort to fasten her, cursing him in the foulest language, daring him to hang her. Still the staunch Thomas refuses to be intimidated. Although she deals him a blow which almost knocks him out of the cart, he closes with her again. The rope that has pinioned her is lost in the fight, but he snatches off his garters and succeeds at last in binding her wrists. Daunted now by the implacable executioner, Hannah Dagoe makes no further resistance. Yet when the noose is slipped around her neck, she hurls herself out of the cart in a fit of rage before the signal is given, dying without a struggle.

Nevertheless, John Rice, one of her companions on the way to Tyburn, proves a gentle and penitent criminal. He wins the crowd by his pious conduct and there is much weeping. It is said that he is the only stockbroker who was ever hanged. (Perhaps Providence does not always attend to business.)

Mary Blandy on ascending the steps of the ladder asks her executioner not to hang her high for the sake of decency.

The system of strangulation in vogue is favorable to the recovery of life. One John Smith condemned for housebreaking is carried from Newgate to Tyburn to be executed. Some minutes after he is turned off, a reprieve comes for him and being immediately cut down, he soon recovers to the admiration of all the spectators and is brought back to Newgate. Ann Green, who is executed near Oxford for the murder of her child, is cut down and carried according to custom to the anatomy school in Christ Church to form the subject of a lecture. When the corpse is unpacked, it is observed to display signs of vitality and under the care and skill of the anatomy reader and his assistant is restored once more to life.

Margaret Dickson is still another case. After she is hanged, her body is cut down and delivered to her friends who put it in a coffin and send it in a cart to be buried at her native place. But the weather being sultry, the persons who have her body in their care, stop to drink at a wayside tavern. While they are refreshing themselves, one of them perceives the lid of the coffin move, and uncovering it, the woman immediately sits up. Most of the spectators run off in fright. It happens that a person who is then drinking in the public house remembers to bleed her. In about an hour afterwards she is put to bed, and by the following morning she is so far recovered as to be able to walk to her own house. By the Scottish law, a person against whom the judgment of the court has been executed can suffer no more in the future but is thenceforward totally exculpated. And it is likewise held that a marriage is dissolved by the execution of a convicted party. Mrs. Dickson having been thus convicted and executed, the King's advocate can prosecute no further, but he files a bill in the High Court against the sheriff for omitting to fulfil the law. The husband of the revived convict marries her publicly a few days after, and she constantly denies that she has been guilty of the alleged crime. She lives about thirty years after this.

"Executed at Tyburn. Elizabeth Banks for stripping a child. Catherine Conway for forging a seaman's ticket, and Margaret Harvey for robbing her master." They are all drunk, contrary to the express order of the Court of Aldermen gainst serving them with strong liquor.

At Oxford Street: A whole cartful of young girls in dresses of various colors on their way to be executed at Tyburn after having been condemned for burning some houses during the Gordon riots.

A criminal convicted of returning from transportation and afterwards executed, addresses himself to the populace and tells them he wishes they would carry his body and lay it at the door of Mr. Parker, a butcher in the Minories, who it seems is the principal evidence against him. Which being accordingly done, the mob behaves so riotously before the man's house that it is no easy matter to disperse them.

Du Vall, the cavalier thief who foots it on Hounslow Heath in a graceful coranto with one of his victims, is executed at Tyburn in spite of many efforts to secure a reprieve. After the hanging, he is given a lying-in-state at a tavern in St. Giles's, the room being draped in black, relieved with escutcheons. Eight candles burn around him and eight tall gentlemen in long cloaks keep watch. Many ladies of fashion and beauty go masked, with tear stained faces, to see him. He is given a splendid funeral in St. Paul's Church, Covent Garden, and a handsome stone decorated with heraldic achievements, is placed over his grave, and on it this epitaph—

> Here lies Du Vall: Reader, if Male thou art,
> Look to thy purse; if Female to thy heart.
> Much havoc has he made of both; for all
> Men he made stand, and woman he made fall.
> The second conqueror of the Norman race,
> Knights to his arms did yield and Ladies to his face.
> Old Tyburn's Glory; England's illustrious thief,
> Du Vall, the Ladies' Joy, Du Vall, the Ladies' Grief.

Earl Ferrers, condemned by his peers to be hanged for killing his steward in a fit of frenzy, dies in style. The Ferrers landau in which the Earl is seated dressed in a white satin wedding suit, is drawn by six horses and attended by liveried servants. High constables surround the coach, and there are besides two parties of Grenadier Guards. My lord is provided with black silk cushions to kneel upon during prayers and a black silk sash to bind his arms.

Some of the brightest eyes are in tears for tall, handsome Jemmy McLean, the famous highwayman, who has a lodging in St. James's Street when in town and is well known as a frequenter of Button's Coffee House. His gentlemanly deportment is extolled, and a sort of admiration kindles for him in the public mind. His crimes are gaily recounted by those who do not suffer from them. The ladies take great notice of him while he is in Newgate and keep him well supplied with money. He finally makes his exit at Tyburn with the brief prayer, "Oh, God, forgive my enemies, bless my friends, and receive my soul."

After his death broadside and ballads celebrate his exploits.

Ye Smarts and ye Jemmies, ye Ramillie Beaux,
With golden cocked hats, and with silver laced clothes,
Who by wit and invention your pockets maintain,
Come pity the fate of poor Jemmy Maclaine,
        Derry down derry, etc.
He robb'd folks genteely, he robb'd with an air,
He robb'd them so well that he always took care
My Lord was not hurt and my Lady not frighted,
And instead of being hanged, he deserved to be Knighted!
        Derry down derry, &c.

Hundreds come to see Valentine Carrick, son of a retired jeweler, and the Newgate turnkeys reap a rich harvest in fees paid. Such an extraordinary rush impresses even the prisoner who thinks it very stupid. "Good folks," he exclaims, "you pay for seeing me now, but if you had suspended your curiosity till I went to Tyburn, you might have seen me for nothing."

When he comes to the place of execution, he smiles upon and makes his bows to all he knows. Instead of praying with the rest of the criminals, he employs his time in giggling, taking snuff, and making apish motions to divert himself and the mob. When prayers are over, he tells them the Sheriffs have made an order that no surgeon shall touch his body. The Ordinary advises him to consider whither he is going, to which he answers that being a Roman Catholic he has received no sacrament and prepared for death in his own way. And then giving himself some pretty and genteel airs in adjusting the halter about his neck, the cart is drawn away.

William Hawkes, one of the Flying Highwaymen, is greatly honored. He has been condemned on the paltry charge of stealing a small quantity of linen (quite beneath a person of his skill) and like many another fine fellow, receives distinguished company as he lies in his dungeon cell. Rank and fashion, wit and beauty, enliven his days and make them pass cheerfully enough. Among others who call upon him is the eccentric Colonel George Hanger, afterwards Lord Coleraine, who offers him a handsome price for his horse. "Sir," Hawkes warmly responds, "I am as much obliged to you for your proposal as for your visit. But," he adds in a low tone, "the mare won't suit you, perhaps, if you want her for the Road. It is not every man that can get her up to a carriage." Hanger is so exceedingly pleased with this little trait of professional sympathy that he advances Hawkes £50 to enable him to offer bribes for his escape. But all efforts in that direction failing, the highwayman later returns the money with his grateful thanks.

On the morning of his execution while his irons are being knocked off, one of his acquaintances addresses him thus: "How do you do, Billy? Will you have some flowers?" "I am pretty well, I thank you," Hawkes says. "How is Harry Wright? [One of the turnkeys of Tothillfields, Bridewell]. He has been ill of late, I hear." And then while his friend holds the nosegay, he picks out a flower and with great composure places it in a buttonhole of his coat. . . . He is buried in Stepney Churchyard with the following epitaph—"Farewell, vain world, I've had enough of thee."

There is the famous housebreaker John Hall, a chimney sweep, who has his biography written by no less a person than Paul Lorrain, the Ordinary of Newgate. He has a long poetical elegy composed on him, after the fashion of the times—and an epitaph:

Here lies Hall's clay	At Judgment day,	I'd better say,
Thus swept away;	He'd make essay	Here lies Jack Hall
If bolt or key	To get away:	And that is all.
Obliged his Stay	Be't as it may.	

John Smith behaves himself with great resolution, professes himself extremely sorry for his vices and the bloody act which brings him to his shameful end. He especially recommends to all who speak to him to avoid the snares and delusions of lewd women. At the place of execution he delivers the following paper—

Paper Delivered by John Smith at the Place of Execution, I was born of honest parents, bred to the sea, and lived honest till I was led aside by lewd women. I then robbed on ships and never robbed on shore. I had no design to kill the woman who jilted me and left me for another man but only to terrify her, for I could have shot her when the loaded pistol was at her breast, but I curbed my passion and only threw a candlestick at her. I confess my cruelty towards my wife, who is a woman too good for me, but I was at first forced to forsake her for debt, and go to sea. I hope in God none will reflect on her, or my poor innocent children who could not help my sad passion and more sad death. Written by me,

John Smith.

Ebenezer Elliston, a notorious Irish thief, says: "Good people, fare you well. Bad as I am, I leave many worse behind me, and I hope you shall see me die like a man, though a death contrary."

Peter M'Cloud, aged sixteen, on the morning of his death, receives the sacrament in company with the other malefactors who are to suffer with him. When he arrives at the fatal tree, he requests a person to beg that his mother will not unreasonably grieve at his death, as he has hopes that he is departing to the regions of eternal glory.

James O'Bryan, highwayman and street robber, is positively tender, sending his sister verses two days before his execution—

> My loving tender sister dear,
> From you I soon must part, I fear,
> Think not on my wretched state,
> Nor grieve for my unhappy fate,
> But serve the Lord with all your heart,
> And from you He'll never part,
> When I am dead and in my tomb,
> For my poor soul I hope there's room,
> In Heaven with God alone on high
> I hope to live eternally.

Just before Matthias Brindsen, wife killer, is launched into eternity, he desires the Ordinary to read a declaration he has written. "I was born of kind parents who gave me learning: I went apprentice to a fine drawer. I had often jars, which might increase a natural waspishness in my temper. I fell in love with Hannah, my last wife, and after much difficulty won her, she having five suitors courting her at the same time. We had ten children (half of them dead), and I believe we loved each other dearly, but often quarreled and fought. Pray, good people, mind I had no malice against her, nor thought to kill her two minutes before the deed, but I designed only to make her obey me thoroughly, which the scripture says all wives should do. This I thought I had done, when I cut her scull on Monday, but she was the same again on Tuesday.

"Good people, I request you to observe that though the world has spitefully given out that I carnally and incestuously lay with my eldest daughter, I here solemnly declare, as I am entering into the presence of God, I never knew whether she was man or woman, since she was a babe. I have often taken her in my arms, often kissed her, sometimes given her a cake or a pie when she did any particular service beyond what came to her share, but never lay with her, or carnally knew her, much less had a child by her. But when a man is in calamity and is hated like me, the women will make surmises into certainties. Good Christians, pray for me, I deserve death, I am willing to die, for though my sins are great, God's mercies are greater."

Nothing is so neat as the last remark of an atrocious villain, Tom Austin, who when he stands with the rope round his neck, replies to the Ordinary's query if he has anything to say before he dies—"Nothing, only there's a woman yonder with some curds and whey, and I wish I could have a pennyworth of them before I am hanged, because I don't know when I shall see any again."

CHAPTER 13

A MURDERER, A HUMBUG,
AND THREE REBELS

EVERYBODY HAS HEARD THE STORY OF PAR-
son Hackman and Miss Ray. This lady is the maîtresse en
titre of Lord Sandwich. He first sees her behind the counter
of a milliner's shop in Tavistock Street when he is making
purchases there. She is the daughter of a laboring man
living at Elstree, according to one account, although another
makes her father a staymaker in the Strand. The point is
not material. All that concerns us here is that Sandwich,
who is old enough to be her father, seduces her from her
employment and finally takes her to his place, Hinchinbrook, where to the distress of Lady Sandwich, he establishes her as his mistress. Even Bishops with their wives sit
unblushingly through the musical performances with which
the Earl is in the habit of entertaining his neighbors, perfectly aware that the unrivalled songstress to whom they
listen is the paramour of their host and the mother of his
nine children. She has an exquisite taste and ear for music
which her noble lover spares no cost in cultivating. She is
the favorite pupil of Giardini. Large sums of money are
offered to tempt her to sing on the stage. Her performances
in the private theatricals and oratorios at Hinchinbrook excite never failing admiration. Her execution of the fine air
in *Jephthah*, "Brighter scenes I seek above," approaches perfection.

At one of the balls she is introduced to Lieutenant
James Hackman, who instantly falls head over heels in love
with her. He has the most honorable intentions and tries all

his powers of persuasion to induce her to leave Lord Sandwich and to marry him. All sorts of reasons are given for the young lady's refusal—she does not choose to carry a knapsack. He exchanges the army for the cloth, but the cloth has no greater power to change Miss Ray's feeling than the epaulettes, and the Reverend James Hackman, now become Vicar of Wyverton in Norfolk, grows daily more desperate. At last finding all appeals useless and life without Miss Martha Ray a desert, he determines to commit suicide.

"Last night," begins one of the journals next morning, "the following melancholy fate terminated the existence of the beautiful, the favored, and yet the unfortunate Miss Ray. As she was stepping into her carriage from Covent Garden Theatre (she had witnessed a performance of *Love in a Village*), a clergyman whose name we hear is Hackman came up and lodged the contents of a pistol in her head; which done he instantly shot himself and they fell together." Hackman merely wounds himself, but so firmly is he bent upon the entire completion of the fatal business that he tries to dash out his brains with the butt end of the pistol. He is seized by the bystanders and carried to the Shakespeare Tavern where his wound is dressed. The body of Miss Ray is likewise carried to the same place.

A messenger is instantly despatched for Lord Sandwich. He comes about twelve o'clock "in the most lamentable agonies and expresses a sorrow that certainly does infinite honor to his feelings." When Hackman asks his pardon, Sandwich sends him word that as he "looked upon his horrid action as an act of frenzy, he forgave it, that he received the stroke as coming from Providence which he ought to submit to, but that he had robbed him of all comfort in this world."

Miss Ray's body lies at the Shakespeare Tavern for some days, and George Selwyn is said to have seen it there. According to one correspondent, he sits as a mourner in the room, with a long black cloak on, which reaches to his heels, and a large hat slouched over his face. But as a matter of fact Selwyn is in Paris at the time. His friends, however, supply him with details of Hackman's execution.

On the morning of the fateful day, some gentlemen wait on the Reverend Mr. Hackman and accompany him to the Chapel where prayers are read by the Ordinary of Newgate, after which he receives the sacrament. When the sheriff's officer takes the cord from the bag to perform his duty, Hackman says—"Oh, the sight of this shocks me more than the thought of its intended operation." He then sheds a few tears and takes leave of the two gentlemen in a very affecting manner. He is then conducted in a mourning coach to Tyburn, the cart hung in black. On his arrival at the gallows he gets out of the coach, mounts the cart, and takes an affectionate leave of a friend and the Ordinary. He then kneels down and prays with two clergymen. The prayer is so long drawn out that at the end of twenty minutes, Ketch brusquely announces he must set about his business. Hackman replies with dignity that he will drop his handkerchief when he is ready. When the poor man finally drops the handkerchief, it falls under the cart, and Jack Ketch, mindful of his rights and profits, instead of instantly whipping on the horses, runs to pick it up. He then returns to the head of the cart and Jehues Hackman out of the world

The body is exposed to public view at the Surgeons' Hall in the Old Bailey soon after the execution. When the doors are opened so great a crowd is assembled that no genteel person attempts to gain admittance as it is observed that caps, cardinals, gowns, wigs, hats, etc. are destroyed without regard to age, sex, or distinction.

Newspapers have Boswell's name as riding in the coach with Hackman, and Boswell is sorely vexed. He is for going express to the editors or sending to Johnson for advice. He calls Lord Pembroke. But Pembroke declares: "I did not think it you. There are a hundred Boswells." This relieves Boswell at once. "Well," says he, "it shows the importance of a man to himself. I'm not entitled to say *I* was meant."

Then Burke is consulted as a friend. He says it will make it worse if Boswell controverts the statement. They will put in: "Mr. Boswell was not in the coach. But, etc."

Burke. "Was not you in Newgate?"

Boswell. "Yes."

Burke. "Was not you at Tyburn?"

Boswell. "Yes."

Burke. "Why, then, they only sent you in a coach. Besides why be angry at their making you perform one of the most amiable Christian duties: to visit those in prison?"

Boswell sees the execution "quite well." He is near the gallows, for after the execution he interviews the hangman and tries to find out what it is that Hackman said in his last moments to the clergymen who attended him. Ketch (Edward Dennis, who from hanging Sixteen-string Jack Rann and the Perreaus has become a person of prominence) promptly puts him in his place. "I thought it a point of ill manners," he says, "to listen on such occasions." Boswell, rebuffed, goes away and drinks white wine, being so much affected by what he has seen that he is afraid to meet people in the street.

But when he looks that evening into *Lloyd's Evening Post,* he is surprised and vexed to find his name figuring very prominently in the account of the execution. He learns that early in the morning he accompanied Hackman to the prison chapel where Hackman received the sacrament, that he rode in the mourning coach with Hackman to Tyburn, that he even ascended the fatal cart and prayed with Hackman just before he was turned off. In short his name has been substituted throughout for that of the Reverend Mr. Charles Porter, Hackman's friend, who really paid the murderer these mournful attentions. Two other newspapers which appear the next day carry the same story.

Boswell is now "vexed" and "sadly uneasy." But, as usual, having asked advice, he follows the promptings of his own feelings. He goes to the printers of the three offending newspapers and asks them to correct the account. For the *Public Advertiser* he writes "a good paragraph in a tone of waggery." It reads as follows: "It was not Mr. Boswell, but Reverend Dr. Porter of Clapham who so humanely attended the late unfortunate Mr. Hackman. Mr. Boswell had for a day that praise which is so justly allowed to generous tenderness; but he has taken care that it shall be enjoyed by the worthy person to whom it is due."

Johnson highly approves of this declaimer. He is glad, he says, that Boswell did not ride in the coach with Hackman, and glad that he contradicted the story for "people thought (and he thought) that Boswell had put the paragraph in himself"—which in view of Boswell's known proclivities is no unreasonable supposition.

A violent altercation arises between Dr. Johnson and Beauclerk over the affair. In talking of Hackman, Johnson argues that his being furnished with two pistols is a proof that he meant to shoot two persons. Beauclerk says, "No, for every wise man who intends to shoot himself, takes two pistols, that he may be sure of doing it at once. Lord ——'s cook shot himself with one pistol and lived ten days in great agony. Mr. —— who loved buttered muffins, but durst not eat them because they disagreed with his stomach, resolved to shoot himself and then he ate three buttered muffins for breakfast before shooting himself, knowing that he should not be troubled with indigestion. He had two charged pistols; one was found lying charged upon the table by him after he had shot himself with the other."

"Well," says Johnson with an air of triumph, "you see here one pistol was sufficient." Beauclerk replies smartly, "Because it happened to kill him." And being piqued at Johnson's triumphant remark, adds, "This is what you don't know and I do."

There is then a cessation of the dispute. Some minutes intervene during which dinner and the glass go on cheerfully, when Johnson suddenly and abruptly exclaims, "Mr. Beauclerk, how came you to talk so petulantly to me as 'This is what you don't know but what I know.' One thing I know which you don't seem to know is that you are very uncivil." Beauclerk. "Because you began by being uncivil which you always are." The last words are not heard by Johnson. Here again there is a cessation of arms. Johnson waits some time without taking any notice of what Beauclerk has said because he is thinking whether he should resent it. But when he considers that there are present a young Lord and an eminent traveler with whom he has never dined before, he is apprehensive that they may think they have a right to take such liberties with him as Beau-clerk has done, and therefore he resolves not to let it pass—"he will not appear a coward."

A little while after this the conversation turns on the violence of Hackman's temper. Johnson then says: "It was his business to command his temper, as my friend Mr. Beauclerk should have done some time ago." Beauclerk. "I should learn of you, sir." Johnson. "Sir, you have given *me* opportunities enough of learning when I have been in *your* company. No man loves to be treated with contempt." Beauclerk, with a polite bow to Johnson. "Sir, you have known me twenty years, and however I may have treated others, you may be sure I could never treat you with con-tempt." Johnson. "Sir, you have said more than was neces-sary." Thus it ends, and Beauclerk's coach not coming for him till very late, Johnson and another gentleman sit with him a long time after the rest of the company are gone. He and Bozzy dine at Beauclerk's on Saturday the week following.

Selwyn is sorely grieved at not witnessing Hackman's exit at Tyburn, but fortunately, as he writes from Paris, "we have a Miss Ray of our own, a sinister story with a dif-ferent catastrophe . . . Our Hackman here has destroyed himself with a coup de couteau when his pistol failed. What is become of the lady his wife I do not know. She was wounded in the breast. It happened in the Luxembourg Gardens the day after my arrival from Lyons . . . Hackman I find has died with a better character than Lord S. lived with. I never thought his lordship would be inconsolable—il n'est pas fait de cette étoffe."

George is already famous for his morbid interest in see-ing traitors beheaded and malefactors turned off. When he is out of town, his friends are enjoined to send him minute details. He is certainly present when the rebel lords are executed on Tower Hill. He hires a window in a house on the Hill and invites his friends to view the spectacle with him. Here is the voucher—

Tower Hill
14th August 1746

Sir,—As you are unknown to my servants, you will please shew them this, when you will be let into my house. I am, Sir, Your most humble Servant, S. Bethell

2.

The hills of Scotland echo with the sound of bagpipes and pibrochs. The clans are rising.

The arrival of Prince Charles Edward, the Young Pretender, on the coast of Scotland is the signal. He goes to Glenfinnan with high hopes, expects to see the valley alive with plaid and steel, and a sea of bobbing bonnets, eagle feathers, and white cockades. He finds instead a deep silent glen—no warriors, no banners, no lifted swords. The Vale of Glenfinnan is a picturesque but desolate place—overhung with rugged mountains and watered by a slender stream leaping over sleepy rocks. For the first time Charles is discouraged. Two hours he waits, doubting, wondering. Suddenly a wild far away note pierces the stillness—and then on the crags above him are the bright red tartans of six or seven hundred Camerons who rapidly descend the steep hillside. Shouts ring among the mountains, and bagpipes scream their loudest to bid him welcome. Old and feeble Tullibardine with much ceremony unfurls the Stuart standard of white, blue, and red silk, and as the folds are shaken out to the breeze, pibrochs scream louder than ever, Highland bonnets fly up in the air like a dark cloud, and clansmen shout madly.

"Go, sir," says Bonnie Prince Charlie to one of his prisoners, "Go and tell your general that Charles Stuart is coming to give him battle."

Charlie is tall and fair, has exquisite manners, a boyish shyness and the ladies adore him. He is gay and waves his hand to the chieftains and smiles at the pretty girls who come up to watch the army pass.

[161]

Oh, to see his tartan trews,
Bonnet blue, and laigh-heeled shoes;
Philibeg aboon his knee,
That's the lad that I'll gang wi'.

He is cheered and hurrahed. Bells are rung, bonfires lighted at night in the streets, thousands wear the white cockade. Women run out of houses to snatch a kiss of the Chevalier's hand.

At Prestonpans he meets the King's forces under Sir John Cope. "Follow me, gentlemen," cries Prince Charlie, as he leads his men to the charge, "and by the assistance of God, I shall this day make you a free and happy people." The Highlanders then pull off their bonnets, look up to heaven, make a short prayer, and rush on. In seven minutes, by the claymore alone, they sweep Cope's well trained dragoons from the field in hopeless confusion.

The young Chevalier's troops are eager to advance; they are flushed with victory; their hearts are high; they believe in the sanctity of their cause; they believe the Lord of Hosts is on their side, and such a belief strengthens their hands.

On to Penrith, Kendal, Lancaster, and Preston. The army of six thousand reaches Carlisle, reaches Manchester. On December 4, 1745 it is at Derby, only one hundred and twenty seven miles from London.

Panic prevails in the city. There never was so melancholy a town. No kind of public place is open but the play-houses and they look as if the rebels have just driven away the company. Inhabitants flee to the country with their most precious effects and all the shops are shut. Jacobites come forth from their lurking holes and corners and openly avow their preference for the House of Stuart. Seditious meetings are put down by proclamation. The gates of Temple Bar are now shut on sudden alarms two or three times a week— as if the closing of these rotten portals could in any way impede the progress of the rebellion. The Lord Mayor is mighty busy calling out train bands and having them drilled in Moorfields for the defence of the City. The weavers offer the King a thousand men, the lawyers form a regiment. Guards at all the posts at the Court end of the town are doubled. Cannon are run out, matches kept lighted, whole battalions maintained under arms, drawbridges pulled up and port cullises lowered with a great clanking of chains and gnashing of old iron teeth. A run on the Bank of England is met by a simple ruse, that of employing agents who present notes and ask to be paid in sixpences. These agents go out at one door with the specie they have received and bring it back by another. Thus the Bank literally faces its creditors.

People fear the dreaded pibrochs may be heard at Charing Cross. The Royal family is in tears and swooning. King George orders his yachts, in which he embarks all his most precious effects, to remain at the Tower quay in readiness to sail at a moment's warning.

The crown of England is in the hollow of Prince Charlie's hand, and he opens his hand and lets the prize fall from it. The Highlandmen start back into Scotland— the singing dies—the pipes are silenced. And then happens that short but tremendous fight of Drummossie Moor, commonly called the Battle of Culloden, where claymores and Lochaber axes clash and glint for the last time against English broadswords and bayonets. To the stirring notes of bagpipes, the Highlanders cross the Moor, running uphill, their targets held high over their heads, their bright swords flashing, their sporrans swinging, and hurl themselves against a wall of steel. When the remnants with undiminished ardor charge the second line they are met by a triple row of muskets. The rebels are hotly pursued—no quarter is given. After this there is what is called the pacification of the Highlands, meaning that the Duke of Cumberland and his dragoons devastate all before them with fire and sword. Murder, rape, torture, hold high carnival. Cumberland wins the thanks of both houses of Parliament, a grant of £25,000, and a place in song as "hero" of Handel's famous triumphal chorus.

In the end Westminster Hall is brilliant with scarlet hangings and crowded with an illustrious company to witness the trial of the three most important of the captive rebels—Lords Cromarty, Kilmarnock, and Balmerino.

Horace Walpole and George Selwyn are both present. "I am at this moment," writes Walpole to Sir Horace Mann, "come from the conclusion of the greatest and most melancholy scene I ever yet saw! You will easily guess that it was the trial of the rebel lords. As it was the most interesting sight, it was the most solemn and fine: a coronation is a puppet show and all the splendor of it idle, but this sight feasted one's eyes and engaged all one's passions . . . The first appearance of the prisoners shocked me; their behavior melted me."

Lord Kilmarnock is tall and handsome, dignified, pale; Lord Cromarty dejected and sullen, Lord Balmerino robust, gallant, careless. At the trial Balmerino asks to have his wife, his pretty Peggy with him in the Tower. Cromarty weeps every time anything of his fate is mentioned to him. Lady Cromarty only sees her husband through the gate, not choosing to be shut up with him as she thinks she can serve him better by her intercession without. She is big with child and very handsome. When the prisoners are brought from the Tower in separate coaches, there is some dispute in which the ax must go. Old Balmerino cries, "Come, come, put it with me." At the bar, he plays with his fingers upon the axe while he talks to the gentleman gaoler. One day, somebody coming up to listen, he takes the blade and holds it like a fan between their faces. A little boy is near him but not tall enough to see; he makes room for the child and places him near himself.

A great intercession is made for the two Earls, Kilmarnock and Cromarty. The Duke of Hamilton, who has never been at Court, designs to kiss the King's hand and ask Lord Kilmarnock's life. The King is much inclined to mercy, but the Duke of Cumberland is for the utmost severity. In the end Lord Cromarty is reprieved. The Prince of Wales asks his life and his wife's also. The Duke's intercession rather hurries Lord Kilmarnock to the block.

Unlike the others, Balmerino declines to admit that he has committed a crime or to sue for mercy. When he learns

that they have petitioned the King, he remarks caustically
that as they must have great interest at Court, they might
have squeezed in his name with their own. He recognises
at once that his case is desperate, for as he says himself,
he has been concerned in both rebellions (1715 and 1745)
and has been pardoned once already. To the last, therefore,
he is constant to his Jacobite principles.

He keeps up his spirits to a high pitch of gaiety. In his
cell at Westminster he shows Lord Kilmarnock how he
must lay his head, bids him not wince, lest the stroke should
cut his skull or his shoulders, and advises him to bite his
lips. When getting into the coach, he says to the gaoler,
"Take care or you will break my shins with this damned
axe." The keepers stop up one of his windows because he
talks to the populace; thus he has only one which looks
directly on the scaffold. Still he is jolly with his Peggy. They
bring in the death warrant at his dinner and his wife faints.
He says—"Lieutenant, with your damned warrant you have
spoiled my lady's stomach."

It will be difficult to make you believe to what heights
of affectation and extravagance my Lady Townshend carries her passion for my Lord Kilmarnock. When he is put on
trial, my Lady Townshend is present and falls in love with
him on the spot. She stays under his windows, sends mes-
sages to him, gets his dog and his snuffbox, takes lodgings
out of town and then goes to Greenwich, forswears conversing with the bloody English and takes a French master.
She has Lord Hervey promise her he will not sleep a whole
night for my Lord Kilmarnock and in return says, "Never
trust me more if I am not as yellow as a jonquil for him."
She says gravely, "Since I saw my Lord Kilmarnock, I
really think no more of Sir Harry Nesbitt than if there was
no such man in the world." When she hears her husband
vote—*Guilty upon my honour*, she remarks, "I always knew
my Lord was *guilty*, but I never knew that he would own it
upon his *honour*."

George Selwyn dines with her. Not thinking her affection so serious as she pretends, he talks rather jokingly of
the execution. She bursts into a rage and flood of tears,

tells him she now believes all his father and mother said of him, and with a thousand other reproaches flings upstairs. George coolly takes Mrs. Dorcas, her woman, and makes her sit down to finish the bottle. "And pray, sir," says Dorcas, "do you think my Lady will be prevailed upon to let me go and see the execution? I have a friend that has promised to take me, and I can lie in the Tower the night before."

As the clock strikes ten on the morning of the execution, they come forth on foot, Lord Kilmarnock all in black, his hair, unpowdered in a bag, supported by Dr. Forster, the great Presbyterian, and by a young clergyman, his friend. Lord Balmerino follows alone in a blue coat, turned up with red, and brass buttons, his rebellious regimentals, a flannel waistcoat, and his shroud beneath, their hearses following. They are conducted to a house near the scaffold. The room forward has benches for the spectators; in the second Lord Kilmarnock is put, and in the third backwards, Lord Balmerino; all three chambers are hung with black. Some wine and cakes are provided for them. Lord Kilmarnock by much entreaty takes two glasses, Lord Balmerino of his own account drinks three, eats a good deal of cake, praises both, and says he believes it is near dinner time. Being importuned to go on the scaffold, he requests to see Lord Kilmarnock to take his last farewell of him. In this he is indulged. He observes Kilmarnock is greatly discomposed, which makes him say he expects his lordship will bear his fate with more fortitude. He then asks Kilmarnock upon his honor, whether or no the vanquished army at Culloden had any orders to give the Duke's army no quarter, to which Kilmarnock replies, "Upon my honor, there was no such orders." Balmerino answers, "It was a lie raised to excuse their barbarity to us."

Soon after this they are informed the hour is near elapsed in which time they are to suffer and are desired to prepare immediately. To which Balmerino answers he will not delay them an instant. Lord Kilmarnock and he have a most affectionate embrace and Balmerino says, "My Lord, I wish I could suffer for both." Then he turns to the Sheriffs and asks them, "Where shall I go now?" He is brought to the same apartment he came from, and there ensues a great hurry and clearing the scaffold.

Lord Kilmarnock remains an hour and a half in the house and sheds tears. At last he comes to the scaffold, pale and terrified, but with a resolution which prevents his behaving in the least meanly or unlike a gentleman. He walks slowly, looking about as if he expects a reprieve. He takes no notice of the crowd, only to desire the executioner to lift up the baize from the rails that the mob may see the spectacle. The executioner, John Thrift, is in a dreadful state of panic. He dislikes his employment intensely. Being no politician, he disapproves of the axe and the block, as every good hangman should, believing that a stout hempen rope affords ample protection both for church and state. And his nervous, simple soul is thrown into an agony of consternation. When they dress him all in white and bring him to the scaffold and stand him beside the block, he is so dismayed by the terrific spectacle that he faints away. After a draught of wine he recovers and is able to stand at attention. The appearance of the young and comely Lord Kilmarnock distresses him so deeply that he bursts into tears. Once more he is revived with a glass of wine, but when led forward to beg his victim's forgiveness according to custom, he falls upon his knees and weeps bitterly. Lord Kilmarnock speaks to him gently, while he slips into his hands a more effective restorative than strong drink—a purse full of guineas. At last the hangman-headsman recovers his self control and dignity.

Lord Kilmarnock stands and prays sometime with the priest, who weeps over him and exhorts and encourages him. The Earl delivers a long speech to the Sheriff, declaring he wishes that all who embark in the same cause may meet the same fate. Then he takes off his bag coat and waistcoat, and after some trouble puts on a napkin with black ribbons. The neck of his shirt is unbuttoned and tucked down to his shoulders. He then several times tries the block, the executioner out of tenderness concealing the axe behind himself. At last the Earl kneels down with a visible unwillingness to depart, lays his head on the block and prays for some time, the executioner continually posing the axe over his neck. After five minutes the Earl drops his handkerchief, the signal, at which the executioner raises the axe as high as he can and gives him a deadly stroke, the body springing very high with a cloud of blood. The head is cut off at once, hanging by a bit of skin, and is received in a scarlet cloth by four of the undertaker's men, kneeling, who wrap it up and put it into the coffin with the body, orders being given not to expose the heads as is the custom with traitors. The scaffold is immediately strewn with sawdust, the block new covered, the executioner new dressed, and a new axe brought.

Then comes old Balmerino treading with the air of a general. As soon as he mounts the scaffold, seeing his coffin there, he says, "I must look at it to see whether they have put my title right." He then surveys the spectators, who are in amazing numbers, even to the masts of ships in the river, and pulling out his spectacles, reads a treasonable speech, which he delivers to the Sheriff, and says the Pretender is so sweet a Prince that flesh and blood could not resist following him. Lying down to try the block, he adds, "If I had a thousand lives, I would lay them all down here in the same cause!" He says, if he had not taken the sacrament the day before, he would have knocked down Williamson, the Lieutenant of the Tower, for his ill usage of him. He takes the axe and feels it, and asks the headsman how many blows he gave Lord Kilmarnock to which he answers one. "Oh," says Balmerino, "that will do well for me," and gives him three guineas. Two clergymen who attend him, coming up, he says, "No, gentlemen, I believe you have already done me all the service you can!" But he embraces some friends very cheerfully, the smack of his kisses being heard up to where Hanbury Williams is. Then he goes to the corner of the scaffold and calls very loud for the warder in order to give him his periwig, which he takes off, and puts on a night cap of Scotch plaid, and then pulls off his coat and waistcoat and lies down. But being told he is on the wrong side, he vaults round and immediately gives the sign by tossing up his arms as if he were giving the signal for battle. He receives three blows, the first certainly takes away all sensation. His last words are: "Oh, Lord! reward my friends, forgive my foes, bless King James, and receive my soul." He is not a quarter of an hour on the scaffold; Lord Kilmarnock above half a one. As he moves along from prison to execution, he hears someone in the crowd inquire with anxious curiosity, "Which is Lord Balmerino?" With goodnatured politeness, he turns half around and says, "I am Lord Balmerino, gentlemen, at your service." Seeing every window and top of house filled with spectators, he cries out, "Look, look, how they are all piled up like rotten oranges."

The multitude disperses and forms into small companies reasoning for and against these executions. On the way home one Captain Bradstreet sees two men boxing. The cause of the quarrel is: one insists the executioner intended to favor Lord Balmerino by giving him three strokes instead of one to despatch him; the other violently contradicts him.

My lively Lady Townshend will go nowhere to dinner for fear of meeting with a rebel pie, for, she says, everyone is so bloody minded that they eat rebels. Nearly a year afterwards she picks up a little stable boy in the Tower whom the warders palm off upon her as a bastard son of Lord Kilmarnock and takes him into her own house.

3.

George Selwyn's next execution is that of Simon Fraser, Lord Lovat. He attends the trial in Westminster Hall, and on one morning lends his ticket to a friend Vincent Mathias by which he has "one of the best seats in the hall and I lost not a word of all that was said." Lovat is executed on the 8th of April, 1747, and dies with a dignity which would have done credit to an ancient Roman. Selwyn is again at Tower Hill on this occasion, perhaps in Mr. Bethell's window.

Lovat has an interesting and stormy career. He has been mixed up in every plot for the bringing back of King James ever since the Old Chevalier's father gave up the ghost at St. Germain's. Yet he has somehow managed to escape scot free from attainder and confiscation. When a young man he is appointed a captain in Lord Tullibardine's regiment, but he resigns his commission in order to prosecute his claim to be chief of the Frasers. In order to effect this, he lays a scheme to get possession of the heiress of Lovat, who is about to be married to a son of Lord Salton. He raises a clan who violently seize the young lord, and erecting a gibbet, show it to him and his father, threatening their instant deaths unless they relinquish the contract made for the heiress of Lovat. To this, fearing for their lives, they consent. But still unable to get possession of the young lady, Simon seizes the mother, the Dowager Lady Lovat, in her own house, causes a priest to marry them against her consent, cuts her stays open with his dirk, and assisted by his ruffians, tears off her clothes, forces her into bed, to which he follows her, and then calls his companions to witness the consummation of the outrageous marriage. In the next room bagpipes are played furiously to drown the lady's squeals. For this breach of the peace, he is indicted, and a sentence of outlawry is pronounced against him. Fleeing to France, he turns Papist, ingratiates himself with the Pretender, and is rewarded with a commission. But he is apprehended on the remonstrance of the English ambassador in Paris and lodged for some years in the Bastille. He secures his liberty by taking priest's orders under color of which he becomes a Jesuit. In the rebellion of 1715 he returns to Scotland and assists the King's troops, for which service he gets the title of Lovat, is appointed to a command, and has other favors conferred on him.

At Castle Downie he holds a sort of court and several public tables and has a numerous body of retainers always attending. He keeps open house and even the raggedest ruffian of the clan can dine at the castle. The ranks and orders of men, however, are strictly observed, and with due regard to economy. At the head of a long table sits Simon and near him the distinguished guests. For them there is claret and French cookery. Lower down comes the more important class of vassals, enjoying solid beef and mutton and inferior wine. At the lower end are crowded the inferior vassals with sheeps' heads and ale or whiskey before them. And on the Castle Green in summer and in winter in the outhouse are the lowest class of clansmen. Servants waiting on the table have no food except what they carry off in the plates. The consequence is that the guests have to keep a watchful eye on their plates, for if they lay down their forks and knives and turn to address their neighbors, hey, presto! the plates are whipped off the table in an instant.

Simon shows dexterity in soothing ruffled feelings. "Cousin," he will call out from the head of the table to some dissatisfied Fraser at the lower end, "I told my lads to bring you claret, but I see you like ale better. Here's to your roof-tree!" Those who molest Simon are hung by the heels for hours.

He keeps Lady Lovat a naked and half-starved prisoner. The circulation of his blood being defective, he finds it necessary to have recourse to animal heat in the form of buxom young women to keep him warm. His vigor is remarkable. He is ill with fever, ague, scurvy, and minor ailments. And yet after all his diseases, he is fit and ready at the age of sixty-five to romp with wenches on the floors of taverns. He believes in the efficacy of a cold bath and has a passion for dancing which he never loses.

He is generally more loaded with clothes than a Dutchman with his nine or ten pairs of breeches. He has a large mouth and short nose, with eyes much contracted and down-looking, and a very small forehead, almost all covered with a large periwig. He says God bless you! with a kind of fiendish yowl quite horrible to behold.

In the rebellion of 1745 he tries to hoodwink both parties. Finally he turns sides and joins the Pretender, a step treacherous in the extreme. When taken he is old, unwieldy, and almost helpless. Yet on the way to London he kisses every one of his hostesses and talks of saluting them on the way back. He petitions the Duke of Cumberland for mercy, recapitulating his former services. However, the evidence proving his guilt to be of no ordinary character, he is convicted, and sentence of death is pronounced.

His pleasantry during his trial is very remarkable. On

each day of the trial he kneels and on each occasion Lord Chancellor Hardwicke solemnly says to him, "My Lord Lovat, your Lordship may rise." When asked if he has any questions to put to Sir Everard Fawkener, who is one of the strongest witnesses against him, he answers, "I only wish him joy of his young wife." And when, after sentence of death is pronounced upon him, he is retiring from the bar, he says, "Fare you well, my Lords, we shall not meet again in one place."

On his way to the Tower after his condemnation, an old woman thrusts her head into the window of the coach which conveys him and exclaims, "You damned old rascal, I begin to think you'll be hanged at last." "You damned old bitch," Lord Lovat replies, "I begin to think I shall."

On the night before his execution, one of the warders expresses his regret that the morrow should be such a bad day with his lordship. "Bad!" replies Lovat, "for what? Do you think I am afraid of an axe? It is a debt we must all pay and don't you think it better to go off in this manner, than to linger with consumption, or gout, dropsy, or fever? I die as a Christian and a Highland chieftain should do—that is, not in my bed." The same night he eats a hearty supper, and on the following morning he dresses himself with care and sits down to breakfast with the lieutenant of the Tower and a few of his own friends, with whom he converses with usual cheerfulness and ease. "It would have been better," he says, "to have sentenced me to be hanged, for my neck is so short and bent that the executioner will be sure to strike me on the shoulders."

His thoughts revert to the Highlands that he has in his fashion loved. He says he wishes to be buried in the church of Kirk Hill, a few miles from Castle Downie, and that he once intended that all the pipers from John o' Groats to Edinburgh should pipe at his funeral, and that even now he hopes the coronach will be heard over his grave. "And then," says he, "there will be crying and clapping of hands, for I am one of the greatest chiefs in the Highlands."

Arrived at Tyburn he looks sadly up at the gallows and with a heartfelt sigh exclaims, "O Jesus!" One of the platforms erected for the convenience of the spectators falls, several persons being killed. "The more damage," remarks Simon, "the better sport." As he is going up to the scaffold, assisted by two warders, he looks round and seeing so great a concourse of people, says, "God save us, why should there be such a bustle about taking off an old grey head that cannot get up three steps without three bodies to support it?" Turning about and observing one of his friends much dejected, he claps him on the shoulder, saying, "Cheer up thy heart, man! I am not afraid; why should you be so?" As soon as he comes upon the scaffold he asks for the executioner and hands him a purse remarking, "Here, sir, is ten guineas for you. Pray do your work well, for if you should cut and hack my shoulders and I should be able to rise again, I should be very angry with you." He then desires to see the axe, feels the edge of it, and says he believes it will do. After that, he goes over to his coffin and reads the inscription thereon—*Simon Dominus Fraser de Lovat, decollat. April 9, 1747, Aetat. suae 80*. Then sitting down in a chair which is placed for him, he repeats from Horace: "Dulce et decorum est pro patria mori." And after a pause adds from Ovid:

> Nam genus et proavos, et quae non fecimus ipsi
> Vix ea nostra voco.

(For our ancestral line and our ancestors—and anything which we ourselves have not made, I hardly call our own.)

He desires all the people to stand off except his two warders who support his lordship while he says a prayer. His last words are addressed to Mr. James Fraser who is in attendance—"My dear James, I am going to heaven, but you must continue to crawl a little longer in this evil world."

Some women scold Selwyn for going to see the execution and ask him how he can be such a barbarian to watch a head cut off. "Nay," says he, "if that was such a crime, I am sure I have made amends, for I went to see it sewed on again!" When he is at the undertaker's, as soon as they have stitched Lovat together and are going to put the body into the coffin, George, in my Lord Chancellor's voice, says, "My Lord Lovat, your lordship may rise."

An execution breakfast is arranged by Gilly Williams to watch Harrington's porter make his exit. Everything comes off as planned for Gilly reports to Selwyn who is in Paris— "Harrington's man was hanged last Wednesday. The dog died game, went in the cart in a blue and gold frock, and as an emblem of innocence, had a white cockade in his hat. He ate several oranges in his passage, enquired if his hearse was ready, and then, as old Rowe used to say, was launched into eternity." And Henry St. John adds—"What served to encourage my writing was the curiosity which you expressed to hear of Wisket, the porter's execution, which my brother and I went to see at the risk of breaking our necks by climbing up an old rotten scaffolding, which I feared would tumble before the cart drove off with the six malefactors. However, we escaped and had a full view of Mr. Wisket, who went to the gallows with the same hardness as appeared through his trial."

Many of Selwyn's friends are thus eager to assure him that they only patronize executions so that they may satisfy his curiosity. "Hullo! Here's a hanging," they seem to say with an engaging air, "let's go and see it, and describe it to George."

Selwyn interests himself in two other well known criminal cases. One is that of the Kennedys which excites considerable attention. Two brothers, Matthew and Patrick Kennedy, are indicted for the wilful murder of John Bigby, a watchman, in a riot on Westminster Bridge, of which offence, after an eight hours' trial, they are convicted and sentenced to be hanged. But the Kennedys have a pretty sister who is "no better than she ought to have been," and her brothers owe their lives to the efforts she makes with her paramours on their behalf. Anyway George Selwyn interferes in the Kennedy affair to oblige two of his friends who keep the young lady, and he gets the brothers off with a sentence of transportation for life. On the pardon being reported to the Privy Council, Lord Mansfield objects, and Matthew Kennedy is again ordered for execution. Upon this George Selwyn himself waits upon the King who again commutes the sentence. Matthew is actually on board ship on his way to a penal colony when the widow of Bigby lodges a fresh appeal against the brothers and both Pat and Mat are once more brought to Court. But influence is used, a memorial to the King is drawn up, and when the next sessions at the old Bailey come on, the widow is bought off and allows the appeal to be dropped. When she goes to receive the money (£350), she weeps bitterly and at first refuses to touch the money that is to be the price of her husband's blood, but being told that nobody else can receive it for her, she holds out her apron and bids the attorney who is to pay it, sweep it into her apron.

George Selwyn takes the keenest interest in the case and does perhaps more than any other man to help the unfortunate brothers. And why? Because he has a kind heart. But brutal Junius has not. "The mercy of a chaste and pious prince," he says, "extended cheerfully to a wilful murderer, because that murderer is the brother of a whore."

The other criminal case which impresses Selwyn is that of the pious humbug, Dr. William Dodd.

As a clergyman the Reverend Dr. Dodd is on the whole very successful. As a forger, however, he is a complete failure. It is his lack of success in this direction that causes him to make a lamentable exit by dangling from a public gallows.

He is a popular preacher, and while he holds the pulpit, the Magdalen, a charity hospital, draws all the town. Mayfair as well as Mile End sit under him regularly. There are prayers, then psalms and a sermon. He harangues in the French style, very eloquently and touchingly. He apostrophises the lost sheep who sob and cry from their souls. Lady Hertford follows their example and Dodd writes a poem upon the Countess's tears. Of the Magdalens themselves, Walpole, who visits the Hospital, is struck and pleased with the modesty of two of them who swoon away with confusion at being stared at.

The hospital is delighted with their shepherd and sing his praises lustily. But they give him a beggarly sixty guineas

a year. The result is, the reverend doctor is often hard put
to it to meet his requirements. These are not modest, for
he lives in considerable style. Accordingly he plies a busy
pen—turns out columns of newspaper articles, writes a number of theological works as well as poems and pamphlets
by the dozen. Altogether he is responsible for more than
fifty volumes. His *Beauties of Shakespeare* elicit the high
praise of Goethe.

He insinuates himself into the graces of Bishop Samuel
Squire. The first fruits are a prebend's stall and a chap-
laincy to the King. Squire soon does more, for he obtains
for Dodd the tutorship of Philip Stanhope, godson and heir
of Lord Chesterfield, with a salary of £200 a year. We
next find the Reverend Doctor with a house in the suburbs
where he teaches classics and mathematics to a select number of young gentlemen of good families. In this he is
helped by Mrs. Dodd, who has a stroke of luck and wins
the handsome prize of £1000 in a lottery. (The manner
in which Mrs. Dodd comes by this lottery ticket shows that
politeness is never wasted. A year or two earlier she happens
to be at an auction where she bids for a cabinet. Just as it
is being knocked down to her, a lady bids against her, on
which Mrs. Dodd makes a curtsy and stops. The successful
competitor is so pleased that out of gratitude she presents
her with the lottery ticket that afterwards secures the
prize.) She dutifully hands over the proceeds to her husband, who lays them out in the purchase of a chapel in
Pimlico, called Charlotte Chapel, after the Queen.

He attracts a vast congregation together with an income
of £600 a year. This ought to be enough for Doctor Dodd,
but it is not enough. The fact is, Dodd's personal extravagance is his besetting sin. He lives above his means, he
entertains like a prince, he keeps open house, he has a big
retinue of liveried flunkeys eating their heads off, and his
stables are always full of carriages and horses. Nor can
he keep away from the card tables. When he loses, as he
nearly always does, he attempts to adjust things by a flutter
in stocks and shares. The voice of scandal is also busy with
him. There are disquieting whispers, that leaving his cler-

ical costume behind, he will occasionally slip off to Paris accompanied by a lady who is certainly not Mrs. Dodd. No wonder the wits of the coffee house dub him "The Macaroni Parson."

To indulge his secular tastes, Dr. Dodd runs up big bills with obliging tradesmen. When they stop being obliging, he gets into the hands of the money lenders. He is now in a desperate position.

At this juncture the important Crown living of St. George's Hanover Square suddenly happens to fall vacant. Dr. Dodd, forgetting the precept of the tenth commandment, which he expounds with such unction to fashionable audiences every Sunday, looks upon the rectorship with covetous eyes. It will be just the thing, he feels, to set him on his legs again, for there is a salary of £1500 a year attached to the post, together with handsome pickings in the way of marriage fees, etc. Also there are christenings.

He gets Mrs. Dodd to send an anonymous letter to the wife of the Lord Chancellor strongly recommending himself for the post and offering her a bribe of £3000 if he is selected. This is going too far. The Keeper of the King's Conscience takes the suggestion amiss. He makes inquiries into its authorship and soon discovers from whom the letter came. Thereupon he complains to his Majesty and as an inevitable consequence, Dodd is promptly struck off the list of Royal Chaplains. It is a thousand pities.

His fortunes decline rapidly; he is stripped of all he possesses. As a result he sees the inside of a sponging house and is only released from its discomforts through the good offices of a feminine admirer whose gentle heart is touched by the tale of his misfortunes.

To help himself out of his embarrassment, he is put to all sorts of shifts. He is even said to sink so low as to edit a newspaper. Harassed by creditors, who come down on the poor reverend doctor like a pack of wolves, he forges a bond for £4200 in the name of his patron the Earl of Chesterfield. After paying out on it, the bankers are troubled by qualms as to the genuineness of the signature and take the bond to Lord Chesterfield for verification. When disowned by him they procure a warrant for Dodd's arrest. Thereupon he voluntarily surrenders £3000 and offers to give security for the balance, provided further proceedings are dropped. But they are not dropped, and Dodd is brought before the Lord Mayor. The Earl of Chesterfield is unwilling to prosecute. As a matter of fact, he offers to put the bond in the fire and say no more about it. Also he says flatly that he does not want to be bothered.

"Pray, my Lord Mayor," begs the miserable Dodd, "consider my case, and as there is no prosecutor, release me. I am sure my lord Chesterfield does not want my life. I hope he will show clemency to me. Mercy should ever triumph over justice."

Sir Thomas Hallifax, the Guildhall magistrate, will not hear of such tenderness. There have been too many forgeries during the past few months. It is high time they were stopped. He is a banker himself. The result is, the wretched man is brought to trial. Although he has able counsel, he cannot divest himself of the pulpit manner and insists on making most of the speeches for them. However, the evidence is so clear that it does not leave a loophole through which Dodd can wriggle. In ten minutes the jury returns a verdict of guilty, and the sentence of death is pronounced upon him.

While languishing in Newgate the despairing man has some pangs of remorse. Thus he makes a clean breast of his misdeeds, refunds the stolen money, and delivers sermons in the prison chapel.

Attempts are made to obtain a pardon. The conversation in every circle is of poor Doctor Dodd. Grub Street rallies to his cause. The press teems with minute descriptions of every act of his sad hours. Meetings are held to consult upon measures to avert the severity of justice. The Countess of Huntingdon intercedes for him. A petition containing twenty-three thousand signatures (the first being that of the foreman of the jury) is drawn up and laid at the foot of the throne. Lord Percy sends another. There is a third from the Common Council of London. A "Last Solemn Declaration" and a number of other documents are composed for the criminal. "Led astray from religious strictness by the delusion of show and the delights of voluptuousness"—the hand is the hand of Dodd, but the voice is the voice of Dr. Johnson.

Yet all to no effect. The Privy Council, guided by Lord Mansfield, deprecates any commutation of punishment as a dangerous precedent and recommends that the sentence be carried out. George III no sooner hears the opinion pronounced by Lord Mansfield than he takes up the pen and signs the death warrant.

On the morning of his execution, a wet and stormy one, after waiting some time for the officers, Dodd says—"I wish they were ready, for I long to be gone." He requests his friends to pray for him to which he is answered by two of them, "We pray more than language can utter." He replies, "I believe it." On his seeing two prisoners looking out of the windows in the yard, he goes to them and exhorts them so pathetically that they both weep abundantly. He says once, "I am now a spectacle to men and shall soon be a spectacle to angels."

After he is bound, the Ordinary offers to assist him with his arm, but he replies with seeming pleasure, "No, I am as firm as a rock." When he comes near the street where he has formerly dwelt, he is much affected and sheds tears. But it is a weakness, he says, he cannot help, and not cowardice. And he adds, "I hope I am going to a better home."

As he draws near the gallows, a woman in the crowd calls out mockingly, "Well, your reverence, where is the Lord thy God now?" The condemned man looks at her. "Woman," he says, "you will find the answer in the tenth verse of the seventh chapter of Micah."

This verse for those who have not a Bible at hand reads: "She that is mine enemy shall see it and shame shall cover her which said unto me, Where is the Lord thy God? Mine eyes shall behold her: Now shall she be trodden down as the mire of the streets."

The Lord's vengeance is quick and sure. A few minutes later, the woman who jeered in this fashion is herself knocked down and trampled to death.

The doctor to all appearances is rendered perfectly stupid from despair. His hat is flapped all around and pulled over his eyes, which are never directed to any object around nor even raised, except now and then lifted in the course of his prayers. When he leaves the coach and enters the cart, a very heavy shower of rain falls. An umbrella is held over his head, which Gilly Williams, who is present, observes is quite unnecessary as the doctor is going to a place where he may be dried. He is a considerable time in praying, which some people standing about are rather tired with. The wind, which is high, blows off his hat, and this rather embarrasses him, for it reveals his face which until then scarcely anyone could see. His hat, however, is restored to him, and he goes on with his prayers. He prays for himself, his wife, and a fellow criminal who suffers with him. He declares that he dies in the true faith of the gospel of Christ, in perfect love and charity with all mankind and with thankfulness to his friends. When he finishes, he stands up and delivers a long sermon on Sin and its consequences. Then the executioner takes off his hat and wig at the same time; why he puts on his wig again we do not know, but so he does and the doctor takes off his wig a second time, and then with a faint smile ties on a nightcap which does not fit him, and very soon afterwards there is an end of all his hopes and fears on this side the grave.

Dodd will not suffer his legs to be pulled, and his body is hurried away to a house in the city where some friendly surgeons put him in a hot bath and try to restore animation. The efforts come to nothing if for no other reason than that the excessive curiosity of the crowd is responsible for much delay in the coach journey from Tyburn.

CHAPTER 14

PARLIAMENT

SELWYN'S LIFE IS ON THE WHOLE EVENT-less; it has few dates of any importance. But perhaps 1747, when he first enters the House of Commons, is one of these. For Selwyn is a genuine House of Commons man. He sits there for the long period of three and forty years. He hears or sleeps through nearly all the principal debates; he votes solidly for one hardly knows how many successful minis-tries.

He sits in the same house with William Pitt the elder and Henry Fox and hears both of these men in their prime, hears the early speeches of their sons also and lives to take his last and most lucrative sinecure from the hand of William Pitt the younger and to call his once good friend Charles James Fox, "Mr. Fox." He sees England win an empire under Chatham and lose another empire under North, is mobbed by patriots in the days of Wilkes, is "ill-treated" (according to himself) by at least two prime min-isters, and finds "Bourk" a very civil person until the Irish-man takes to depriving decent people of their places.

For years he writes an almost daily letter to his friend Lord Carlisle and his political jottings in this correspond-ence are not encouraging. "Cursed tiresome debate," says he on one evening. On another: "Charles spoke well."

He enters the House as M.P. for Ludgershall, a little vil-lage of small red cottages and thatched roofs lying among the Wiltshire downs. It has a quiet out of the world look, and there is a marketplace with a cross in it. Once upon a time it was a place of some importance, with a substantial

Norman castle. But its importance, like its castle, has vanished. Nothing is left of the castle but a few stones.

But one valuable privilege it still retains: the right namely of returning two members to the House of Commons. John Selwyn purchases this right and Ludgershall becomes the Selwyns' "pocket borough." The representation is as much in their hands as the trees in the adjoining field.

Pocket boroughs have their advantages. There you have none of the wear and tear of a contested election: no hustings, no speeches, no mobs. If there are any voters (and there are some at Ludgershall) you request them politely to return your candidate to Parliament and they do so, thinking they have no option in the matter. Or you make an ad hoc assignment of property to your steward and your gardener and your footman, who thus become free and independent burgesses and do their duty on the polling day. Or happiest of all, you may own a borough without a single house or a single burgess—Old Sarum, for instance. There the procedure is of the simplest. The steward comes down one afternoon, erects a tent under a spacious elm tree, and nominates William Pitt, Esq. as parliamentary candidate for the ancient borough of Old Sarum. No rival candidate appearing, William Pitt, Esq., is declared duly elected and the thing is done. (Sarum is a sheep walk, but Droitwich is an abandoned salt pit, and Dunwich is half under the sea. A handful of Cornish fishing villages with a total electorate of fourteen hundred can outvote the representatives of the capital.)

But how many other privileges do pocket boroughs not possess! You can put your sons or other relatives into them, as George Selwyn does; or you can dispose of them for a consideration as George Selwyn does more than once; or if you are truly patriotic or have a lively anticipation of favors to come, you can put the seat at the disposal of the Prime Minister, as again is the case with George Selwyn.

Consider for a moment the history of Ludgershall in the Selwyn period. Here is a list of its members from 1741 to 1791.

	Major Charles Selwyn		Lord Melbourne
1741	Thomas Hayward	1774	Lord George Gordon
	George A. Selwyn		George A. Selwyn
1747	Thomas Farrington	1780	Lord Melbourne
	Sir John Bland		George A. Selwyn
1754	Thomas Hayward	1784	Sir N. W. Wraxall
	Thomas Whately		George A. Selwyn
1761	John Paterson	1790	W. B. Harbord
	Lord Garlies		
1768	Penistone Lamb, first Lord Melbourne		

Thus George Selwyn himself sits for Ludgershall in four Parliaments, three of his uncles have each a turn, and the rest are strangers. But the strangers mostly pay for the privilege. Thus it is said that in 1768 George Selwyn gets no less than £9000 for the double seat. He is not the man to give them away.

The buying and selling of seats is notorious. Lord Chesterfield offers £2500 for a secure seat for his son, but he is laughed at, as the price of boroughs goes up to four or five thousand pounds in consequence of the determination of the rich East and West Indian nabobs to enter Parliament. But this in the end is relatively cheap. A contested election for the borough of Northampton costs the Earl of Spencer no less than £70,000. Some boroughs commission attorneys to ply about the country as jobbers.

Selwyn enters Parliament at an interesting time politically. The long Walpolian struggle is over. Sir Robert, beaten but not disgraced, has retired as the Earl of Orford to the obscurity of the House of Lords. Others have tried to govern in his stead and have failed dismally. Then comes the broad bottomed administration—Newcastle and Pelham and Henry Fox and William Pitt the elder, and it is when this government is in office that Selwyn first enters the House.

Under Mr. Pelham and the Duke of Newcastle, the private member dozes his time away happily on the back benches. He has no political enthusiasms, and he never makes speeches. There are Mr. Fox and Mr. Pitt and Mr.

Murray to do that. His duty is to eat his dinner and drink his port and serve on a committee occasionally and vote steadily with his party.

It is a lazy life, nor do the habits of the House make for strenuousness. It meets early, twelve o'clock, and seldom rises later than nine or ten—time enough for George Selwyn and his friends to get back to White's for supper and a game of picquet.

The Commons is rather a mean, dingy, little building that not a little resembles a chapel. It has a cavernous air with five tiers of green covered horseshoe benches carried back to the wainscotted walls, strips of gallery running overhead along each side and at one end, and chandeliers hung not high near the ceiling but low down in mid-air. It is a contracted, unadorned, well packed apartment, composed of fire, flatulence, and fog.

In the middle of the room there is a table and clerks in wigs and gowns writing upon it. Behind the table stands a high chair (not unlike a pulpit) whereon sits the Speaker clad in a black gown with an enormous bushy powdered wig. Members dress as they choose; they even come into the House in their great coats, with boots and spurs. It is not at all uncommon to see a member lying stretched out on one of the benches while others are debating. Some crack nuts, others eat oranges, or whatever else is in season. There is no end to their going in and out.

As often as anyone wishes to go out, he places himself before the Speaker and makes him a bow as if, like a schoolboy, he asks his tutor's permission. Those who speak seem to deliver themselves with but little gravity. All that is necessary is to stand up in your place, take off your hat, turn to the Speaker (to whom all speeches are addressed), hold your hat and stick in one hand, and with the other hand make any such motions as you fancy necessary to accompany your speech. If it happens that a member rises who is but a bad speaker, so much noise is made that he can scarcely distinguish his own words. Even the favorites, who speak often and speak well, have to struggle to obtain silence.

Laughter, hooting noises, stamping of feet, shouts of *Oh! Oh!* Heedless of the tumult a fat swarthy man stands near the table; upon it he bangs and thumps his fist, turns his face towards the high chair and the enormous wig, waves his arms. At length his voice rises above the din, the noise of *Oh! Oh!* dies away, the cry of *Hear him! Hear him!* resounds instead.

The members are always demonstrative. When one statesman leaves the house after the repeal of the Stamp Act, he is greeted by three cheers. On the other hand, hisses and catcalls assail Grenville. Swelling with rage and mortification, he seizes the nearest man to him by the collar, but the fellow has more humor than spleen. "Well, if I may not hiss," says he, "at least I may laugh,"—and laughs in Grenville's face.

There is no regular division into Government and Opposition benches; there is merely a bench reserved for members of the Privy Council, and on this are usually seated, side by side, the leaders of both the Government and the Opposition. It is quite a common thing for a member, after indulging in the bitterest sarcasms on the conduct of some individual statesman to take his seat again by the side of the object of his invective and inquire how he has done. Which inquiry the latter will answer with the utmost good nature ere rising to return the hail of words which rattled so savagely about his ears. Once Sir Robert Walpole, sitting down near to Pulteney after an earnest appeal to the House, is informed by his enemy in a whisper that he misquoted Horace. Walpole bets him a guinea he has not. The matter is referred at once and decided against the minister, who tosses a guinea to Pulteney. The latter catches it up triumphantly and, holding it up to the House, cries, "This is the first public money I have received for many years, and it shall be the last,"—a sarcastic allusion to the gratifications bestowed on Walpole's supporters.

There are numerous resolutions against the continued absence of members. Once it is formally resolved that those who stay away are neglecting their duty. But even this scathing rebuke is ineffectual. The claims of the East India

Company give way to tiger baiting. Private theatricals, fêtes champêtres, races, any kind of amusement, lure away the House and cause the postponement of public business. Walpole adjourns the House from Friday night to Monday in order not to miss his Saturday's hunting at Houghton.

Reports of the proceedings are prohibited. Notes jotted down surreptitiously in the Gallery, containing the drift of argument and an occasional metaphor inserted like a flower, culled here and there, are taken to the nearest tavern where they are spun into a connected story. Reporters mangle the speeches of those they dislike or slip into them comic passages. Mr. Wilberforce is made to lament to his brother members that when a child, not enough potatoes were given him—and this is Wilberforce's reason. "For potatoes, Mr. Speaker, potatoes, sir, make men healthy. Potatoes make men tall. More especially do I feel this because being under the common size, I must ever lament that I was not fostered under that genial vegetable, the potato." Often the wit and eloquence of one side are due to the talents and political sympathy of the writer. Dr. Johnson, who compiles a large number of speeches in *The Gentleman's Magazine*, glories in the fact that he never lets the Whig dogs have the best of the argument.

The accounts are often scurrilous. Colonel Onslow complains of two newspapers which misrepresent his conduct in the House and hold him up to contempt by describing him as "little cocking George." Disregarding a warning from Burke as to the folly of entering into a quarrel with the press, the House orders the printers arrested, and afterwards reprimands them. In retaliation the newspapers attack the various members, especially Onslow, who is described as "a paltry insignificant insect" and so on. When the quarrel is renewed for the press by the city reformers, and the Lord Mayor and one Alderman Oliver are committed to the Tower, the agitation against the Commons is so great that an angry mob storms the House, interrupts its business, pelts several members, and roughly handles North and Charles Fox, who are conspicuous as defenders of privilege, and breaks their carriages. The prisoners are visited in the Tower by Rockingham, Burke, and other members of the Opposition. On their release, at the end of the session, they are saluted by a cannon of artillery and by the huzzas of the populace—and the city is illuminated.

The House also wages a losing battle to support the right of compelling such delinquents as are called to its bar to fall down upon their knees and to remain in that degrading position while the Speaker is addressing them. In 1751 a Mr. Alexander Murray incurring the hot displeasure of the House by something he has done or is charged with having done, it is voted that he shall be sent to Newgate and further that he shall be brought to the bar to receive his sentence on his knees. Murray enters the House with an air of confidence, composed of something between a martyr and a coxcomb. The Speaker calls out, "Your obeisances, Sir, your obeisances!" Then, "Sir, you must kneel." Murray replies, "Sir, I beg to be excused. I never kneel but to God." The Speaker repeats the command with great warmth. Murray answers, "Sir, I am sorry that I cannot comply with your request. I would in anything else." The Speaker cries, "Sir, I call upon you again to consider of it." Murray answers, "Sir, when I have committed a crime, I kneel to God for pardon, but I know my own innocence and cannot kneel to anybody else." The Speaker orders the seargeant-at-arms to take him away and secure him. He is going to reply, but the Speaker will not listen to him. The prisoner being removed, a warm debate ensues, the Speaker telling them that if a party may behave thus with impunity, there is an end to the dignity and power of the House. One member proposes that Murray be kept in Newgate without pen, ink, and paper. Another hints that it may be well to send him to the dungeon called Little Ease in the Tower. A third will have an Act of Parliament passed for the special punishment of such audacious conduct. At last, after naming a committee to consider the matter, the House adjourns at near two o'clock in the morning.

It is an age of party, and almost everything takes its

shape and hue. By its means the columns of the newspapers are continually flooded with libels; by its means also the streets are filled with riots and tumults. Heads of families neglect their wives and their children, tradesmen forsake their counters and divines their pulpits that they may bear their part in the interminable political discussions of the coffee houses and clubs. The one thing needful is political support, and that it may be secured nothing is grudged. In order to secure fidelity every office in the State, from the Prime Minister down to the humblest fellow in the Post Office or the Customs, is conferred.

More than half the members of Parliament hold offices, pensions, sinecures. Sir Robert Walpole's estimate of political honesty is very similar to his estimate of female virtue. He bribes George II by obtaining for him £100,000 a year more than his father, bribes the Queen, bribes the Dissenting ministers. When the members of Parliament are invited to his dinners they occasionally find a five hundred pound note folded up in their napkins. All these men, he says, have their price, and he is obliged to bribe them for their conscience. He is accustomed to ask young men who enter Parliament whether they are going to be saints or Romans. And so in ten years no less than a million and a half pounds are expended in secret service money. Sir Robert is not thought honest until he is out of power.

Peerages are an essential commodity for satisfying the claims from the House of Commons. So much so that when on the eve of a general election George II shows himself obdurately German in his blue blood prejudices, Newcastle tells him: "If his Majesty expects that I should be employed in choosing a new Parliament, I cannot do it if I have not the power to oblige the first gentlemen in the countries." It is easier to create peers than to raise money for places and pensions.

George III reduces bribery to a fine art. When in Parliament the number of placemen is reduced to eighty-nine, it does not mean that there is less corruption. On the contrary ministerial influence is carried to such lengths that Sir Robert Walpole would have stared. Parsimonious as His Majesty is in his own affairs, he has no hesitation in buying the patron of a borough or in paying the debts of a man who is willing to stand as the King's Friend at the next election. "If the Duke of Northumberland," he writes to North, "requires some gold pills for the election, it would be wrong not to give him some assistance."

The ways and means of election are public money, promises, titles, contracts, preferments, places, and by threatening to displace, etc., besides liquor and the current coin of corruption. A few guineas each to the common voters are enough to assure their support. And landlords usually expect their tenants to vote as they direct. Then again voters are pleased to receive a personal letter from a great Duke like Newcastle—it pleases their vanity and pins the basket. Better than a letter is a government position. They wish to be dockyard carpenters, clerks, excise men, postmasters, officers in the army and navy, consuls in foreign countries, even lord chief barons of the exchequer Competition for better church places is very keen. Three candidates for the Deanship of Chichester write Newcastle before the old Dean dies. Many are not too particular—they want an easy berth anywhere.

Voters have to be taken care of when they get into difficulties. Houses have to be bought at the seller's price in order to win votes. In a dozen rotten boroughs any one who can prove himself possessed of a hearth by coaxing a kettle to boil (pot walloping) has the vote. Before an election men can be seen repairing a doorway, for a door is evidence of householding, lighting a fire, spreading a table in public to prove their electoral qualification. In Prestons any man who sleeps there the night before is a voter. The electoral rights of clergymen are recognised by statute. A chorister of Ely Cathedral, the butter and brewer of Westminster Abbey, the bell-ringer, the gardener, the cook and the organ blower all vote by virtue of their superior ecclesiastical office.

Candidates depend more upon the strength of their liquor than their arguments, and the merits of a treat often recommend a member who has no merits of his own. At election time: alehouses crowded with people, eating, drinking, smoking, swearing, singing, drunkards reeling about the taverns, hawkers distributing satirical papers, butchers enchanting the souls of all true lovers of music with discordant sounds of marrow bones and cleavers, gangs of men parading the streets with banners, companies marching up to the hustings to vote with cockades stuck in their hats. Add to this, window smashing, free fights, pealing of church bells, and a banquet when the results are made known—and the picture is complete.

Articles consumed at dinner only by voters of a small borough on the day of electing members—independently of veal, mutton, poultry, pastry, etc., and a preparatory breakfast which alone costs £750:

        980 stone of beef
        315 dozen of wine
         72 pipes of ale
        365 gallons of spirits (converted into punch.)

Candidates are expected to mix readily with the crowd at the parties and to drink freely. One Mr. Warren is so liberal with his drink that his own mob grows very troublesome to him, beginning first to plunder the victuals, ale, and wine, then to breaking the bottles, glasses, pots, chairs, etc., till at last his friends are forced to send for the constables.

Some recreant electors venture to oppose Lord North's nomination of their Mayor shortly before the annual dinner to which his lordship is in the habit of sending venison. The old steward while carving it sends plenty of fat to the obedient voters but makes the rebels sensible of his displeasure by exclaiming as he despatches their respective plates—"Those who didn't vote for my lord's mayor shan't have none of my lord's fat."

In the borough of Wendover voters agree to return two candidates against the Earl of Verney's interest and influence for the sum of £6000. This being settled, a gentleman is employed to go down and meet the electors at a mile from the town. The electors ask the stranger where he comes from. He replies, "From the moon." Then they ask, "What news from the moon?" He answers that he has brought from thence £6000 to be distributed among them. The electors being thus satisfied with the golden news from the moon choose the candidates and receive their rewards.

People in the Cornish boroughs have been bribed before and now get together to fix their prices. The electors of Shoreham combine and resolve themselves into a joint stock company. Sir George Yonge inherits £80,000 from his father; his wife brings him a like amount; the government pays him £80,000, but Honiton swallows it all. In the same borough one of the independents says to Lord Dundonald, who is canvassing the electors: "You need not ask me, my lord, who I vote for? I always votes for Mr. Most."

Bill of Costs for the late Tory election	£	s	d
Imprimis, for bespeaking and collecting a mob	20	0	0
Item: for scores of huzza men	40	0	0
For roarers of word Church	40	0	0
For several gallons of punch on Church tombstones	30	0	0
For a majority of clubs and brandy bottles	30	0	0
For bell-ringers, fiddlers, and porters	10	0	0
For a set of coffee house praters	40	0	0
For extraordinary expense for cloths and lac'd hats on show days to dazzle the mob	50	0	0
For Dissenters' damners	40	0	0
For demolishing two houses	200	0	0
For committing two riots	200	0	0
For secret encouragement to rioters	40	0	0
For a dozen of perjury men	100	0	0
For breaking windows	20	0	0
For law and charges in the King's Bench	300	0	0
For pot ale	100	0	0
For a set of notorious lyars	50	0	0

In France the Chevalier des Grieux whenever he finds himself without means or provision from the State or Church can think of nothing better than card sharping, or else his lady-love Manon Lescaut has to sell herself to the highest bidder. In England the range of employment for gentlefolk is much more extensive. Gentlemen go into trade, to the Colonies, to India, etc. But the most natural thing for a pretty young man of gentle birth and small means is to look for provision directly to the state. If the family is sufficiently great or has borough influence, he will be returned to Parliament and on the strength of his seat in the House will seek and obtain some place under the government—*quelque chose de par le roi.*

Daniel Finch, second Earl of Nottingham, has by his second wife Anne thirty children (the burden on the state, however, is not that heavy—seven are stillborn and ten die young). The fourth son, Henry Finch, educated at Cambridge, becomes Fellow of Christ's College, but after ten years at the University, meeting with disappointment, he has to look out for some other settlement in life. The question is debated in the family whether Henry shall be sent abroad to learn languages and rub off the academical rust which in the course of ten years he must have gathered, or whether a provision out of Parliament will be most agreeable to his circumstances. Ultimately both expedients are adopted. He is sent for some time to the Hague, and when a vacancy occurs in a pocket borough of his brother-in-law, Henry Finch is chosen for it. He is soon made Receiver General of Revenues for Minorca (which he never visits), Surveyor General of His Majesty's Works (which he never surveys), and finally is given a secret service pension of £900 p. a. Truly he has achieved a provision out of Parliament.

Everybody who has influence in Parliament or at Court uses it for the express and avowed purpose of making or repairing his fortune. One nobleman has £8000 in sinecures and the colonelcies of three regiments. Another as auditor of the Exchequer (inside which he never looks) has £8000 in the years of peace and £20,000 in the years of war. A third with nothing to recommend him but his outward graces bows and whispers himself into four great employments from which thirteen or fourteen hundred British guineas flow monthly into the lap of his Parisian mistress. The racing friend, the French cook, the children's tutor, the led captain, the hired poet and the inspired pam-

GEORGE SELWYN, RICHARD EDGECUMBE, and "GILLY" WILLIAMS

From an engraving by J. Scott, after the painting by Sir Joshua Reynolds

HORACE WALPOLE
EARL OF OXFORD

From an engraving by Thomas Lawrence, 1796

MADAME DU DEFFAND

From an engraving by Carmontelle

phleteer are all paid with nominations or pacified with reversions. Thus when Lord Holland goes to Italy, he thinks it necessary to provide for his son's tutor, and so obtains for him a pension of £300 a year. The Duke of Grafton procures £500 a year for an old Newmarket race track acquaintance who has squandered his fortune. Bute's hackwriter has a pension from the public of £600; his poet, one Dalrymple, is gratified with the Attorney Generalship of Granada.

There are highly endowed posts whose functions can be performed while seated at a whist table of White's or Brooks's. An English Duke is made Lord Treasurer of Ireland. Virginia and her sister colonies are not supposed to know what is best for their own interests, or at any rate for the interests of their masters, and plenty of gentlemen are soon drinking their claret and paying their debts out of the savings of the fishermen of Maine and the farms of New Jersey. America is for many years the hospital of England.

The stranger who for the first time throws his eyes round the House of Commons can distinguish at a glance the

> Patriots bursting with heroic rage

from the

> Placemen, all tranquillity and smiles.

With everything to get and nothing to trouble him a minister regards office as a paradise from which no man of sense would be so infatuated as to banish himself on any grounds of public duty.

Interest rules the Church as it rules Parliament. While the inferior clergy starve upon stipends of £25 to £50 a year, the greater men scramble for every gift they can extort from their privileged friends. Cowper describes a parish priest as

> Loose in morals and in manners vain,
> In conversation frivolous, in dress
> Extreme; at once rapacious and profuse,
> Frequent in park with lady at his side,
> Ambling or prattling scandal as he goes,
> But rare at home and never at his books.

George Grenville considers bishoprics of two kinds: bishoprics of business for men of abilities and learning and bishoprics of ease for men of family and fashion. Among the first are Canterbury and York, London and Ely; Durham, Winchester, Salisbury, and Worcester are among the second. There is Dr. Taylor with his prebend in Westminster, his London benefice and his great comfortable house at Ashbourne with no park but a little enclosure behind his house in which there are about thirty bucks and does, his bullocks and runts (young cows)—he is just the man towards whom preferments seem naturally to flow, and who will hurry up to London in his large roomy postchaise drawn by four stout plump horses and driven by two steady jolly postillions to urge his claim on the ministry for a deanery. "Sir, I love him," Dr. Johnson says, "but I do not love him more. My regard for him does not increase. As it is said in the Apocrypha, his talk is of bullocks. I do not suppose he is very fond of my company. His habits are by no means sufficiently clerical. This he knows that I see, and no man likes to live under the eye of perpetual disapprobation."

A true Irish bishop has nothing more to do than to eat, drink, grow fat, rich, and die. Paley is a notorious pluralist. Dr. Watson of Cambridge, who plants trees and blasts rocks on his estate, is all the happier because he is Bishop of Llandaff, Regius Professor of Divinity, and Rector not a few parishes away in the less desirable Midlands. He never visits his parishes or his diocese.

Among the clergy there are poachers and fox hunters who, having spent the morning scampering after the hounds, dedicate the evening to the bottle and reel from inebriety to the pulpit. With the exception of the Methodists there is a general indifference to religion, and even a good churchman like Dr. Johnson despises and dislikes the Revivalists. "I had a walk in New Inn Hall Garden with Dr. Johnson, Sir Robert Chambers, and some other gentlemen," says Lord Eldon. "Sir Robert was gathering snails and throwing them over the wall into his neighbor's garden. The doctor reproached him very roughly and stated to him that this was unmannerly and unneighborly. 'Sir,' said Sir Robert, 'my neighbor is a Dissenter.' 'Oh!' said the Doctor, 'if so, Chambers, toss away, toss away as hard as you can.'"

Advertisement—"Wanted, a curacy in a good sporting country, where the duty is light and the neighborhood convivial."

CHAPTER 15

SORROWS OF A PLACEMAN

GEORGE SELWYN SITS FOR LUDGERSHALL
for seven years—the full space of one Parliament. It is
probable that on his father's death in 1751 he might have
become junior member for Gloucester if he had so chosen.
John Selwyn had been M. P. for that borough for seventeen
years and had won the respect and esteem of all good citizens in that time. A deputation from the Corporation of
Gloucester waits upon George in London "to consult with
him concerning a representative in the room of your dear
and ever honored father." But it is not until the general
election of 1754 that he himself becomes a member for
Gloucester City.

Selwyn begins his career as M. P. for Gloucester with
all the omens favorable. His family is well known in the
city; his father was immensely popular; and he himself is
not disliked. But his parliamentary connection with Gloucester is anything but untroubled. During the first Parliament from 1754–61 he has no difficulty with his constituents
and he is reelected in 1761 without opposition. But in 1768
all this is changed. For some reason or other George loses
his popularity and is in imminent danger of losing his seat.
Can we account for this sad state of things? It is not difficult to do so. George Selwyn is a thick and thin government man, a contemner of Wilkes and Liberty, a fervent
supporter of the privileges of the Crown. Now there is
always a good deal of sturdy radicalism in Gloucester, even
from the days of the Commonwealth. The good burgesses
are loyal and law abiding, but they admire John Wilkes and

think the squint-eyed patriot a sadly persecuted man. (Wilkes and Liberty are everything with the people. The mobs insult his Majesty with "Wilkes forever, and no Jack Bute." "Wilkes and Liberty" is such a byword that people commence their letters with "Sir, I take the Wilkes and liberty to assure you," etc., etc. Such is Wilkes' popularity that his likeness is made to swing on the signboards of half the ale houses in the kingdom. He himself relates that one day, walking behind an old lady, he hears her exclaim as she glances up to one of these evidences of his popularity—"Ah! he swings everywhere but where he ought.") Above all the burgesses have their "feelings," which George steadily refuses to consider. He is essentially an aristocrat who regards constituents as necessary nuisances, nasty people who unfortunately have votes and things of that sort and who must therefore have some little attention paid them. Now an M. P. of this type may be very virtuous, but he is bound in time to achieve unpopularity. And he invariably complains bitterly when the storm breaks. The storm breaks upon Selwyn at the general elections of 1768.

A third candidate appears in the field. If this person were a lord or a member of a county family, things would not be so bad. But he is a low tradesman, a timber merchant. Conceive the just indignation of Mr. George Selwyn and his friends at White's. "I am heartily sorry, my dear George," writes Gilly Williams, "that this damned carpenter has made matters so serious with you." "Why did you not set his timber yard afire?" remarks Carlisle from Turin. "What can a man mean, who has not an idea separated from the foot square of a Norway deal plank, by desiring to be in Parliament?" That is the way Selwyn's friends look at it. Well, Selwyn wins the seat again. He gives, says Gilly Williams, the carpenter a duster—but only after a tremendous battle. (Selwyn takes no risks, however. He gets himself nominated and returned for a pocket borough belonging to Lord Garlies' family but elected to sit for Gloucester.)

The next election is 1774. Selwyn passes through the same horrible pangs of doubt and anxiety concerning his seat as he has done in 1768. He puts off his journey to

Gloucester as long as possible. "My heart fails me," he writes, "as the time of my going to Gloucester approaches . . . But there will be no trifling at the end of next week. Then the judges will be met, a terrible show, for I shall be obliged to dine with them and be in more danger from their infernal cooks than any of the criminals who are to be tried. How long I shall stay, the lord knows, but I hope in God not more than ten days at furthest, for I find my aversion to that part of the world greater and more insuperable every day of my life." He reaches Gloucester at last and is consoled for a few days by the presence of Horace Walpole. He feels a "'monstrous oppression of spirits" and has serious thoughts of "a total renunciation of Parliament, Ministers, and Boroughs"—and "'the emoluments attached to these connections." But he opens his trenches before the town "'as one who intends to humbug them for one seven years more." He gives a dinner to the Corporation, makes a speech (which he is glad nobody hears but themselves), and prophesies as a result a peaceable election. He is right. No third candidate troubles him on this occasion, and on the seventh of October, 1774, he is returned as M. P. for Gloucester for the fifth time.

And so he does "'humbug the town for one seven years more," or more accurately for six. As the General Election of 1780 approaches, Selwyn seems to realize that he cannot possibly hold the seat at Gloucester. He has sinned too deeply ever to be forgiven. There is the disgrace of the American War of which George, mindful of his places and his Negroes, has been a determined supporter. Like Burke at the neighboring city of Bristol, he has been "How-de-do'd" out of all hopes of success at the election by an enterprising candidate, Mr. Webb, while he, Selwyn, was attending to his parliamentary duties (and emoluments) in London. To be more apt, while he slept an enemy has been sowing tares. But the time comes when he has once more "to engage in the bustles and disputes of that abominable town of Gloucester." He goes down to Matson early in August whence he writes to his nephew Charles Townshend: "I thank you for wishing me out of my difficulties.

The most oppressive one to me is that of breathing. I find
my cough but very little better, and my nights are the most
uncomfortable in the world. I am the more dispirited because I have here no advice but that which I brought from
London upon which I can depend. There are but two
Apothecaries, and they are both in opposition to me. One is
so violent that I cannot trust him to make up the medicine
which Dr. Robinson has prescribed, and the other is afraid
of coming to my house lest he should give umbrage to his
party. I was in hopes that change of air would supply the
best of other remedies, but it has done me as yet little
good that I perceive. I must have patience . . . Pray write
to me a line now and then. I long to hear how things
are likely to go in the West Indies, or more properly are
gone. Yours most affectly."

Again on the 31st of August: "That I have kept my seat
six and twenty years is much more astonishing than that I
am obliged to resign it now." In another letter to Carlisle:
"I wish to God that it was all at an end—

> What sin, to me unknown,
> Dipped me in this, my father's or my own."

The answer is, entirely his own. It is his intention "to resign
all thoughts of being a candidate at the next election"—
so he informs Lord North—because he is ill, and it will cost
money which he cannot spare, and above all: "I have subjected myself to the humours of these people till I am quite
tired of them." Lord North, however, persuades him to
stand together with Sir Andrew Hammond in the government interest. The opposition candidates are Mr. Charles
Barrow and Mr. John Webb. So many freemen of Gloucester live in London that the candidates on both sides
make special efforts to secure the London vote. Selwyn's
nephew Charles Townshend works indefatigably. But in
vain. The election ends on the 14th of September, 1780,
when Mr. Webb and Mr. Barrow are returned. This is a
grievous blow to Selwyn and his friends who have been
hoping for a different result. "I have so strong a presenti-
ment of your success," writes Dr. Warner, "that I am almost

tempted to give you joy of the event tomorrow." Alas, on the morrow, George is hurrying to London with an angry mob at his heels.

DEAR CHARLES—I am this evening setting out for London. I was yesterday burned, and today hung in effigy upon a sign post. The election for the County is today and the Town full of ale and mob, and I have received information that they intend when it is dark to make a visit to this house. What they will do here, the Lord knows . . . I have left behind me a dying speech which is now printing off, and of which I shall bring you a copy. I shall hear tomorrow by the servants if a House at Matson remains or not.

Yours most affectionately,
G. S.

Matson remains, but Selwyn has had enough of Gloucester. "That infernal place," he calls it. "It has been truly a cittá dolente to me." On the 6th of November he resigns his position as Alderman of the City (he has been Alderman for many years and twice elected Mayor), but the Corporation refuses to accept his resignation. From Gloucester he goes to Ludgershall where he is received with ringing of bells and bonfires. "Being driven out of my capital and coming into that country of turnips where I was adored," says Selwyn, "I seemed to be arrived in my Hanoverian dominions."

Selwyn keeps his seat in the House by returning himself together with Lord Melbourne for the borough of Ludgershall. And it would be pleasant now to record that his parliamentary troubles are over, that in the shelter of his Wiltshire pocket borough he remains free from all anxieties about votes and interests for the rest of his days. Alas, it is not so. For who would think that the modern spirit would penetrate to Wiltshire in time for the election of 1790, that the free and independent voters of Ludgershall, tainted with the heresies of the French Revolution, scorched by those flying sparks which Selwyn dreads so much, should begin to murmur about their "rights," should fail to appreciate their grand old privilege of supporting whomever the lord of the manor commands them to support? Yet so it is.

[200]

Once again sympathy is being invited for this poor harassed gentleman whose most cherished ideas on the subject of property and of politics are being thus rudely attacked. To Mary Townshend: "I thought nothing of this kind could have happened, having had so much reliance upon the nature of the borough and supposing that whatever was wanting to confirm our property in it would be supplied by the vigilance of others. Weak princes are always supine and lose by security what could not have been extorted from them if they did not think themselves secure. This misfortune I undergo and share with my most christian brother Louis XVI. The Poissards of Paris or of Ludgershall were too much despised by us, and I shall not be surprised if, instead of being at the head of the poll, my head may be upon one before the election is over, for I am told that the democrates at Ludgershall are already very riotous and may overpower les troupes de ma maison."

But in spite of the "democrates" Selwyn is on the 12th of June, 1790, again returned for Ludgershall.

Fortunately there is nothing complex about George's political creed. His is the simple faith of the Vicar of Bray and he holds it with the same engaging candor and firmness. In short George is a placeman who holds that it is the first duty of all placemen to keep their places and to annex as many more as circumstances (and a friendly Prime Minister) will permit. His creed may be reduced to the following—

1. Government is an important body of persons to whom a mysterious Providence has confided the patronage of a large number of well-paid sinecure Places.

2. It is better to have a Place than not to have a Place. Remember this when what you call your convictions trouble you.

3. All governments should be supported while there is the slightest chance of receiving a Place in exchange for a Vote. Death-bed repentances on the part of governments are not unknown; therefore be careful how you withdraw your valuable support from a Minister. A Placeman should keep his eye upon the eleventh hour.

[201]

4. You may abuse an Opposition as much as you like. When it becomes a Government, however, treat it with respect. It is pedantic to carry your prejudices into the Opposition Lobby.

5. Subject to the foregoing, the King should be master in his own house.

The fifth article is added out of fairness to Selwyn. He is a Placeman, it is true, but he is a King's man also. Perhaps he is a King's man because he thinks that the King will always and eventually win against aspiring politicians. But he has also an hereditary attachment to the royal house which is unselfish and genuine. "If I only see his (the King's) hat upon the throne," he cries once in an ecstasy of loyalty, "and ready to be put upon his head when he can come and claim it . . . I shall be satisfied." Can King worship be more touching than this?

As to whether Selwyn is a Whig or a Tory, what does it matter? The placeman knows not these political distinctions. They mean nothing to him. Selwyn is a Whig by birth, but he is a "discoloured" Whig. No matter, he is a Government man. Newcastle and Pitt, Bute and Grenville and Rockingham—Selwyn votes for them all, with possible qualms of conscience when the liberal Rockingham is in office. He rejoices at the Pitt-Grafton coalition (1766–1770), acceptable as it is to the King, and is soon in negotiation with the Duke of Grafton about a place. "I had yesterday morning my conference with the D. of G. He has assured me that I should have the place of Treasurer to the Queen, added to that which I already have . . . The two places together, if I am not mistaken in the estimate, will be near £2300 per annum. I'm much obliged to the D. for his liberal and kind manner of treating with me. I have succeeded better, I find, in negotiating for myself, than when I employed another, but I have this time to deal with a person who seemed willing to comply with anything which I could propose in reason and has even gone beyond my proposals. And I have reason to flatter myself that His Majesty has not that reluctance to oblige me which his Grandfather had and has certainly a much better opinion of me."

But George is never appointed Treasurer to the Queen. "I do assure you, my dear Lord," he writes to Carlisle in 1773, "my spirits are very much below par for a variety of reasons, and I wish that I could go from hence to change the scene. The ill treatment which I have met with from the D. of G. and Lord North has been very ill-timed, and the altercation there has been about it very disagreeable to me." It is certainly very unkind of the Duke of Grafton, who has often entertained Selwyn at Euston and relieved him of a good deal of money at cards. Why visit great houses and play the deuce with your fortune if nothing results? But never mind. Grafton has failed him; he will try North. "Except North take me by the hand, poverty is to be *juncundus amicus in viâ pro vehiculo* [a pleasant male companion on the road instead of a vehicle]." But Lord North has so many people to take by the hand. Selwyn, however, goes on steadily supporting his lordship's administration, steadily voting with him on the American War. There is nothing else to do, for is not the Opposition proposing all kinds of terrible innovations in the ancient constitution of the realm?

There is Burke's Bill, for example. Burke has been very civil to Selwyn, notwithstanding political differences. But what is a poor placeman to do when civil persons take to depriving him of bread and butter? Conceive Selwyn's feelings on listening to a certain Speech on Economical Reform in 1780. Burke begins by attacking the King's household, the wardrobe, and kitchen, and the rest. Well, that does not affect us. We are not Lord Chamberlain or Groom of the Stole. But now the terrible man turns to the Board of Works of which institution we happen to be Paymaster. "The good works of that Board of Works are as carefully concealed as other good works ought to be; they are perfectly invisible . . . *That office too has a treasury and a paymaster of its own*"—tut, tut—"*and lest the arduous duties of that important exchequer should be too fatiguing, that paymaster has a deputy to partake his profits and relieve his cares . . .* I propose, therefore, along with the rest, to pull down this whole ill-contrived scaffolding, which obstructs, rather than forwards, our public works." Well, we have heard the worst. We mop our brow and think regretfully of our threatened four hundred a year. Four hundred a—but what is that? "The mint, though not a department of the household, has the same vices." (Sensation in the bosom of the Clerk of the Irons and Surveyor of the Meltings: a poor thing, sir, that post.) "It is a great expense to the nation, chiefly for the sake of members of Parliament." Is it any wonder, then, that years afterwards, when the King's madness declares itself, Selwyn should exclaim in the bitterness of his soul: "That I should live to speak of my master at last as a lunatic! Burke walking at large and he in a strait waistcoat!"

(For Selwyn it is pleasant to think that Burke recovers his sanity on the fall of the Bastille. But it is also necessary and only honest to report that the great Orator and "Reformer" has clay feet despite the soaring eloquence. An odor of financial adventureship surrounds Burke's domestic ties. If his friends' schemes had succeeded, he would himself have been enriched, and in this respect it is impossible to palliate his conduct by relating it to the morality of the age. Burke's Bill for Economical Reform deals a blow at eighteenth century corruption. But between Burke's intentions and his actions there is a wide gulf which no amount of sophistry can ever hope to bridge. He is overwhelmed by the intensity of his family connections and is temperamentally incapable of seeing what would be clear as daylight to any lesser intelligence. He shows a serious lack of responsibility. For instance he approaches Lord North in the matter of his brother Richard's shady land speculations at a time when he is threatening that minister with impeachment (Richard, too, is a welcher in his debts); he attempts to further the schemes of his kinsman William in India when he is impeaching Warren Hastings (William trails a reputation of chicanery from England to India; his juggling with Indian exchange is scandalous); besides he attempts to obtain for his son the second fattest plum on the Exchequer when he is laboring to force through Parliament a series of bills for suppressing such abuses and for putting down jobbery and corruption. At the Literary Club Hawkins once attacks him for stockjobbing. His friend, the Bishop of Chester, describes his house as a "hole of adders." His friends and relatives—to him—are God's noblemen, their adversaries unmitigated scoundrels. His welfare is involved in the dealings of William and Richard Burke, for the household is a financial unit and all within share in the failures or successes of any member. Should the dreams of William and Richard in East India stock come true, there will be no financial problem for the Burkes. They constitute one household, one treasury, one secretariat.

(We need only mention in passing Burke's salaried service as agent of the State of New York during the agitation of repeal of the Stamp Tax and the matter of conciliation with the Colonies, (though one biographer indulgently calls that employment a lucrative "side-line activity" that hardly affects his main interests, purposes, and conduct in public life) and his large loans from members of his party—with no record of repayment—"the mastery of living on nothing a year," as Thackeray calls it. The worries of being a debtor weigh less than the prestige and pleasure of being a landed gentleman. The purchase of his estate, Gregories, when he has no money to speak of, is consummated by loans or mortgages from friends to the tune of £20,000. And at his magnificent country estate he entertains lavishly—and borrows chronically. He even turns to Garrick for a loan of £1,000.

To put it mildly, Burke is imprudent, and the imputation is always that he is an Irish adventurer, a ne'er-do-well and upstart—and that is one of the reasons he never attains cabinet rank. But to return to our honest placeman.)

As Lord North's government verges to its decline in 1782 Selwyn finds himself between the devil and the deep sea. He has served the devil faithfully but for naught; the deep sea of the Opposition is about to overwhelm him. He undergoes all the racking agonies of the placeman—the pangs of alternate hope and fear, the sad remembrance of promises broken and vows unfulfilled. He sees the storm coming and awaits it philosophically. "I have only desired, if they are resolved to turn me out, to have three months' warning, that I may get into another place, which I shall certainly have if I go with the same character which I had in my last. I am sober and honest and have no followers, and although I used to be out at nights and play at the alehouse, I have now left it off." He is filled with horror and indignation at the talk which he hears at White's—Charles Fox's talk and Richard Fitzpatrick's and that of the other young bucks of the Opposition. However: "No future minister can hurt me, for none will I ever trust. Lord North and his Secretary have acted such a part by me that I should never have believed anything but a couple of attorneys of the lowest class to have done." While the cabinet making is going on, George's spirits rise and fall daily. "When I left the House, I left in one room a party of young men, who made me, from their life and spirits, wish for one night to be twenty. There was a table full of them drinking—Young Pitt, Lord Euston, Berkley, North, etc., etc., singing and laughing à gorge deployée. Some of them sang very good catches; one Wilberforce, an M. P., sang the best."

But George is in no humor for singing catches. He goes home and writes to Carlisle: "I utter no complaint, but I feel the danger I am in, and the distress which it may occasion to me, and still more Lord North's abominable treatment of me." It is quite like North's insensibility to sing catches while people's places are in danger. Yet on another day: "Burke was last night in high spirits. I told him that I hope, now they had forced our entrenchments and broke loose, that he and his friends would be compassionate lions, tenderhearted hyenas, generous wolves. You remember that speech of his; he was much diverted with the application." Again: "The juncture of time"—'tis the eleventh hour, friends—"the abominable treatment which I have received from the late ministry, and the little expectation of any favor from the present, hold out to me a most melancholy prospect . . . I long to see you, Lady Carlisle, and the children. This is the only balm in this infernal business." But our nephew Tommy Townshend is

Secretary of State in the new ministry, and really . . . you never know. "If any favor is shown to me, it must come to me in a becoming manner, or I shall not accept it." The eleventh hour has struck. North the villain has gone out without a word, and the Opposition at length has become a Government. Away, therefore, with pedantry! Away with prejudice! "The new government, for it is more than a new administration, has given me quite a new system for my own conduct. If they have by violence, etc. got into places from whence I would have excluded them, if now they should behave rightly in them, and the country becomes better and safer for their conduct, *it would be folly not to assist them.*" Truly George is the Perfect Placeman.

Well, Fox and his friends come into power for a few months. Burke's Bill becomes an act, and the Paymaster of the Works loses his place. But the balm is not long delayed. Rockingham dies, Shelburne falls, Mr. Fox (late Charles) and Lord North form their fatal coalition; that too disappears. And then young Mr. Pitt comes into power. "A premier at the starting post," Selwyn calls him once—and so he is. Besides the Selwyn family is on terms of personal friendship with the Chatham family—"Mr. Townshend and the family at Frognal desire to join with Mrs. Selwyn in congratulations to Lord and Lady Chatham, the Lady Pitt and the Mr. Pitt on this occasion."

This agreeable friendship bears fruit after many days. Mr. Pitt becomes Premier on December 18, 1783. Nine days afterwards *The Morning Chronicle* announces that George Selwyn has been appointed Surveyor General of Crown Lands. Let us leave the member for Ludgershall in his last and most lucrative place, calmly enjoying his £800 a year, doubly sweet after the long bitterness of waiting.

There is no record of Selwyn's ever having made a speech of any length or importance during his forty-three years of parliamentary life. Ordinary members are content to leave speechmaking to the gladiators of the Front Bench. But Selwyn attends the House steadily, does his duty in the Lobby, and sleeps profoundly through the long debate.

But even then there are duties to which the private member, however somnolent, has to attend. There are lawyers wanting judgeships, country gentlemen yearning for peerages, deans waiting preferment, and humbler citizens desirous like their betters of snug berths under the government. Finally there is the lamprey pie to be presented every year to the Prince of Wales from the Corporation of Gloucester.

The annals of Selwyn's quiet life in Parliament include his work on Private Bill Committees. As chairman of one of these committees, George seems to admire his own performance prodigiously. But no sooner does he begin to read the preamble to the Bill (Sedgemoor Enclosure) than he finds himself in a nest of hornets. "The room was full, and an opposition made to it, and disputes upon every word, which kept me in the chair, as I have told you. I have gained, it seems, a great reputation, and am at this moment regarded as one of the best chairmen on this stand." But in spite of George's talents, the Bill is lost. "It is surprising," says he, "what a fatality attends some people's proceedings. I begged last night, as for alms, that they would meet me to settle the votes. But my advice was slighted and twenty people were walking about the streets who could have carried this point.". . .

Burke is making one of his confounded harangues in the House on economy and Selwyn is tired. "I've had enough of it," he says to his friend Wraxall, "shall we go upstairs?" So bowing to the Speaker the two men leave the chamber and mount the stairs to the committee room where there is an arm chair and a fire. There Selwyn gossips about the old days at Court, about Molly Lepell and Mrs. Howard and Mary Bellenden, about the Duchess of Portsmouth even, Charles II's mistress. She knew a lot about the Stuarts, that queer old lady. What's this she said once about Charles I's executioner? She asserted that Charles was not beheaded either by Colonel Pride or Colonel Joyce, though one of the two is commonly considered to have performed the act. The Duchess claimed, says Selwyn, that the man's name was Richard Brandon. When on a sunny afternoon in January, 1649, Charles stepped upon the scaffold, he was confronted by two masked executioners. One of these was Brandon. He wore a black crape stretched over his face and had no sooner taken off the King's head than he was put into a boat at Whitehall Stairs together with the block, the black cloth that covered it, the axe, and every article stained with blood. Being conveyed to the Tower, all the implements used in the decapitation were immediately reduced to ashes. A purse containing a hundred broad pieces of gold was delivered to him after which recompense he was discharged. Brandon survived the transaction many years, but divulged it a short time before he expired. . . .

The talk drifts on until it gets dark, and the narrator begins to nod when Wraxall steals away, leaving Selwyn quietly sleeping.

CHAPTER 16

PARIS: FASHION

SELWYN SUCCUMBS TO WHAT THE ENGLISH
papers call the French disease—going to Paris. In this he
resembles the majority of young men of fashion who with
but little persuasion will forsake the clubs of St. James's
Street or the waters of Bath for the many dear delights
of the French capital. The leaders of society are as much
Parisians as Londoners. They get from France their dress,
their carriages, their trinkets, their drink, and their morals.
"They are indeed," writes Lady Hervey of the French, "a
charming people, inhabiting a delightful country. Oh, that
my lot had fallen in that fair ground! I had then a goodly
heritage."

Paris is the sightseer's paradise. It is the home of polite
manners. The English come there in droves. Within two
years of the peace of 1763 no less than forty thousand pass
through Calais. They make friends in Paris and the more
they make friends, the more they are induced to go. Lady
Mark Coke is present at a dinner where there are eighteen,
all English. General Conway makes ninety acquaintances
in a few weeks. Fox finds the younger members of the
French aristocracy quite congenial companions; Garrick
goes and establishes a friendship with the leading members
of the French stage. Adam Smith talks political economy
with Turgot and Dr. Burney, music with L'Abbé Arnaud.
Wilkes displays to the French nobility the vices of an English macaroni, Fitzpatrick shows them how to gamble, Shelburne learns economics. The Duchess of Northumberland
pays court to Mme. du Barry, Georgiana of Devonshire

excites Mme. du Deffand and her circle with the charms of English beauty. Lord March dines out night after night, once with the Prince de Soubise, another with Mme. de Choiseul, a third with the Duc de Chartres. Lord Carlisle sups one day at Mme. Aiguillon's, another time at Mme. du Deffand's, and then has a posse of people to dine with him. And so it is with all.

Englishmen move about freely (even in times of war), though subjected to discreet police supervision. Parisian hostesses are anxious to make their guests feel at home. Thus the Maréchale de Villars in the middle of a vast dinner in honor of the Duchess of Bedford, suddenly exclaims in tragic accents—"Oh, Jesus! They have forgot! Yet I bespoke them and I am sure they are ready. You English love hot rolls." And the guests have to do justice to an enormous dish of hot rolls swimming in melted butter. When the Parisians get hold of a real philosopher: "I eat," says David Hume, "nothing but ambrosia, drink nothing but nectar, breathe nothing but incense, and tread upon nothing but flowers."

The air is light and stimulating. It has a pleasant effect on the spirits similar to that of good champagne, only far more abiding.

Paris stands for three things: fashion, the Court, the salon. England is a provincial town; it must wait to see what is done at Paris. Paris is the centre of fashion. It sets the tone for dress, for manners, for the art of living generally. An English gentleman does not consider himself dressed unless he wears the latest Parisian designs in velvets and ruffles and wigs. When he comes to Paris, he cannot appear until he has undergone a total metamorphosis. He must even change his buckles and the form of his ruffles and (though at the risk of his life) suit his clothes to the mode of the season. Neither old age nor infirmity will excuse him for wearing a hat upon his head either at home or abroad. The good man who is used to wear a plain English cloth suit and a bob wig all the year round must here provide himself with a camblet suit trimmed with silver for spring and autumn, with silk clothes for summer, and cloth laced with gold or velvet for winter, and he must wear his bag wig à la pigeon. Footmen and coachmen wear scarlet and plumes and gold and silver. Their cravats are worn so short that they can scarcely be seen. At present they are to the neck and hang down like Bologna sausages.

When excessive cold and sharp weather comes in, on a sudden all the world gets into muffs, some so large and unwieldy as to oblige the owners to have a sort of belt of the same skin come over one shoulder to support their enormity. Some are as big as a mastiff dog. Even beggars and mumpers in the streets have their muffs.

Shoes are an artistic production. Extravagant as they are in price, yet it is impossible to speak of such marvels of workmanship as dear. The cordonnier of the day—to translate him into shoemaker is to drag him from his pedestal— is truly an artist.

Young ladies take to using long gold-headed canes which they hold in the middle like the suisse at the door of a nobleman's residence. This leads to the introduction of very costly canes made of scented wood, tortoise shell, and ivory.

When coiffures continue to increase, they at last reach such a pitch that ladies find the roof of the carriage too low and are either obliged to put their heads out of the window or to ride in a kneeling posture. Scaffoldings of hair are crumped, curled, frizzled, plaited, and surcharged with feathers, ribbons, gauze, wreaths, flowers, fruit, pearls, and diamonds. There are coiffures representing landscapes, gardens, mountains, and forests—and fancy names are given to them—the oisseau royal, chien couchant, hérisson, hats à l'enigme, à la mont-desir, à l'économie du siècle, au desir de plaire, poufs à la Pierrot, parterres galants, caps au becquet, aux clochettes and à la physionomie, bonnets anonymes, coiffures à la candeur, au berceau d'amour, au mirliton, etc. To have the beauty of their headdresses, the ladies introduce a parasol or umbrella of silk which covers them in summer from the sun and in winter from the rain.

It is unpardonable not to have "vapours," for only market women have the right to be in robust health. All ladies of fashion make a point of being affected with these vapors as an excuse for their yawning and headaches. "You feel your head heavy," says the doctor in *Le Cercle* to one of his lady patients, "you feel disinclined to do anything which requires effort . . . I understand there is a certain amount of giddiness and fibrous impatience. These are all 'vapours'; the nervous fluid is electrified by the heat." (Vapours are not stylish, though, in salons.)

Men compete with the women in fashionable matters. Fops provide an example for the beaus in England. They wear earrings and chat of ribbons, pompons, and other feminine fal-lals, do tapestry work, and receive in bed at noon. They interrupt serious conversations to speak to a poodle, talk to their own reflection in the glass, caress their laces, work themselves in a passion for a broken ornament, and fall into a fit over a sick parrot.

But the women think a great deal and rule. They are queens in the drawing room: it is their right. They flock to lectures on anatomy and physics, and one enthusiast actually travels with a corpse at the back of her coach for dissecting purposes.

Paris is the home of culture, the mother of intellect, the center of good society. At Paris an article on the Patriarchs by Voltaire makes as much noise as an attack upon the minority by Charles Townshend ever makes in London. And the mere rumor that Rousseau is likely to walk in the Luxembourg Gardens will draw larger crowds than in England assemble at a horse race. "People may talk of ancient Greece as they please, but no nation is ever so fond of genius as this."

Paris is the schoolhouse of Europe to which the youth of Russia, Germany, and England resort to become civilized. Lord Chesterfield never tires of reminding his son of this and of urging him into these drawing rooms to remove his Cambridge rust. Gustavus III, beaten by the Russians, declares he will pass his last days in Paris in a house on the boulevards. This is not complimentary, for he sends for plans and an estimate. A supper or an evening entertainment brings people two hundred leagues away. Some friends of the Prince de Ligne leave Brussels after breakfast, reach the Opera in Paris just in time to see the curtain rise, and after the spectacle is over, return immediately to Brussels travelling all night.

At Venice the Carnival lasts six months; in Paris it lasts the entire year. The town rings with the clatter of fine equipages. It is a swarm of liveries, uniforms, costumes, as brilliant and varied as in a picture. Drawing rooms are two stories high, saloons vast, ballrooms immense, galleries so long that they run out of sight, and staircases gigantic. In fact the people live solely in order to entertain. Foreigners are overcome with admiration when they see the houses so tastefully arranged and so charmingly decorated.

Paris provides more public amusements than any other place in the world. Little theatres are set up in the country around Paris. Those of highest rank set the example. Masked balls at the Opera are mobbed. Ladies of fashion appear in black dominoes and masked to the eyes, and the disguise covers their feet and hair. They arrive in sedan chairs and go home in wheel chairs. Gentlemen leave their swords at the door, and it is considered bad form to address a mask as Thou. Conversation is carried on in low tones, and as the men are not masked, half the company knows the other half but are themselves unknown. Thus the ladies are able to mystify and intrigue the gentlemen.

The world crowds to see and hear the famous dancers and singers—Jelotte and La Guimard, la Théodore, Dupré, and Vestis (*le Diou de la* dance, who once exclaims—"I know of only three great men in Ourope: the King of Proussia, Voltaire, and myself.") The applause is loud and unceasing when Dupré appears and sings the lovely songs of Naïs—"les Indes galantes." And there are always fireworks. There is nothing more amusing than to let off small fireworks on the table.

Chevalier Gluck, composer and Knight of the Papal Order of the Golden Star, makes his appearance in Paris. He is common, unpolished, and much disfigured by the scars and seams of smallpox. He is arrogant and insolent. He subjects his orchestra and singers to a German drill, and finally, on August 4, 1774, his *Iphigénie* is produced

on the operatic stage in triumph. It is a triumph also for
Marie Antoinette on her first public appearance as Queen.
When therefore the Grand Chorus—*Chantons, célébrons
notre reine*—first bursts on the ear, all eyes are instantly
turned towards the royal box. The audience rises and with
spontaneous enthusiasm salutes the young Queen in the
words of the chorus—*"Chantons, célébrons notre reine."* The
choir, the principal singers, Iphigénie herself, follow the
example of the audience, bowing to the Queen and singing
with an energy that delights the heart of Gluck. The King
too is present, though it is his custom to be in bed by
eleven and up at five to transact business.

At the second representation of the opera, the audience
is even more numerous than at the first. It is indeed a less
courtly and more noisy one, but the opinions of amateurs
are more decidedly expressed. The men stamp, wave hats,
shout as if delirious—*Vivent Gluck et Iphigénie*. Soldiers are
placed at the entrance to restrain the energy of those who
are determined to wedge their way in. Women throw their
gloves, fans, and laced handkerchiefs on the stage. Others
in more tender emotion, sigh, sob, and faint. But this may
be due to the uproar and confusion around them more than
to the charm of the music. (To see ladies with highly
plumed coiffures and the turnips, beet roots, cherries, car-
rots, and cabbages of the *belle jardinière* take to fainting
with emotion, and the scaffolding and various appurten-
ances of these yard and a half edifices come tumbling down
is a pretty scene indeed.)

A celebrated amateur is there the second night who
squeezes himself into a niche at the farthest corner of the
salle. Those who observe him closely and see the enthusiasm
with which he applauds, are of the opinion that he actually
does for a while forget the existence of his own interesting
self to revel in a dream of music. As soon as he is recognised, he has the mortification of hearing his name coupled
with that of the famous German composer—*Vive Rousseau!
Vive l'auteur du 'Devin du Village!' Vivent Rousseau et
Gluck! Vive l'Iphigénie!* Recalled to himself by these un-
wonted acclamations, Jean Jacques, apparently much morti-

fied, makes a hasty retreat. Doubtless he thinks it a conspiracy to deprive him of the pleasure of hearing the opera to the end.

Piccinni and Marmontel succeed Gluck, and Italian music becomes the rage. The ladies declare it full of sweetness, charm, and grace.

Is anyone old in these days? It is the Revolution which brings old age into the world. People are handsome, elegant, neat, gracious, perfumed, playful, amiable, affectionate, and good tempered to the day of their deaths. There are no troublesome infirmities. If one has the gout, he walks along all the same and makes no faces. There is not that absorption in business which spoils a man and dulls his brain. It is thought much better to die at a ball or at the play than in one's bed between four wax candles and horrid men in black.

When after enjoying the delights of Paris, Galiani has to leave it forever, he writes to Mme. d'Epinay on his return to Naples—"I am still inconsolable even at Naples! at having left Paris . . . Paris, my Love, and even though I have been exiled, I shall return . . . It is not merely a question of my pleasure but of my very existence. Every day I feel and experience, more and more, that it is physically impossible for me to live away from Paris. Weep for me as for the dead if I do not return."

(The ladies of Paris have the most enchanting airs and vivacious eyes in the world, but they make themselves hideous by great blotches of paint upon their cheeks which in some cases are as red as the Saracen's Head upon a sign post.

(The English regard the French as lacking in delicacy and decency. A French lady's knee is as modest as the elbow of an English lady. And the people have a habit of spitting up and down their houses and churches. Madame with all her affected airs is constantly hawking and spitting upon the floor during the whole time of dinner. Even the greatest ladies and men of the first fashion are doing so or what is still nastier pulling out their white handkerchiefs and spitting half snuff and half something else into them, for every Frenchman is a snuff-taker. Even Mme. du Deffand in the middle of a dinner, while talking of the Dauphin's little prospect of recovery, assures the company that his Royal Highness has a greater chance than they are aware of—for she has that very morning been informed from Fontaine-bleau that he had a very stinking and fetid stool the evening before and that in great abundance.

(But the English carry their delicacy in this and many other points to too great lengths, particularly in the practise of not going to the necessary conveniences, especially among the ladies, when it is dangerous often to abstain from it.

(In crossing the Channel a French kitchen maid enters into conversation with a servant of the Reverend William Cole and makes herself so talkative, pert, and forward that her tongue runs on at an immoderate rate. At last she addresses the minister himself, as understanding her language, to desire him to beg one of the sailors to give her a chamber pot. Upon which, thinking she is sick, as many are upon deck, he advises her to go to the side of the ship and adds that his servant will hold her by her gown to prevent her from tumbling overboard. But she directly tells him that however practicable such a situation may be for them, it will not suit her at all, and without more ado or further ceremony—sans façon, à la Française— she plainly tells him she wants a chamber pot *pour faire lacher l'eau.* These are her words, so the Reverend Cole forthwith gets her accommodated with one which she, with as little shame and delicacy as ceremony, makes immediate use of, before all the company—and then gives it with the utmost sangfroid and indifference to Cole's servant to empty it overboard for her. The Irish maid cries out, Jesu Maria! and two other maids are quite abashed at the woman's impudence. Her Ladyship is vexed and chagrined at such indecency. But the woman when she sees Cole and some others of the company laughing at her action talks as reasonably and sensibly upon the occasion as anyone can—asks in plain, *gras* and indelicate words what any of them would do if a sudden griping should take them and they should want to go to the necessary house.)

Dr. Tobias Smollett who visits Paris in the course of his travels sneers at French manners and customs. That stout old Saxon travels through France and Italy in true British style, damning and denouncing most heartily the inferior ways of the foreigner, so that Mr. Sterne who follows him considers himself bound to weep copiously at every opportunity in order to prove to the foreigner that all Britons are not so unsympathetic.

But George Selwyn and his friends have none of the prejudices of Dr. Smollett. When Selwyn visits Paris, he realizes his chief aim of wasting time as gracefully as possible. When he wearies of salons, churches, palaces, gardens, theatres, operas, he sips coffee, tea, or chocolate at one of the cafés. Or drinks the popular wines of France—Bon Vin Vieux de Beaune, Preignac, Frontignan, Caste Rotie, or Hermitage. He flits from one lady's dressing table to another, paying his respects, delivers his opinion and exquisite judgment on some snuff box or suit, then escorts some languishing Duchess to the opera, talks scandal with the lady and hunting or dogs with the commander, and then demolishes a bird with the little Marquise. He sees La Grève but is disappointed—it is small. He witnesses several executions. They hang differently in France. The culprit makes his confession and then is privileged to have his dinner—an omelet and a bottle of wine. Notwithstanding the ordeal which he has to pass, he takes care to finish his bottle and then makes his entrée accompanied by the priest and Monsieur le Bourreau. The ladder is placed against the gallows, Monsieur mounts first, the culprit follows. The rope being fixed to it, the French Jack Ketch gives him a sort of Cornish hug, the ladder is taken away, and they both swing together. The Churchyard of Les Innocents is full of coffins and bodies. Selwyn looks into one, and there is a man sewed up in coarse sacking, but one of his feet is out. In his walk he sees two very pretty French women unpainted, which is a greater curiosity than any he has yet seen in Paris.

George is laden with commissions to buy the things for which the city is famous: Velvets, silks, satins, laces, watches, engravings, buckles, snuffboxes, china, glass, furniture, wines. George with the utmost good nature buys them all and sends them (or carries them) to his friends in England. Lord March asks for "a dozen pair of silk stockings for the Zamperini of a very small size and with embroidered clocks. She is but fifteen." "Vous êtes charmant pour les commissions," he observes elsewhere, which George certainly is. As for Gilly Williams, that sprightly person is always in need of velvets and point ruffles, while Henry St. John wants a library. These articles ordered from Paris are, of course, not brought to England openly; they are smuggled. George Selwyn is personally, as he informs his niece, not a great but a very successful smuggler. And if he is making a long stay in France, there are certain "smuggling captains" known to Gilly Williams and himself who can always arrange for the safe despatch of silks and laces from Calais to London without the formality of the Dover customs.

Two days before the Houses meet for the winter sessions, a string of British legislators will be walking on board at Calais in their brand new satin coats and embroidered waistcoats, which they dare not leave among their luggage, cursing the absurd customs laws which they themselves helped frame and learning more political economy in one day than they hear at Westminster in a twelve-month. Mr. Rigby brings one fine suit of clothes which he saves by wearing it when he lands. Mr. Elliot saves a coat and waistcoat, but not taking the same precaution with his breeches, they are seized and burned. All March's stockings are seized by not being taken out of the paper and rolled up which would have made them pass for old stockings. "You must wear your gold," says the Earl of Tyrone, "for not even a button will be admitted." The gentlemen of England are smugglers all. It is no sin with them to cheat the state.

CHAPTER 17

PARIS: THE COURT

PARIS POSSESSES THE MOST BRILLIANT COURT
in Europe. The English Court under George II is dull. Its
ornaments are vulgar German women, half educated peers
and their still less educated wives, and pompous and com-
monplace ecclesiastical hangers-on. But Versailles! All day
long an unbroken stream of carriages rolls between Paris
and Versailles. At the Palace there are crowds of fine ladies
and gentlemen—silks and satins, laces and ruffles, lights and
jewels and laughter.

When the King holds a "grand appartement," when play
or dancing takes place in the gallery of mirrors, four or five
hundred guests, the elect of nobility and of fashion, range
themselves on the benches or gather round the card and
cavagnole tables. An endless shining hall with arched windows and tall mirrors, and blazing chandeliers suspended
from sculptured ceilings peopled with sporting Cupids.
Light from three thousand wax candles streams down on
the glittering diamonds, the white shoulders, the shameless
bright eyes, on silver and gold hilted swords, garlanded
dresses, rows and clusters of rubies, buckles, cravats and
ruffles of lace, silk coats of the hues of fallen leaves or of a
delicate rose tint or of celestial blue embellished with gold
braid and embroidery. There are silver punch bowls set on
silver tables, pedestals of porphyry, silver perfuming pans,
ebony cabinets inlaid with copper, columns of jasper, agate,
and lapis lazuli, curtains of white silk embroidered with
fleurs-de-lys in gold, white blossoms and gold fruit among
green marble and white and mauve pilasters, and on golden

console tables baskets fashioned of glistening silver, silver stands, silver branching candlesticks, orange trees in silver boxes, silver vases, silver lustres. The great space of floor is covered with Savonnerie carpets woven in designs symbolical of kingly power.

There are pickpockets present, says de Luynes; he also grumbles at the draughts which blow out a number of candles and give several distinguished persons colds. But these are trifles. In the center of the gallery sits the King playing lansquenet and shuffling the cards for La Pompadour. The Duke of Luxembourg has the honor of standing behind the King's chair. Around the table are the Dauphin and his wife, Louis's daughters, and a great number of persons distinguished in rank. At the further end of the room the Queen has her gaming table and a number of other tables are scattered about.

The King's orchestra is in blue dominoes. After cards there is dancing to the airs of Auvergne. Ladies and gentlemen dance in circles holding each other by the hand. A lady engages her partner by offering him a bouquet. There are other fashionable dances: the *pavane* replaced by *la courante,* and that in turn giving way to the *passe-pied,* a lively Breton dance which enjoys a long run of favor. The left foot is advanced along the floor like the paw of a kitten. Ladies do not dance after reaching the age of twenty-five.

Balls on state occasions, called bals parés, are magnificent. Ladies can only appear en grande toilette with enormous paniers. The weight of heavy material on their shoulders is so great that they can hardly lift their arms. They wear narrow pointed shoes with high heels, their dresses immensely long and their hair arranged in a high coiffure loaded with precious stones. A heavy cluster of diamonds hanging from their ears completes the costume. The men wear richly ornamented coats, embroidered down all the seams—and a sash.

On days of reception the throng is so great that it is only possible to talk to two of three people close to where one is standing. One is literally hemmed in, and only with difficulty can one manage to pass from one room to another.

The heat is suffocating and the hubbub tumultous. All France fills the great reception room.

The multitude of people of various occupations following the King on his travels resembles the progress of an army. On the King's journey to Chantilly there go with him over two hundred servants employed in the kitchen besides sixty Swiss whose business it is to assist in serving—in all there are seven hundred persons to feed. The pomp of a royal progress is not unworthy of the dignity of an Egyptian or Assyrian monarch. Trumpets sound loudly to announce his presence. He is attended by bodies of gentlemen proud to serve as soldiers of the Queen and by companies of Swiss guards curiously and richly dressed and armed with gorgeous weapons. When the King hunts, besides the ladies on horses and in vehicles, besides the officers of the hunt, of the guard, the equerry, the cloak bearer, gun bearer, surgeon, bone setter, lunch bearer, and we know not how many others, all the gentlemen who accompany him are his permanent guests. When the dauphin is a child of seven, more than one hundred persons are required for his care. And when Marie becomes the wife of Louis XV over four hundred offices are at once created to be filled by those devoted to her service, from ladies of honor to postillions and pastry cooks.

The main thing for the first personages in the kingdom, men and women, ecclesiastics and laymen, the first duty in life, the true occupation is to be at all hours and in every place under the King's eye, within reach of his voice and of his glance. The true courtier follows the Prince as a shadow follows its body. To approach the King or to be a domestic in his household, an usher, a cloak bearer, a valet, is a privilege that is purchased for thirty, forty, and one hundred thousand livres. Old courtiers are found who, eighty years of age, have passed forty-five in the antechambers of the King, of the Princes, and of the ministers. They have only to do three things— say nice things to everybody, solicit every post that is likely to become vacant, and sit down when they can. The highest nobility is attached to Versailles like an oyster to its bed. The Duc

de Saint Simon gives up his regiment of which he is Colonel
to shut himself up at Versailles in a hole in the entresol
without any air or light so as to be near to the rays of the
sun.

Hence the King has always a crowd around him. On
getting up and on retiring, on his walks, on his hunts, His
Majesty has always around him at least forty or fifty seigniors and generally a hundred, with as many ladies, besides
his attendants on duty. People watch for him, walk by his
side and speak with him on his way from his cabinet to
the chapel, between his apartment and his carriage, between his carriage and his apartment, between his cabinet
and his dining room. The passion evinced by men at court
to be noticed by the King is incredible. When he deigns to
cast a glance at certain of them, the one who receives it
thinks that his fortune is made and boasts of it to the others
saying—"The King looked at me."

Great nobles strive for the honor of handing Louis his
cane, his snuffbox, his gloves. Ministers of religion dispute
as to who should say grace at his Majesty's meals. And to
prevent mistakes they all say it together. When his Majesty
speaks it is the voice of God. "One cannot," writes the Duc
de Luynes, "'one cannot be too much impressed by all the
marks of piety and goodness in the King." On this occasion
the piety and goodness of the King consists in the admission that even he is mortal and must die.

The King amuses himself and he amuses his guests.
There is something for every day of the week. Every evening there is a play and a reception in the King's apartments, in his daughter's, in his mistress's, in his daughter-
in-law's, besides balls, operas, excursions, grand suppers,
gaming. It really resembles an Italian carnival; there is
nothing lacking. They play, they laugh, they dance, they
dine, they listen to music, they don costumes, they get up
picnics (fêtes champêtres), they indulge in gossip and gallantries. Dances sometimes last till 8 A.M. and for several
days hardly anyone is ever out of bed in daylight. In summer promenades in gondolas with music on the canal,
promenades in the Orangery, promenades in the Gardens,

on foot, on horse, in carriages, collations and concerts at the Menagerie or at the Trianon. Banquets are spread, sweet music breathes among the trees, and fireworks are reflected in the waters of the lakes, and nymphs emerge from illuminated grottoes to sing the praises of the great King.

Mme. de Pompadour—eyes grey, skin delicate, lovely, a perfect nose, charming mouth, handsome teeth, fascinating smile, and light auburn hair. Tall, slim, elegant—makes her appearance among the cavaliers of the King's escort. One day in a blue dress contrasting with the rose colored lining of her carriage. The next in a rose colored costume on cushions of azure.

The most popular and exciting outdoor amusement is hunting. The Bourbons are all mighty hunters before the Lord, and the forests that surround Paris are full of game. The King hunts and shoots tirelessly. Today he hunts the stag at Fontainebleau, tomorrow he goes to kill partridges in the plains of St. Denis. When he is not hunting, the court is heard to say quite seriously—The King is doing nothing today. (The latest tribute royalty receives is the corpse of a huge wolf, recently killed at Gevandun, which is put on view in the Queen's antechamber and exhibited to the visitors with as much parade as if it were Mr. Pitt.)

Never is there solitude. It is the custom in France, says Horace Walpole, to burn your candle down to its snuff in public. The grandees imitate their monarch. The mansion of the Duchess de Gramont is besieged at daybreak by the noblest seigniors and the noblest ladies. Five times a week under the Duc de Choiseul's roof, the butler enters the drawing room at ten o'clock in the evening to bestow a glance on the immense crowded gallery and decide if he shall lay the cloth for fifty, sixty, or eighty persons.

At the Palais Royal those who are presented may come to the supper on opera days. At Chateauvilain all those who come to pay court are invited to dinner, the nobles at the Duke's table and the rest at the table of his first gentleman. At the Temple one hundred and fifty guests attend the Monday suppers. Forty or fifty persons, says the

QUIZ-ZING a FILLY

"OLD Q"

LORD MARCH, FOURTH DUKE OF QUEENSBERRY

After a caricature by James Gillray

SATIRE ON THE
FASHIONS OF 1776

"A MACARONI"

An English dandy of the 18th century
who affects foreign ways

Duchesse de Maine, constitute "a prince's private company." The prince's train is so inseparable from his person that it follows him even into camp.

Where women are concerned, it is not sufficient to be polite; it is important to be gallant. Each lady invited by the Prince de Conti to Ile-Adam finds a carriage and horses at her disposal. She is free to give dinners every day in her own rooms to her own friends. Mme. de Civrac, obliged to go to the springs, her friends undertake to divert her on the journey. They keep ahead of her a few posts and at every place where she rests for the night, they give her a little fête champêtre disguised as villagers and in bourgeois attire, all singing and reciting verses.

Richelieu is the arbiter of fashion. When appointed ambassador to Austria, his entry into Vienna is almost fairy-like. There are running footmen, lackeys in splendid livery, pages in Hungarian costumes, and his coach is decorated with symbolical figures and drawn by horses sumptuously caparisoned. Their shoes are of silver and so loosely attached that the people are able to pick them up as the dazzling Ambassador continues on the way. Voltaire calls him "the Alcibiades of France." And adds: "He is blessed with virtue, honor, and debts."

The King no longer imposes that stillness around him which lets one hear a fly walk. The great are less concerned in overawing than in pleasing. They seek less than applause. Even around the throne the style is easy and cheerful. The King asks M. de Brèvre, chief punster at the court, to make a pun. "On what subject, sire?" "It does not matter. On me if you like." "Your Majesty is not a subject," is de Brèvre's prompt reply.

Louis XV eats astoundingly although his stomach is extremely elastic. His meal consists of the following:

Soups
Two grand soups of partridge and capon,
Two ordinary soups, bisque of pigeons and cocks' combs;
Four side soups of hashed capon, partridge, and lentils,
stuffed chicken, and boiled capon;

Grand Entrées
Quarter of veal and pigeon pie

Ordinary Entrées
Fricasèe of chicken and salmi of partridge

Side Dishes
Six side dishes of roast partridges, brazed pigeons,
gulled turkeys, truffled chickens, whole and in hash;

Large Dishes
Two large dishes holding fat capons, chickens, pigeons,
partridges and pies
Two dishes of woodcock, teal, young capons,
and partridges.
Vegetables, salads, creams, rissoles, and beignets.
Burgundy, champagne   mocha, coffee.

His Majesty spends the sum of 399 livres, 18 sous, 11
deniers (about £16) for his three meals of breakfast,
dinner, and supper. He never remains very long at the table
and gets into the habit of eating very fast. Often he has
boiled eggs (gourmand as he is) served at his table because
he is very adroit in striking off the Crown of the egg with
his fork. He then dips two or three sippets of bread into
the egg much to the delight of the worthy burghers of Paris
who return from Versailles full of what they have seen at
the King's dinner table.

It is very dishonorable not to be in the King's service,
but it is no dishonor to keep public gaming houses. At least
one hundred and fifty people of the first quality in Paris
live by it. You may go into their houses at all hours of the
night and find hazard, pharaoh, etc. Even the princesses of
the blood have shares in the banks kept at their houses.

Several of the leading members of the Court are frenzied
gamblers. The clergy is not free from the common taint.
The Archbishop of Rheims loses two thousand louis in a
carriage while nominally following a boar hunt. Heavy
losses ruin more than one life. Reineville, lieutenant of the
guards, who has a career before him, is obliged to disap-

pear and is found years afterwards serving as a common trooper in the army of the Elector of Bavaria. Permillac, another officer of promise, shoots himself through the head in bed. M. de Rostaing allows himself to be maintained by his mistress; M. de Muret leaves Court to become a cab driver at Lyons: he is an honorable gentleman.

With the ladies the passion for cards amounts almost to a mania. Mme. de Clérambault cares for little else in life. One superb day, on the way back from Mass, she stops on the bridge that leads into the gardens, turns slowly round in all directions, and then says: "For today I think I have had enough exercise. Ho, bien! Let us hear no more about walking but sit down to cards at once." Thereupon she produces a pack of cards, only breaks off the game for short intervals to eat a meal, and is indignant when the company leaves her at two A.M.

Mme. de Pompadour, lively and sprightly, gambles for the purpose of playing the wanton.

Games of skill are less popular than games of chance, but billiards always has its votaries. Even bishops do not despise the cue. One Bishop of Langres, after being beaten and losing heavily (for he is a great gambler), retires to his diocese for six months to practise the game in private. When he feels himself thoroughly proficient, he returns to Court, where he is at once challenged to a fresh trial of skill by his former antagonists, who expect another easy and profitable victory. The bishop at first declines, saying that he has too vivid a recollection of his former defeat, that he is, moreover, out of practise, as for the last six months, he has been seeing nobody but canons and curés. Finally he allows himself to be persuaded, plays intentionally bad at first and has the stakes doubled. In the end he shows his true form and wins back much more than he lost on the first occasion. He is assuredly, as Saint Simon remarks, a man not designed by nature to be a bishop.

Louis XV has his mistresses, but he does not allow them to ride in the same coach as the Queen.

George Selwyn when in Paris makes his bows to Majesty.

'Tis very convenient to gobble up a whole royal family in an hour's time instead of being sacrificed one week at Leicester House, another in Grosvenor Street, a third in Cavendish Square, etc., etc. The Queen takes great notice of foreigners. No one says a syllable. George is let into the King's bedchamber just as his Majesty puts on his shirt; he dresses and talks good naturedly to a few, glares at strangers, goes to Mass, to dinner, a-hunting. The good Queen, who is like Lady Primrose in the face and Queen Caroline in the immensity of her cap, is at her dressing table attended by two or three old ladies. George spends a few moments chatting with her. Thence he goes to the Dauphin, for all is done in an hour. He scarce stays a minute. The Dauphiness is in her bedchamber but dressed and standing—she looks cross and is uncivil. The four Mesdames who are clumsy, plump, old wretches stand in a bedchamber in a row with black cloaks and knotting bags, looking good humored and not knowing what to say. The ceremony is very short. Then George is carried to the Dauphin's three boys who, you may be sure, only bow and stare. The whole concludes with seeing the Dauphin's little girl who is as round and fat as a pudding.

The King is wondrous shy to strangers, awkward at a question, or too familiar. For instance, when the Duke of Richmond is presented to him, he says: "Monsieur le Duc de Cumberland boude (pouts at) le Roi, n'est ce pas?" The Duke is confounded. The King persists. "Il le fait, n'est il vrai?" The Duke answers very properly, "Ses ministres quelquefois, Sire, jamais sa Majesté." This does not stop him. "Et vous, milord, quand aurez-vous le cordon bleu?" George Selwyn who stands behind the Duke says softly, "Answer that if you can, my Lord." To Lord Holland, the King says, "Vous avez fait bien du bruit dans votre pays, n'est ce pas?" His answer is pretty too: "Sire, je fais tout mon possible pour le faire cesser."

Lord Holland is better diverted with the Duchess d'Aiguillon. She gets him and Lady Holland tickets for one of the best boxes to see fireworks on the Peace and carries them in her coach. When they arrive he finds he has forgotten the tickets. She flies into a rage and *sans marchander* abuses him so grossly that Lady Holland colors and will not speak to her. Not content with this, when her footman opens the door of the coach, the Duchess before all the mob says aloud, "C'est une les meilleurs têtes de l'Angleterre et voici la bêtise qu'il a faite," and repeats it. Lord Holland laughs, and the next day she recollects herself and makes an excuse.

Louis XV's queen is Marie Leszczynski, daughter of Stanislaus, King of Poland. She is George Selwyn's intimate friend, and Selwyn admires her with a great admiration. The Earl of March at Fontainebleau writes to him: "I dine today at what is called no dinner at Madame de Ceingnies. The Queen asked Mme. de Mirepoix, si elle n'avait pas beaucoup entendu médire de M. Selwyn et elle? Elle a répondu, oui, beaucoup, madame. J'en suis bien aise, dit la Reine."

And George Selwyn passing through Paris in 1778 sees Marie Antoinette at Versailles who wakes memories in him of the other Marie—"I dined this day sevennight," he writes to his niece, "at Versailles and was there comme une Beguille, staring at a Royal family, and I had the honour, I believe, to be stared at too by the Queen, for Mme. de Darport, who was in attendance upon her, and was so good as to reconnaître me, told her, as I imagine, who I was. But she must not expect me to be in love with her as I was with the late Queen, although she is really one of the handsomest women of her Court and seems the happiest, which, I am sorry for it, could not be said of ma pauvre Reine defuncte."

History has no stranger tale than that of how Maria Leszczynski comes to be Queen of France. Her father Stanislaus is by the grace of Charles XII, King of Poland. After Pultowa he loses his throne and flees to France where they give him a small pension. Stanislaus lives the life of a country gentleman at Weissembourg with a ragged crew of Polish retainers. He hopes that his daughter Maria will make a good match, say with a German margrave or a French Duke. He never in his wildest moments imagines her

Queen of France. But Louis XV wants a wife, or rather, it is necessary that he should marry. He is not particular in his choice and only bargains that the Lady should be passably good looking. All other troublesome details he leaves to the Duke de Bourbon, who in turn leaves them to his mistress Mme. de Prie. This woman decides that Marie Leszczynski shall be Queen. She thinks that the daughter of Stanislaus, who is poor and simple, will not forget the person to whom she owes her throne and that she will thus retain her influence.

Conceive the raptures of Maria's father and Maria's mother and of Maria herself. On hearing the news, the ex-King of Poland assembles his wife and child and tells them to kneel down, and without any explanation, thanks Heaven for this crowning mercy.

"Ah! my father," says Maria, "then you are recalled to the throne of Poland?"

"No, Heaven is far more favorable to us," says Stanislaus, "You are Queen of France." Maria is twenty one, the King fifteen.

(Stanislaus is in no position to provide his daughter with a trousseau. Not only has he been obliged to pawn his jewels, but he has to appeal to a friendly Marshal to enable him to redeem them. Maria's wardrobe is in such a deplorable state that Mme. de Prie actually sends her a present of chemises. She has not even a presentable pair of shoes to serve as models for those which are to be made for her.)

The Duc d'Antin coming to Weissembourg to make a formal demand for the hand of the Princess with a guard of one hundred and fifty strong, with grooms and footmen and pages in scarlet, with ten carriages, each drawn by ten horses, Stanislaus gathers his ragged regiment of Polish servants and goes out to meet him in a carriage hired perhaps from the nearest livery stable. He has two pages whereas etiquette requires that he should have six, and he has scarcely enough room for the little company he takes with him. His reply, however, to the ambassador's ceremonial address is brief and dignified—"I am greatly obliged to the King, Sir," he says, "not only for having given me an asylum in his realm but even more for giving me a place in his heart which I esteem more than the brilliant crown which he places on my daughter's head."

Maria is married at Strasbourg and journeys through rain and storm and mud to Paris to begin her sad life there. Marie (she is now French) is not beautiful: chestnut hair and full lips, but her nose is too long. Her heavy shoulders and breadth of body make Louis' slenderness the more noticeable. However, she has a lovely complexion, so lovely that fresh water is the only paint it requires. And she is sweet and pious; she is fond of needlework and makes altar-pieces for churches. She is called nothing but the Good Queen. She mixes her wine with a good deal of water.

When presented with a velvet cask embroidered with gold containing the splendid trifles which are called the corbeille (wedding gifts), she distributes them to her household saying, "This is the first time that I have been able to make presents."

She reads at first nothing but the celebrated Conseils, written by her father, which begins with the scriptural reminiscence—"Hearken, my daughter, behold and give ear. Forget thy people and thy father's house." Stanislaus warns his daughter of the dangers she will encounter at Court, such as grandeur and prosperity and flattery. He enlarges upon these three subjects with emotion. "Prosperity," he says, "is the more dangerous in that it is practically unknown to you. Since infancy you have participated so full in my adversity that, as you are aware, there is nothing like the experience of misfortune to guard us from abusing our happiness." Flattery inspires him to some wise precepts—"You must realize that you will be surrounded by those who will vie with one another to pay court to you. There will be no one who will not be prepared to obey you, to sacrifice his goods, his life, for your service, but there will be no one who will tell you the truth or who will not think that if he did so he would displease you and risk his fortunes. Though you are surrounded by those who are devotedly attached to you and are most attentive in your service, yet, on this point, you are left to yourself, and have nothing to rely on but your own good sense and reason."

Marie is not without wit, but it is her pleasure to shun the society of courtiers. It is her fate to sit passively by and watch other women please the King and rule both him and the country. She is often alone, but she always makes good use of her time. Her mornings are passed in prayers and serious reading. Then after a short visit to the King, there come recreations, especially painting. (The good Queen is not a master, and she is not even highly gifted. Her pictures seen at the Trianon are retouched by some obliging artist.) She also loves music—she plays the guitar, viol, and the harpsichord, and is the first to laugh at her own false notes. At half past twelve she makes her toilet, which is followed by the daily mass and dinner at which twelve ladies in waiting attend. After dinner she retires to her private apartments and is no longer Queen but an ordinary mortal. She does her embroidery and speaks of her morning's reading (which malicious tongues say she does not always understand). Her favorite books are historical ones, which she reads in the original language—French, Polish, German, Italian, etc.—for she knows them all. About six the Court assembles in her apartments. Afterwards every one tries to escape the eternal game of cavagnole at the Duchess de Luyne's where Marie spends her evenings and sups. Etiquette is banished from this society. The Queen allows people to argue with her.

> We think that games of chance distract,
> But boredom comes with measured steps
> To sit between two Majesties
> At Cavagnole.

There are ten children of whom seven survive: the Dauphin Louis and six daughters: Mesdames Elisabeth, Henrietta, Adelaide, Victoire, Sophie, and Louise (Mlle. Dernière). Mlle. Adelaide rules the family—she has a high pitched voice. Papa Roi (the King) calls her "the duster." They are all devout. But the King loves them, visits them of an evening on his return from hunting and brings them dainties prepared with his own hand. Louise the youngest dies a Carmelite in the pious hope of atoning for the sins of her father.

Stanislaus is created Duke of Lorraine with an annual pension of two million livres. He keeps at Luneville the simplest and most idyllic court in Christendom. He hates pomp and ceremony, goes to bed at nine o'clock, keeps a dwarf whom they once bake in a pie, reads history and philosophy, patronises men of letters, and studies politics. "I would ask," he writes to General Lee, "why it is that the right of sending representatives to the British Parliament is not accorded to the Colonies. Representation and taxation would then go together, and the mother and daughters would be indissolubly united. Otherwise I see no alternative but oppression or complete independence."

Mme. de Boufflers is Queen of the Court of Stanislaus. She has a baby face with a sparkling whiteness of complexion. She speaks little, reads much—not for instruction but to forego the need of speaking. Her reading is limited to a few books which she frequently reads again. She rules the Court because she rules the master by the force of her gaiety, originality, and variety. She keeps her two sons and her daughter with her at Lunéville, which shows she is a good mother, though, perhaps, not altogether a wise one. The younger son is educated by a tutor, the Abbé de Porquet, who becomes an acquisition of the Court. He is so amusing that much is forgiven him. When one day he reads the Bible to Stanislaus, he falls in a doze and waking with a start reads—"God appeared to Jacob en singe." "What!" cries Stanislaus, "you mean en songe." "Ah, sire," replies Porquet quickly, "is not everything possible to God?"

When Stanislaus retires to his chamber at nine o'clock, all the persons of his court and household sit down to faro, the domestics of the palace down to the very turnspits or scullions crowding round to stake their écus on the cards over the heads of the company.

The King, who is nearly seventy, makes love to his charming guests as though he were only of their own age, which they think delightful. Hénault describes his host as "a model for all Princes." Montesquieu and Voltaire visit him, and Voltaire celebrates his arrival by falling seriously ill—too ill to express his usual conviction that he is on the point of death. Stanislaus sends his own doctors and pays a visit to the philosopher's bedside. As soon as he is restored to health, a series of festivities is arranged to amuse him. Plays are acted and concerts given. "It is true I have been ill," Voltaire writes to his divine Angels, D'Argental and his wife, "but it is a pleasure to be so at the King of Poland's. There is certainly nobody who takes more care of his invalids than he." The King's troupe plays *Mérope*. And Voltaire adds: "Believe me, madame, they cry here as much as at Paris. And I who address you, I forgot myself sufficiently to cry like any of the others."

Everywhere is feasting and liberty. Voltaire sums up the Court in a phrase: "Lansquenet and love."

One winter's day in 1766 Stanislaus, wearing a wadded pelisse embroidered by his daughter and a wadded camisole, stands up in front of a blazing grate in order to wind up a clock on the mantlepeiece. His garments take fire and he is burnt beyond recovery.

Sitting to the Chevalier de Bouffler for his picture when very fat and near four score, Stanislaus observes: "I am but an unworthy model for a painter." The Chevalier says: "It is true, Sire, that your Majesty is a model more for Kings than for painters." (*Il est vrais, Sire, que votre Majesté est un modèl plûtot pour les rois que pour les peintres.*)

Horace Walpole to George Selwyn (March 7, 1766) on "your old passion," after the recent deaths of the Dauphin and Stanislaus: "Have not you felt a fright lately? If you have not, there is no *sentiment* in you. Why! the Queen has been in great danger, received the *viatique* . . . But be easy. She is out of danger. La Maréchale de Luxembourg saw her the night before last and congratulating her recovery, the Queen said, 'I am too unhappy to die!' "

CHAPTER 18

PARIS: THE SALONS

But in addition to the attraction of
the French Court there are for Englishmen the attractions
of the Salon. It is the golden period of the salon in Paris.
In George II's time there is of course nothing approaching
a salon in London. There are only dinners and card parties
and balls given by patrician ladies of an inconceivable dullness. But when George Selwyn and his friends cross the
Channel to Paris, they find many salons open to them.

Women in the decline of their beauty reveal the dawn
of their intellect. Salons are brilliant, versatile, free, lax,
sceptical, full of intrigue and wit. It is Voltaire who gives
the tone, and even Voltaire is not radical enough for many
of these iconoclasts. "He is a bigot and a deist," exclaims
a feminine disciple of D'Holbach. The maxims of La Roche-
foucauld are the rule of life. Wit counts for everything, the
heart for nothing. Women love with their minds, not with
their hearts. The only sins that cannot be pardoned are
stupidity and awkwardness.

To be agreeable is the cardinal aim in the lives of these
women. To lead others to talk wittily and well is their
crowning gift. Men of letters find companions and advisers
in women, consult their tastes, seek their criticism, court
their patronage, and establish a sort of intellectual comrade-
ship. Mme. de Tencin advises Marmontel before all things
to cultivate the society of women if he wishes to succeed.
Diderot and Thomas fail of the fame they merit through
their neglect to court the favor of women.

A stream of English pour through their drawing rooms
and listen with interest or with alarm to the philosophers

who are busily pulling down God and the King. Here are a few of the houses which Selwyn and his friends patronize. There is for example the house of Helvetius, the encyclopedist, one of the many apostles of futility. Again there is Baron D'Holbach who keeps "the café of Europe." Selwyn is fairly intimate with D'Holbach and visits him many times at his town house in the Rue Royale, known as "The Synagogue."

D'Holbach is not shy and retiring like D'Alembert, nor wild and imprudent like Diderot. He has a well stocked mind, an enormous income, a fine library, a pretty wife, a first rate cook, and an admirable cellar. Celebrated men of letters meet in an informal way to enjoy the good cheer and good wines of this maître d'hôtel of philosophy and to discuss the affairs of the universe. The learned and free thinking baron is agreeable, kind, entertaining, a bon vivant with the most pleasing weakness for a little gossip and scandal. He is lavish in his hospitality. The guests dine well and a long time. They talk of art, of poetry, of philosophy, and of love, of the greatness and vanity of their own enterprises, of Gods and Kings, of space and time, of death and of life. They say things to make a thunderbolt strike the house a hundred times if it strikes for that. Morillet demonstrates that all restrictions on trade should be abolished, Diderot proves that a belief in God must be done away with, Galiani, most sceptical of all, is not even certain of the non-existence of a Creator.

Mme. D'Holbach is pretty, gay, and charming. She plays on the lute, worships her husband and children, and hates philosophy. If her guests like to talk it—well, by all means so they should. The D'Holbach children are adorable. There are two little boys and a couple of little girls, the elder as pretty as a cherub and the younger a ball of fat, all pink and white. Then there is an ami de la maison, a Scotsman by the name of Hope and nicknamed Père Hoop, a shrivelled, withered person who, says he, suffers from life weariness.

There are generally three or four guests staying at the house and sometimes very many more. Diderot is here often for weeks together and sometimes for months. It is partly owing to his influence that the Baron entertains Englishmen so largely. Sterne accepts his hospitality so often that he can say the Baron's house is his own. The broad unmeaning face of Hume is to be seen here and Garrick, Walpole, Wilkes, and Selwyn.

The Baron has a charming chateau at Grandval just near enough to Paris and just far enough away. At half past one the host and guests meet in the salon and go in to dinner—the famous dinner—exquisitely arranged and appointed—servants numerous, the most delicate wines, and the most irreproachable of chefs. There are generally twelve to fifteen at the table and sometimes more. Good as the food is, the only intoxication is ideas.

The talk ranges from the history and customs of the Chinese to the final annihilation of the human race. Sometimes it lights on *Clarissa Harlowe* and the company is for and against sentiment as understood by the bookseller Richardson. In 1759 the *Candide* sets the table in a roar of delight. Or in 1762 the *Social Contract* of our impossibly impassioned Jean Jacques—Man is born free and is everywhere in chains. Or it is D'Alembert out of his shell again with his *History of the Destruction of the Jesuits.*

After dinner a walk in the beautiful gardens. When the walkers return, it is evening, and there are lights and cards on the table. Some play picquet, some billiards, some tric-a-trac. Some visit their host's picture gallery or his famous cabinet on natural history.

Then supper about nine—wit, gaiety, champagne. Then more conversation until the party breaks up or goes to bed still ardently philosophizing with their bedroom candlesticks in their hands.

The Baron is an author also. Although forty-five works are attributed to him, not one of them is published during his lifetime in his own name. The manuscripts are printed in Amsterdam.

His *System of Nature* attracts howls of rage and imprecation while its author sits in perfect peace and comfort in his pleasant garden at Grandval, beloved by all his fellows, safe, unsuspected, serene. Voltaire pronounces the work a philippic against God and a sin against Nature. La Harpe calls it "this infamous book." Young Goethe flees from it as from a spectre. It causes Frederick the Great to break with the philosopher's party. But Diderot says—"I like a philosophy that is clear and frank and definite, and such you have given us in *The System of Nature*. The author is not an atheist on one page and a deist on the next."

It is the fashion to dine or sup with Helvetius on Tuesday, with Madame Geoffrin on Wednesday, with D'Holbach on Thursday, and with Madame du Deffand on Sunday.

But now we have mentioned the names of two of the most distinguished salonières in Paris—both intimate friends of George Selwyn.

They each keep a salon which has its own circle of visitors, though many like Walpole and Selwyn patronize both houses. Mme. du Deffand's is aristocratic, Mme. Geoffrin's affects the aristocracy of intellect only. At Du Deffand's may be found the best blood of France and England; at Geoffrin's—"*les philosophies étaient chez eux.*" Mme. du Deffand refers to her rival's salon as "une omelette au lard." History unfortunately has not preserved Mme. Geoffrin's retort.

At Mme. du Deffand's you will meet fine ladies and gentlemen, wits, leaders of fashion; at Madame Geoffrin's sculptors, musicians, painters, philosophers, the Encyclopedists. The wise man distributes his favors impartially. This is George Selwyn's plan. But Selwyn is really of the Du Deffand faction and only pays flying visits to the camp of the enemy. Mme. du Deffand is much the more fascinating woman of the two, but nobody can love Mme. du Deffand, however much one may admire her, whereas Mme. Geoffrin is a kind little bourgeoisie who is regarded with affection by those whom she befriends.

A little girl in a flat mob cap of dainty muslin goes regularly to Mass. She is as pretty as an angel and clasps the most delightful hands in all the world before the altar. A rich man observes her, falls in love with her, and marries her. Thérèse Rodet is fourteen, M. de Geoffrin a widower of forty-eight. The union is hardly a suitable one. For seventeen years Thérèse seems satisfied with her unassuming household. Then she begins her social career. Now she is rich and honored, establishes her kingdom in the Rue St. Honoré. All Europe stands three deep round her chair, waiting for a word or a glance.

Mme. Geoffrin cannot be presented at the French Court, but she numbers Catherine of Russia and Gustavus III of Sweden among her friends, and Stanislaus, King of Poland, loves to call her *Maman*. Boucher, La Tour, Van Loo are among her friends. Rameau plays on her clavecin, and of course she scoops the young prodigy Mozart when he comes to Paris.

She is in no sense a luminary. She has no claim to intellectual preeminence. She has neither rank, beauty, youth, education. To an Abbé who wishes to dedicate a grammar to her, she replies—"To me? Dedicate a grammar to me! Why, I do not even know how to spell!" But she has tact, a persistent will, and a great deal of common sense, and she protects artisans and authors.

Hers is the most complete, the best organized and best conducted of the salons. "Do you know why la Geoffrin comes here?" remarks the famous Mme. de Tencin on her deathbed. "It is to see what she can gather from my inventory." It is the same lady who advises Geoffrin never to refuse a man, for, says she, though nine in ten will not care a farthing for you, the tenth may live to be a useful friend. La Geoffrin does not adopt or reject the whole plan but fully retains the purport of the maxim.

Her faults as well as her virtues are quite obvious. Her humor is forever expressing itself in homely maxims which suggest the lore of the peasants. Her keen intelligence enables her to understand the philosophers at least as well as they understand themselves, to advise them, to be their "Mother," to push them into the Academy. She scolds and pushes, punishes and rewards, decides disputes with a word. She spends with an open hand. Her great desire is to be of help to her children. But she never forgets that in her own house she alone is mistress.

All the hotheads of the *Encyclopedia*—Duclos, Grimm,

Caylus, Diderot—obey her like a school or seminary. When she says, "Violà qui est bien" ("Enough of this"), this call to order ends the conversation. Duclos draws in his claws and Diderot his thunder. Mme. Geoffrin is a born parliamentarian; it is she who ought to be called the Presidente.

She catches Hume's faults and vanities and impositions so quickly and explains them to him so clearly and convinces him so easily that "The next time I see her," says Hume, "I believe I shall say: 'Oh! Common Sense, sit down. I have been thinking so and so. Is it not absurd?' "

Mme. Geoffrin is tall, dignified, with silver hair concealed by her coif. Modest and simple. She likes sombre colors and fine lace. She carefully avoids all violent passions and all controversies. To her lawyer who is conducting a suit that worries her, she says, "Wind up my case. Do they want my money? I have some, and what can I do with money better than to buy tranquility with it?" *Donner et par-donner* is her device: to do all the good possible—but to respect all the conveniences. She is sensible. She has no melting moods.

Whether from malice or inattention, one who is in the habit of lending books to the husband of Mme. Geoffrin sends him several times in succession the first volume of the *Travels of Father Labbat*. M. Geoffrin always reads the book over again without perceiving the mistake. "How do you like these travels, sir?"—"They are interesting, but the author seems to me somewhat given to repetition."

However deficient M. Geoffrin is, the poor man is permitted to sit down to dinner at the end of the table upon condition that he never attempt to join in the conversation. A foreigner who is very assiduous in his visits to Mme. Geoffrin, one day not seeing him as usual at the table, enquires after him. "What have you done, Madam, with the poor man whom I always used to see here and who never spoke a word."—"Oh, that was my husband—he is dead."

To speak with Mme. du Deffand is to witness the triumph of mind. She is a remarkable woman. Born Marie de Vichy Chamrond, she marries at the age of twenty-five the

Marquis du Deffand, who is only remembered as the husband of his wife. Yet he does not occupy that position (except in name) for long. Soon after her marriage Madame is spoken of as the mistress of the Regent, the Duke of Orleans. Her second alleged liaison is with no less a man than Voltaire. She is young, beautiful, fascinating. It is then that Voltaire writes—

> Qui vous voit et qui vous entend
> Perd bientôt sa philosophie,
> Et tout sage avec du Deffand
> Voudrait en fou passer sa vie.

Yet Mme. du Deffand is careful in her amours. She is never ostracised by her class—ell n'etait jamais complétement déconsidérée. So early as 1730 she begins her last and most faithful attachment—that with Charles François Hénault, President of the French Academy. This is an extraordinary liaison. It is never very passionate or sentimental—"on ne saurait lui faire cette injustice"—but it is based on an affinity of the mind and the connection lasts until Hénault's death in 1770. Hénault, famous for his suppers, his chronology, and his verses, is full of sweetness and harmony. Women often take him for an amiable ignoramus, philosophers for a savant, and the jolly God of the table for a most fastidious connoisseur. He discourses gravely with the Encyclopedists and writes serious works: for example, *L'Histoire Abregé Chronologique*. There is something of the quack about him, but he suits Mme. du Deffand enough because he has no nonsensical views about love and the domestic virtues. As for Madame herself, none can resist her brightness and charm. She talks on an equality with Voltaire and Montesquieu and Rousseau and D'Alembert. Her conversation is brilliant, charming, gay, rapid. She is a monster of wit. She has a most vigorous flow of language. "Écoutez! Écoutez!" Walpole constantly exclaims trying to get in his points. But in vain. She writes letters which gain the highest praise of the eclectic Sainte Beuve a hundred years later. And she has courage too. She goes stone blind in middle life. Yet it does not change her mode of living. She continues her salon; she keeps her old friends and makes many new. She retains all her vivacity, wit, memory, judgment, agreeableness. She goes to operas, plays, suppers, and Versailles, gives suppers twice a week, has everything new read to her, makes new songs and epigrams, and remembers every one that has been made in four score years. She continues her correspondence with Voltaire, dictates charming letters to him, contradicts him, is no bigot to him or anybody, and laughs both at the clergy and philosophers. She still disputes with all sorts of people on all sorts of subjects and is never in the wrong. She humbles the learned, sets right their disciples and finds conversation for everybody.

She lives too strenuously. If she is back by one o'clock in the morning from a supper in the country, she proposes a drive in the Boulevards because it is too early to go to bed. Hour after hour she is busy pulling to shreds old fragments of silk and separating out the threads so that they can be woven up again into new pieces which she gives to her friends.

And yet with all her apparent gaiety, she is bored. And why, *pourquoi?* Because people are selfish, self centred, incapable of real affection. "I am like the late Regent," she writes to Walpole, "I can see nothing but fools and knaves . . . All the same I have nothing better to do than to live among them." Her heart is as dust and ashes within her. About her she can only feel duplicity and hatred; she has no faith in man or in God. "Men and women appear to me as puppets who go, come, talk, laugh, without thinking, without reflecting, without feeling." She confesses that she has a thousand troubles in assembling a choice company of people who bore her to death. "One sees only masks, one hears only lies" is her constant refrain. She does not want to live but is afraid to die. She says she is not made for this world, but does not know that there is any other. She tries devotion but has no taste for it. She sees the emptiness of existence. "All conditions appear to me equally unhappy, from the angel to the oyster."

She is always sceptical and critical—always doubtful of

the sincerity of those dearest to her. Writing to Hénault she says—"As for me, I am sorry not to see you, but I support it with a degree of courage because I believe that you do not share it much and that it does not matter to you."

Literature no longer interests or amuses her; she finds philosophy poisoned by affection; she is bored by all the historians and is glad when she can lay down the first volume of Gibbon. She never really interests herself about Rousseau, nor admires him. His eloquence cannot captivate her, for she hates eloquence. She gets hold of the *Memoirs of Saint Simon* in manuscript, and these amuse her enormously, but she is so disgusted by the style that she is very nearly sick. She asks no style but Voltaire's and has an aversion to all moral philosophy. She has lived in the age of true taste and allows no one but Voltaire to belong to it. She holds that all the rest have corrupted their taste and language. La Fontaine is her idol: that is, simplicity is.

She despises society and is equally bored with solitude. She hears Gluck's *Orphée* and is bored. She hears *The Barber of Seville* and is bored. She reads the *Iliad* and is bored. There is nothing in life that does not feel this blight.

"Quick, quick, quick, let me tell you about the supper of yesterday which worried me so for fear I should be dull or crabbed or embarrassed. Nothing of the sort. I never remember in all my life being younger or gayer or merrier." "Write disagreeably if you like," she remarks again. "As the man said of the rack, it will help me to pass an hour or two at any rate."

She rarely sleeps more than two or three hours. The greater part of that empty time during which conversation is impossible she devotes to her books. Her reader is an old soldier from the Invalides who comes round every morning early and takes up his position by her bedside.

Mme. du Deffand's salon begins in 1753 when the lady establishes herself in a suite of rooms in the Convent St. Joseph, Rue St. Dominique. Here she quickly gathers about herself the flower of the brightest spirits in France. "I have a very pretty apartment," she writes to Voltaire, "very convenient. I only go out for supper. I do not sleep elsewhere and I make no visits. My society is not numerous, but I am sure it will please you, and if you were here you would make it yours." The good nuns object a little to Voltaire at first, but are finally reconciled to visits of the arch heretic.

The salon is hung with buttercup yellow moiré, with curtains of the same shade relieved with knots of flame. Mme. du Deffand's tiny figure is swallowed up in an easy chair which resembles the tub of Diogenes. Her thin, animated face is framed within frills of lace, and a knot of ribbon beneath her chin fastens a black velvet hood. She wears a jacket also of black velvet which opens over a white dress trimmed with deep ruffles of lace. By her side is her irascible dog Tonton. Tonton grows the greater favorite the more people he devours. One night he flies at Lady Barrymore's face and nearly tears her eye out, but he ends in biting her finger.

Her days begin at six in the evening. The great business of the day is supper—"one of the four ends of man's existence," she says, adding, "I've forgotten the other three." Every evening she has three or four friends and on Saturday and Sunday a large party. It is not good living but good conversation that attracts her friends to her table. Her cook's sauces scandalize President Hénault. "Between him and Mme. Brinvilliers (the famous poisoner)," he sighs, "the only difference is one of intention." Conversation goes on far into the night—but never far enough to suit the hostess. New books, new plays, the last song, the latest word of the philosophers, all are talked about, eulogized, or dismissed with a sarcasm. The wit of Mme. du Deffand is feared, but it fascinates. "What tiresome book are you reading?" she says one day to a friend who talks too earnestly and too long. To someone who is eulogizing a mediocre man, adding that all the world is of the same opinion, she replies—"I make small account of the world, Monsieur, since I perceive that one can divide it into three parts, *les trompeurs, les trompés,* and *les trompettes.*" "I love this woman with all my heart," remarks Montesquieu, "she pleases and amuses me. It is impossible to feel a moment's ennui in her company."

The salon of Mme. du Deffand is not easy of access. Genius alone is not a passport to her favor. Her standard must be reached in every particular—taste, gaiety, good sense are necessary qualifications. A man of letters to succeed with her has to be of the first order. Grimm she never will receive. Of Marmontel she says—"How much trouble he takes, how he exerts himself to be witty. He is only a vagabond clothed in rags." She dislikes the enthusiasm of the philosophers unless hidden behind the arts of the courtier as in Voltaire. Diderot comes once, eyes her epicurean friends, and comes no more. The air is not free enough. "There are no hooked atoms between us," she says of him. She cannot tolerate young people. She declares she does not know what to say to them, and they no doubt are in precisely the same difficulty.

The Maréchales de Luxembourg and de Mirepoix, the Duc de Choiseul, the Prince de Beauvain, all the leaders of the highest society, gather almost every evening around Mme. du Deffand's chair. Here too is Horace Walpole, smart and gouty, with his fluent bad French. Here is President Hénault, clever, very deaf, and not yet openly false. Here are D'Alembert, the Archbishop Touloise, and the Chevalier d'Aydie (who at sixty and over is young in spirit and eloquent), and Fourmont, a friend of Voltaire, who says, "We'll talk of everything and discourse on nothing." Here are the Neckers, my Lord Bath, Gibbon, Selwyn, Lord Carlisle, and a dozen minor celebrities. Nor must we forget Pont de Veyle, in much request as the author of amusing tales and comedies, a childhood friend of the Marquise who has always remained faithful to her. They evolve couplets, quatrains, caractères. The wit is graceful, subtle, delicate, tactful, considerate.

Among the women are the Maréchale de Luxembourg (very handsome, very abandoned, very mischievous), Madame la Duchesse de Choiseul, and the Marquise de Boufflers. Mme. de Choiseul: beautiful, clever, good—a perfect little model, Walpole calls her. She is also a pattern of propriety, delicacy, tact, and womanly dignity. When very young she marries a man who soon tires of the perfection of his wife, but all her life she vainly cherishes the hope of winning his affection, and after his death she retires to a convent to save money to pay his debts. It is not easy to quarrel with Mme. de Choiseul. Du Deffand adores her, calls her grandmama, though she is many years the younger, declares over and over again that her love is all she wants and yet in petulance she writes even of Mme. de Choiseul— "She shows a good deal of friendship, and as she has none for me and I have none for her, it is perfectly natural that we should exchange the tenderest expressions in the world."

Then there is Julie de L'Espinasse. She comes to the Convent of St. Joseph a young lady of fascinating manners. She helps Mme. du Deffand to do the honors—receives the guests if Madame is indisposed, entertains them with her lively wit and humor. But soon the elder lady grows jealous, thinks that Julie is intriguing against her, fancies that the wits and philosophies are coming to see Julie when they ought to be paying their court to Julie's mistress. Finally the rupture comes.

One evening du Deffand rises from her bed an hour earlier than usual, mounts the stairs, and leaning heavily on her two sticks, stands terrible in her wrath on the threshold of the room which echoes with bon mots and pleasant laughter. The gentlemen doubtless feel the necessity of withdrawing at once from the fray—even d'Alembert.

"So, Mademoiselle, you would rob me of my friends!" cries Mme. du Deffand, her nasal voice rising almost to a scream. "It is by such treason that you show your gratitude! You shall remain no longer under my roof. I have had enough of nursing a viper in my bosom." The words détesté, abhorré, humilié, écrasé are used freely. Julie retorts with equal passion and so forthwith that very night perhaps the two ladies part to meet no more.

On the morrow Mme. du Deffand sends for d'Alembert and makes known her view of the situation. "You cannot be both her friend and mine. Choose then between us." And d'Alembert replies—"My choice has been made long ago, Madame. I have the honor to wish you a good day." And he goes out slamming the door. He even goes to live in

Julie's house but without compromising her much, for all Paris knows that when an enthusiastic admirer of his scientific genius exclaims—"He is a God," a calmer spirit retorts— "Come, come! If he were a God, he'd begin by making himself a man."

Many friends come to Julie's aid. La Geoffrin helps her with money and the Marèchale de Luxembourg with furniture, and the result is the opening of a rival salon which carries off many of Mme. du Deffand's favorite guests.

All the reports circulated by envy against Julie do not destroy the reputation she always enjoys for superior talents and wit. Never is anyone more calculated to shine in company. She possesses the art so precious and so difficult to be acquired of bringing forth the talents of others. She makes persons very different amalgamate and draw together in company. If conversation begins to flag, by a single word thrown in with judgment, she reanimates it in an instant. Or if it has run too long upon one subject, so that it begins to be worn threadbare, with a word she turns it and it becomes more brilliant than ever. No subject appears foreign to her; there is none with which she does not seem pleased and that she cannot render agreeable to others. Politics, religion, philosophy, news, stories—nothing is excluded from her *conversazioni*. "She renders the marble sensitive and makes matter talk," says Guibert. It is she who urges the pleasure loving abbés to their brightest sallies.

She is the only woman ever admitted to Mme. Geoffrin's dinners. Women, says Mme. Geoffrin, divert attention from conversation to themselves.

Julie is not rich enough to give dinners or suppers. She contents herself with having her only valet open the door of her salon where from five to nine churchmen, courtiers, soldiers, foreigners of distinction, men of letters, and the army of the Encyclopedia assemble. Her guests know nothing of embarrassment and restrictions; temperament is free there and personalities enjoy the right to be frank. Madame Geoffrin's is the official salon of the Encyclopedia; Mlle. de L'Espinasse's salon is its intimate parlor, boudoir, and laboratory. Mme. Geoffrin is feared, Mme. du Deffand admired, Mme. Necker respected, Julie de L'Espinasse loved.

She is the idol of the world in which she lives. She is ardent, impulsive, charming, tender. She lives more by the heart than by the head. She loves in order to live and lives to love. This is the keynote of her life. To love and pain Julie devotes herself.

She has luxuriant brown hair with a roguish little nose. Tall, slim, well-made.

A young Spaniard, the Marquis de Mora, falls desperately and hopelessly in love with her, and she falls desperately and hopelessly in love with the Comte de Guibert. In the very anguish of her pangs for the sufferings of M. de Mora she is most indiscreet with M. de Guibert. She yields to him in her box at the Opera. For she adores music and it is through her, no doubt, that little Mozart is heard at Mme. de Geoffrin's and that Rameau can be seen there at the harpsichord. De Mora wastes away and dies of his hopeless passion, and so does she. "Adieu, my friend," are her last words to Guibert, "If I ever return to life, I shall still love to employ it in loving you, but there is no more time."

Mlle. de L'Espinasse's will appears somewhat extra-ordinary. She leaves her furniture to M. d'Alembert, locks of her hair to all her intimate friends, and the payment of her debts to the Archbishop of Touloise.

Mme. du Deffand says coldly on hearing of her death— "If she had died sixteen years ago, I should not have lost d'Alembert."

"Pont de Veyle!" "Madame!" "Where are you?" "By the fire." "Have you your feet on the fender in a homely sort of way?" "Yes, Madame." "There are not many intimacies as old as ours!" "That's true." "Fifty years old—and in all that time not a cloud, not even a cloudlet."—"That has often struck me." "But Pont de Veyle, that wouldn't have happened only that at bottom we have always been quite indifferent to each other!"—"I daresay, Madame!"

To speak with Mme. du Deffand is to witness the triumph of mind.

CHAPTER 19

"LINDOR"

GEORGE SELWYN'S VISITS TO PARIS BEGIN IN 1742 during his undergraduate days at Oxford. Between then and 1779 he visits the city more than eight times. In 1742 he spends some months there in an impecunious condition. But in 1762 he travels to Paris in the train of the Duke of Bedford, who is sent to conclude a treaty of peace with France. (When the treaty is signed, by the way, Selwyn is "much obliged to the Duchess for the pen that signed it"—so Henry Fox to the Duke—"which will be looked upon with veneration ages hence, for George is already taking care of its preservation.") It is at this time that George is thought to have a better pronunciation than any one that ever came from England, but this is probably in his own estimation only. George remains in Paris through the summer of 1763, conversing, according to Gilly Williams, "with men of beard and wisdom, while Lord March and I are up half the night with people of a profligate character, singing 'The Blue Bells of Ireland' and other songs equally impure and vulgar." In 1764 George settles for a long stay in Paris. Lord March joins him in August, and the two young men proceed to enjoy life, each in his fashion. Gilly Williams supplies them with news from London—who is dead or dying, who has taken or given up office, what is the latest fashionable marriage. There are the usual commissions. "Dick Cox is here and says if you will buy him a set of dishes and plates of the blue and white china which you brought over last year for your mother, he will give you as many dinners off them as you will condescend to accept of."

By September Selwyn's friends begin to expect him back. By October Gilly Williams is beseeching him to "come and live among your friends who love and honour you."

In November: "I never write to you but that I hope it will be the last and that we are to see you again in your native country, which," adds Gilly, "has its charms."

In December: "God bless you, my dear George! When you have nothing else to do, let me hear from you—see you, I suppose, I never shall."

In January: "It is not I alone but all your friends, nay the King himself, who have expressed themselves with some concern that you still continue to run after gewgaws and hunt butterflies, when your presence is absolutely wanted at Westminster."

Still George remains in Paris, kept there not by Mme. du Deffand but by Lord March. Gilly Williams puts March up at the Old Club at White's, but they swear he is now a foreigner and reject him. Selwyn and March finally get back to London about the beginning of April, Selwyn having been absent nearly a year.

In 1765 Horace Walpole "procrastinating on this side of the water as much as March on the other," takes his long planned journey to the French capital and is introduced to Mme. du Deffand by Selwyn. Friends tell her that Walpole has les plus beaux yeux du monde. At first Walpole goes to Mme. du Deffand out of curiosity to hear about the Regent and the gay society of her youth that laughed, danced, and flirted at the Palais Royal and Saint Cloud. But a few weeks disclose a great change in his sentiments and create a memorable friendship. He remains in Paris seven months and on the day of his return begins their correspondence, which continues fourteen years to the end of her life. She has Wiart, her faithful secretary, taught English that Walpole may be spared the trouble of writing in a foreign tongue. When he is ill she begs him to send a daily bulletin of his health. He is frightened by the passionate accents of her letters. He says to himself that doubtless the secret service opens them, then it will be discovered that he is loved by an old woman of seventy. The thing will become known and cover him with ridicule. Throughout the course of their correspondence the struggle continues between her ardor and his apprehensions. She protests, laments, implores, denies, but ends always by submitting. "*Ne m'inspirez pas tant de crainte, ni de respect,*" she pleads but he pitilessly invokes both. Yet after his fashion he is fond of his "dear old blind woman" and grateful to her. It is for her sake that he returns four times to Paris. Then to feel again his quick little handshake, to hear his drawling "*po-int du tout, au con-tr-aire*" consoles the poor old lady for many snubs. She comes to him the instant he arrives and sits by him whilst he strips and dresses himself for, as she says, since she cannot see, there is no harm in his being stark. She plans many little surprises for him: a drawing room recital by the Clarion, a peep through a borrowed telescope at an elusive comet, or a drive about the boulevards together in the gray of dawn. When Walpole returns he writes her a weekly letter and modestly declares that she loves him better than all France together. To his other friends he speaks of her with affection. When the political events in France threaten her pension of three thousand livres, he beseeches her most earnestly to suffer him to make good the loss. When she is dying, he is genuinely concerned and deplores that there is no possibility of sending her James's Fever Powders in time to save her life. But he does not rush to her side. He loves her as much as one is able to love her and as much as he is able to love.

"You have one weakness," she writes to him, "which is unpardonable, to which you sacrifice your feelings and by which you regulate your conduct—the fear of ridicule." Thus he soon begins to be doubtful as to the view posterity may take of their correspondence, asks for and obtains all the letters he has written to her. Possibly he burns the letters, and if so it is with many a pang. We can fancy him consigning opus 1, opus 2, etc. to the flames.

In October, 1761, Selwyn is again in the beloved city,

this time with his young friend, "petit milord" Carlisle, and is entertained by Mme. du Deffand at supper. Walpole writes to her concerning his friend: "Of all the English whom you see in Paris, Mr. Selwyn has the most wit. But you must draw him out; you must make him speak bad French. He makes so many efforts to speak your tongue like a true academician, that he totally forgets to throw in the ideas. *C'est beau vernis pour faire briller des riens.*" To which Madame replies: "What you tell me of Mr. Selwyn is perfect. I add to it that he has only intellectual brilliancy (de l'esprit de tête) and not a scrap of heart. You will put into language much better than mine what I wish to say."

George lingers in Paris through the winter of 1766 despite the entreaties of his friends. In December Gilly writes: "I cannot take leave of you, my dear George, without desiring you to remember that you are an Englishman." Lord Bolingbroke has similar advice to offer: "For God's sake, return home. Nature never meant you for a Frenchman. Burn your formal bagwig and put on your far more agreeable scratch." He asks George to bring with him two or three pairs of laced ruffles and a suit of plain velvet. By plain is meant without gold or silver. But "there is nothing Mr. Selwyn can import from France that will give Lord Bolingbroke half the satisfaction as the immediate importation of himself."

George finally remembers he is an Englishman and in January leaves Paris. He stays in London for the Parliamentary session but is back again "dans ce cher Paris" in August of the same year. He has March to keep him company and Walpole too. Yet the visit is not a success. The truth is, he is getting tired of Mme. du Deffand. "Poor Selwyn left yesterday at five," writes that lady to Walpole. "He did not wish to see me at all. He wrote me a little grumpy note." When he returns to London he is in no hurry to write. "I haven't had a word from Mr. Selwyn," Madame tells Walpole in December. "Is it because I have bored him also *de mes tendresses?* I am in truth an absurd old woman."

Indeed George is weary of the flirtation. "I have a long

letter, almost every week, from my flame also," he writes
to Carlisle in January, 1768, "Mme. du Deffands, but there
are passions which *non in seria ducunt* [don't lead to serious
ends]. She is very importunate to me to return to Paris by
which if there is any sentiment it must be all of her side. I
should not be sorry to make another sojourn there, but if
I did, and it was with *you*, I should not throw away with
old women and old Presidents, which is the same thing,
some of those hours which I regret very much at this
instant."

Lord Carlisle is at this time on the Grand Tour, and on
his way back he calls at Paris where he sups constantly with
the old blind woman. Once Selwyn encloses in his packet
to Lord Carlisle a short note ("three lines") to Madame,
who is so charmed with it that she sends it to Mme. de
Choiseul, who reads it out at Fontainebleau in a great circle.
This vexes Selwyn considerably, for he is morbidly anxious
that his letters be burned as soon as read. He complains to
Madame, who replies in a spirited way: "I have only shewn
one of your letters, five or six lines long, and very charming. You told me, 'I write you when the fancy takes me,
and the fancy took me on Friday!' Could that make you
ridiculous? It is only in England you need fear ridicule;
in all other countries you are safe from it, and particularly
in France, and still more particularly in my special circle.
Your letters are thrown into the fire as soon as I have replied to them. Besides, your prudence leaves you nothing to
be afraid of. The journals give me much more news than
your letters. So my dear Lindor"—Madame's pet name for
Selwyn—"the fears that you display have rather the air of
seeking a quarrel with me, which would be unfair. I am
charmed with your correspondence, but I only desire it so
long as it is agreeable to yourself."

After 1767 George Selwyn does not see Paris again for
eleven years. He grows more lazy, more content with
White's and the good houses of England. In December of
1768 he almost makes up his mind to another visit. "Tell me
if I shall take lodgings for you," writes young Carlisle in
his enthusiastic way. "Where shall I take them? If you dis-

appoint me, I shall be furious. The blind woman is in raptures." But this is a false alarm. George cannot tear himself away from England. He still keeps up his connection
with Paris by a correspondence with Madame and by letters
from friends staying there. "Madame Geoffrin m'a chanté
la palinode," writes Charles Fox to him in 1770. "I dine
there today. She enquires after you very much. I have
supped at Mme. du Deffand's who asked me if I was *déjà
sous la tutèle de M. Selvin*. I boasted that I was . . . Madame
du Deffand complains that you neglect her."

In 1772 Madame would be "very glad to see Lindor
again; his faculty of falling asleep when he is bored makes
his society very convenient. I wish all my visitors have the
same faculty." But again Lindor is not to be enticed. Three
years later Walpole is in Paris and reports to Selwyn upon
Madame. "The star and I went to the Opera last night, and
when we came from Madame La Vallières at one in the
morning, it wanted to drive about the town, because it was
too early to set. To be sure, you and I have dedicated our
decline to very different occupations. I rake with a women
of fourscore. *N'importe*: we know many sages that take
great pains to pass their time with less satisfaction." As for
Tonton: "Mme. du Deffand has got a favorite dog that will
bite all their noses off."

It is not until 1778 when Selwyn visits Paris on his way
to Italy that the old friendship with Mme. du Deffand is
renewed. France is on the eve of a war with England, but
a fact like that perturbs English travellers in France very
little. There are suppers for Selwyn, visits, protestations of
attachment, shops, commissions, and "all the remise,
ménage, and tout amassé of a great town." But he has time
to visit the old blind woman, shortly after his last visit
paid to her by Voltaire. "That rascal (Benjamin) Franclin
has put notions into their head, which I hope have no
foundation. I have not seen him or Voltaire. I would not
go in search of either, if they had come in my way, well.
Voltaire has been twice at Madame du Deffand's. The first
time he was very good company, and so was she. It was
bien attaquée, bien defendue, et toute la conversation

piquante et intéressante au dernier point, but the second time, l'ennui en était affreuse. They got into philosophical reflections upon the misery of human life, which tired everybody."

As for Madame herself: "She is not veillié d'un jour, and they are so good as to say that I am not changed neither in any respect, and that they are glad of it. I know the contrary, for I know that I have onze ans de plus, and I believe onze dents de moins. But I have enough left to confine my tongue, which I wish my countrymen would consider also, but they tell them everything they know, or don't know. I was afraid that I had lost my language or theirs, more properly speaking. But Mme. du Deffands says, au contraire, il me paraît que vous parlez avec plus de facilité et moins d'accent que jamais; that may be true or not, I do not much care . . . Mme. du Deffands has a carpet fort velouté. I forget what we call that sort of carpet, it is a manufacture with us, introduced a few years ago. She wants to cover the whole room with it, which is about twenty feet square. The colours must be jaune et Crameris chiefly. She wants to know the price of such a carpet. Shall I give you the trouble to ask and to send me word? . . . If you can buy for me at Pickering's a pound of the best Hyson tea, and send it by anybody who comes here, to be carried to her, I should be glad. I do not know what to send them here for all their civilities."

Selwyn does not spend all his time in the Rue St. Dominique. "I was the day before yesterday with the Maréchal Bison in his garden, he had thirty-six persons at dinner . . . The Maréchal's garden, dans son genre, is the finest you ever saw, and the greatest quantity of fruit in it . . . He keeps the best table, in short, on ne peut parler trop longtemps de Monsieur le Maréchal. But I took the liberty to give him my opinion how his garden could be improved, dont il parut ne m'en savoir trop bon gré. The gravel is the worst in the world, and it is rare to have any gazon where the verdure is good, or well-kept. I have never yet seen a roller. Now the Maréchal has plat fermé, and gravel walks, and his gazon is very beautiful; but he chooses that you should walk up to your ankles in bad gravel and has very little of the other." Concluding with a patriotic outburst: "I have told everybody what a vigorous defence we are making in England in case they come there, but ils pensent à rien moins qu'à cela. I am afraid of nothing but that Gunpowder Destains [the French Admiral D'Estaing], and Rodney tells me I need not be afraid of him. I must own that I wish these people to be well drubbed . . ."

Coming back from Milan Selwyn is very attentive to Mme. du Deffand who is then, it must be remembered, eighty-one years of age. He calls every day. On his return to London, however, his letters are very irritating. "He promises to tell me many things and tells me nothing; he only trifles. He pretends that you [Walpole] wished to let me have some of his bon mots but that you could not translate them."

In the following year, 1779, Selwyn pays his last visit to Paris and says farewell to his old blind friend. England is at war with France, and he asks Madame to use her good offices in obtaining his passport. She also tries to procure a house for him, but eventually he lodges in the Hôtel de Bourbon. He arrives on the 14th of April, comes to Du Deffand's salle à manger and as he is in morning dress does not enter. The next day, Thursday, he comes at noon. He brings her a book of Walpole's, some tea, and some small scissors which she has asked him to buy. She expects him in the evening to supper. Friday he comes to supper and brings her razors for her nephew and some fans at twelve sous each. He plays at loto and stops to talk with Mme. de Bouveau, Mme. de Cambise, and herself. He tells them all his projects, his fears, his hopes.

Madame is not in the best of health or spirits. "I think my friend declines very much," writes Selwyn. "But last night although she had not been out of her bed for two days, she had company. Twenty were playing in her bedchamber, and ten at supper in the next room. The hot victuals were brought to her in her bed, and she played at loto by substitute and directed by memory."

Selwyn doubts the sincerity of Mme. du Deffand, and

Madame knows that he doubts it. This note remains to the end. On the 15th of June, 1779, Selwyn leaves Paris and for the last time. "I regret him much," writes Madame to Walpole. "He leaves us content enough with me." "I don't know," she says again, "what account Lindor will give of me. He has said many pretty things, has made a thousand protestations of friendship. All that was like ice . . . He has wit, no doubt, but it is neither wide in range, nor profound, nor even agreeable, unless he is suddenly inspired . . . *Ah! monsieur! que les gens amiable sont rare!* It is useless to look for them; one must learn how to get on without them." In December she complains to Walpole at the absence of letters from Lindor. "He is a curious creature," she remarks. "Only you and your young duke (Richmond) observe the ritual of friendship. All the other English disdain even the appearance of it." Almost the last reference to Selwyn is a similar complaint. "Why does Selwyn keep his promises so badly? What better proof can he give me of his friendship and his gratitude than that of keeping me supplied with news?" This is in December, 1779. On August 24, 1780, Mme. du Deffand dies, brave and worldly to the end.

"Spare me three things," she says to her confessor in her last moments. "Let me have no questions, no reasons, and no sermons." Seeing Wiart her faithful servitor in tears, she remarks as if surprised, "You love me then?" "Divert yourself as much as you can," is her final message to Walpole. "You will regret me, because one is very glad to know that one is loved." She commends to his care and affection Tonton, her little dog.

She dies as she has lived, her room crowded with acquaintances and the sound of conversation in her ears.

CHAPTER 2 0

LADY SARAH AND OTHERS

GEORGE II IS ONE DAY WALKING IN KENS-
ington Gardens when a little red cheeked girl of about
five years old breaks away from her nurse or governess, and
running up to the King, addresses him without ceremony,
*"Comment vous portez-vous, Monsieur le roi? Vous avez
une grande et belle maison ici, n'est ce pas?"* Her audacity
pleases the sovereign who asks her name, and she tells him
it is Lady Sarah Lennox. He becomes very fond of her and
sees her frequently until she is sent to Ireland to her aunt
with whom she remains until she is thirteen. Then she is
invited to Court where the King plays jokes with her as if
she were still a little child. This unexpected treatment embarrasses her. She can find nothing to say and shyly keeps
her eyes on the ground, whereupon the King turns from her
saying, "Pooh! she's quite stupid." The young Prince of
Wales, however, is struck with admiration and pity—in short
then and there falls in love with her. Lady Sarah, who is
not fifteen when she goes to Court in 1759, is indeed a most
lovely girl. Her beauty is not easily described otherwise
than by saying she has the finest complexion, the most
beautiful hair, and the prettiest person that ever was seen,
with a sprightly air, pretty mouth, remarkably fine teeth,
little eyes and blooming cheeks. Half London is at her feet.
At the death of his grandfather, George III makes no effort
to hide his feelings. He rides to and fro in front of Holland
House to catch a glimpse of Lady Sarah. Of course the
Princess Dowager comes to know of her son's attachment,
and she and her minister Lord Bute are aghast at the notion
of the King marrying a girl from the Whig family dominated

by the astute Henry Fox. The affair progresses rapidly—so far that the King confesses his passion to Lady Sarah's friend, Lady Susan Fox Strangways with whom he has the following guarded conversation.

"You are going to Somersetshire. When do you return?"

"Not before winter, sir, or I don't know how soon in winter."

"Is there nothing will bring you back to town before winter?"

"I don't know of anything."

"Would you not like to see a Coronation?"

"Yes, sir. I hope I should come to see that."

"I hear it's very popular, my having put it off. Won't it be a much finer sight when there is a Queen?"

"To be sure, sir."

"I have had a great many applications from abroad, but I don't like them. I have had none at home. I should like that better. What do you think of your friend, you know who I mean, Lady Sarah Lennox. Don't you think her fittest?"

"'Think, sir?"

"I think none so fit. Tell her so and let me have an answer the next drawing room day."

A week later the King asks Lady Sarah if she has heard what he said and she answers in the affirmative. But when he puts the question, "Do you approve?" he receives as an answer only a cross look whereupon in high dudgeon he turns on his heel and quits the room. This brusque repulse is explained by the fact that Lady Sarah is piqued by her lover Lord Newbattle and seeks solace by avenging his offence upon her royal suitor. Lord Newbattle is a vain, insignificant puppy, lively and not ugly, who makes love to all the girls, but is much in love with Lady Caroline Russell. Lady Sarah tries to get him away from her and is so pleased with her success that she grows too much pleased with his lordship. The King hears of Lord Newbattle, and more than is true, but his love soon conquers his dignity and a reconciliation is hastened by the news of an accident in the hunting field to Lady Sarah. Lord Newbattle when told she has fractured a leg says, "It will do no great harm, for her legs were ugly enough before." And this statement repeated to Lady Sarah cures her of her attachment to his lordship and makes her more ready to accede to the King's request to reconsider his proposal.

But ardent as his love is, the King's union with Lady Sarah is not to be. A council is summoned, the voices of prudence and policy prevail, and George III announces his forthcoming marriage with Princess Charlotte of Mecklenburg Strelitz—small, lean, with a flat nose, and a large mouth.

Lady Susan Fox Strangways is more aggrieved than the lady chiefly concerned, for as she remarks, "I almost thought myself Prime Minister." Lady Sarah is not in love with the King, and the shock falls not on her heart but on her vanity. "I did not cry, I assure you, which I believe you will, as I know you were set upon it," she writes to Lady Susan. "The thing I am most angry at is looking so like a fool, but I don't much care. If he was to change his mind again (which can't be though) and not give me a very good reason for his conduct, I would not have him, for if he is so weak as to be governed by everybody, I shall have but a bad time of it." Fox is furious at the disappointment. Half in anger, half in jest, he says to his sister-in-law, "Well, Sal, you are the first virgin in England, and you shall take your place in spite of them all as Chief Bridesmaid, and the King shall behold your pretty face and repent."

THE PROCESSION OF THE BRIDE:

Drums and Trumpets
The Sergeant Trumpeter
The Princess's Servants
A Page
A Quarter Waiter.
A Gentleman Usher between the two Senior Heralds.
Vice Chamberlain
Maids of Honour.
Ladies of the Bedchamber, not Peeresses.
Peeresses.
Unmarried Daughters of Peers.

The King's Vice-Chamberlain—The King's Lord Chamberlain.
THE BRIDE
In her Nuptial Habit, supported by their Royal Highnesses,
the Duke of York and Prince William, her Traine borne by
ten unmarried Daughters of Dukes and Earls, viz:
Lady Sarah Lennox, Lady Caroline Russel, Lady Ann Hamilton,
Lady Elizabeth Ker, Lady Harry Bentinck, Lady Car. Montagu,
Lady Elizabeth Keppel, Lady Louisa Greville,
Lady Elizabeth Harcourt, Lady S. Strangways.

The ten bridesmaids to the Queen are all dressed alike in white lutestring with silver trimmings ornamented with pearls, diamonds, etc. Immediately on the bride and groom joining hands, the Park and Tower guns are fired.

During the whole ceremony the King appears absent-minded but never takes his eyes off Lady Sarah. When the young bridesmaids are drawn up in a line near Her Majesty with Lady Sarah at their head, Lord Westmorland, a very old Jacobite who is purblind and has never appeared at Court since the Hanoverian succession, mistaking Lady Sarah for the Queen, plumps down on his knees and takes her hand to kiss. She draws back startled, and deeply coloring exclaims, "I am not the Queen, sir." This little incident creates a laugh and a little gossip. When George Selwyn hears of it he observes: "Oh, you know, he always loved Pretenders!"

Frederick, fifth Earl of Carlisle, just out of Cambridge and about to make the Grand Tour with Charles James Fox and Lord Fitzwilliam, carries on a reckless flirtation with Lady Sarah after she has become Mrs. Bunbury. Consequently he is in no haste to scamper about Europe with Charles Fox. His attention and politeness flatter Lady Sarah, but she cannot help looking upon him as a schoolboy. Henry Fox, Lord Holland, crystallizes the situation in a rendering of one of Horace's odes which he addresses to Lady Sarah and forwards to George Selwyn for approval:

> Sally, Sally, don't deny
> But for God's sake tell me why
> You have flirted so, to spoil
> That once lively youth, Carlisle?

He used to mount when it was dark
Now he lies in bed till noon;
And you not meeting in the Park
Thinks that he got up too soon.

Manly exercise and sport,
Hunting and the tennis court,
And riding school no more divert,
Newmarket does, for there you flirt!
But why does he no longer dream
Of yellow Tyber and its shore;
Of his friend Charles's favorite scheme
On waking, think no more?

Lady Sarah is quite pleased, but George Selwyn is decidedly not. To George a lord is a lord whose most trifling flirtations are to be spoken of with respect. But Carlisle at length is able to tear himself away from Lady Sarah (or perhaps it is Lady Sarah who is torn away from him). At all events he writes to Selwyn from Brussels confessing that he has been in love with an unmarried girl and what is worse with a German princess. "Excuse all my follies, my dear George, it is better having them at this age than twenty years hence."

Then with his friends on the Grand Tour, faithfully reporting his progress to Selwyn. When they arrive at Cherbourg men and boys half naked and in wooden shoes seize upon every trunk within their reach and throw them into the boats lying alongside. They find French beds stuffed with potatoes rather than with feathers and are eaten up in Italy by the infinite number of gnats, bugs, fleas, and lice. They view the latter country knick-knackically, a danger against which Chesterfield warns his sons. They are in a violent hurry upon the road. (To cover leagues on land and water, to take punch and tea at inns, to speak ill of other nations, and to boast without ceasing of their own—that is what the crowds of English call travelling.) And they have a fondness for spending money which gains them the title of Golden Asses. They come across one Englishman engaged in play with an infamous gamester who strips him in the very first partie; another poxed and pillaged by an anti-quated cantatrice; a third laid under contribution by a dealer in pictures. Perhaps a fourth hires a low Irish wench whom he drives about in a hired chaise to the great honor of himself, his family, and his country.

Lord Carlisle crosses the Alps in a chair, shuddering at every step and tortured by apprehensions for the safety of his dog who ventures now and then to look over the edge of a precipice. The scenery of a fine pass inspires him with horror and melancholy, and he never speaks of beauties until he is safe and warm in the Opera House at Turin. The friends travel with eight servants apiece, noticed by Queens, treated as equals by ambassadors, losing their hearts in one palace and their money in another, and gathering every vice on Christian ground. At Rome Lord Fitzwilliam kisses the Pope's toe. "When he kissed it," writes Carlisle, "he lifted his foot a little which made the old man give such a grunt that almost killed me." Fox tries upon the Italian dandies the effect of his queer little French hat and red heels with which he designs to astonish his brother Mac-aronis of St. James's Street, and before he and Carlisle leave the Continent, the pair of scapegraces drive post all the way from Paris to Lyons in order to select patterns for their embroidered waistcoats.

To return from Italy or France with nothing charac-teristically Italian or French is not to be thought of. They buy a picture or two, some mosaics, a clever statue, and perhaps what they take to be antiquities. (So assiduous are the English in gathering curiosities that the Romans say— "Were our amphitheatre portable, the English would carry it off." They fill great boxes with sham Raphaels and Dom-enichinos and Andrea del Sartos, and ship them to ancestral halls in England.)

During Lord Carlisle's absence the Order of the Thistle is conferred upon him, and the insignia of the order is sent to him at Turin where he is invested by the King of Sar-dinia. Carlisle wishes that the ribband be despatched from England by a proper courier and also that the investment be carried out with all the pomp and circumstance befitting so important an occasion. Selwyn gives the precious packet to the conqueror of India, Lord Clive, who is to bring it to Paris. A special courier, George explains to Carlisle, will cost too much. This news saddens young Carlisle. "By Lord Clive!" he exclaims. "It might as well be sent by a Chelsea pensioner." But the ingenuous youth need not have excited himself. The "Chelsea pensioner" brings the Order only so far as Paris; thence to Turin it is more worthily borne by a messenger of the British embassy. And in a few weeks Carlisle is able proudly to announce to his dear friend George that he is now "a Knight Companion of the Ancient Order of the Thistle. The ceremony was performed this morning in the King's cabinet, the Royal Family and all the principal officers of the Court being present."

Lord Carlisle is the most intimate of Selwyn's later friends. To Carlisle Selwyn is father confessor, a person of experience and worldly wisdom to whom at all times he can turn for counsel and advice. Selwyn for his part has a real affection for Carlisle and his family, not perhaps unmingled with a feeling that it is very pleasant to be father confessor to a peer of wealth and social standing. Selwyn writes hundreds of letters to his young friend, invariably beginning "My dear Lord," and his young friend reciprocates by writing not quite so many letters to Selwyn.

The friendship grows deeper as the years go on. Carlisle marries at the early age of twenty-two, but his marriage makes no difference in his relations with Selwyn, who is always a welcome visitor at Castle Howard. If the Earl is in the country and Selwyn is in town, no day passes without a long letter from Selwyn containing the latest social and political gossip—balls, routs, parties, debates in Parliament, ministerial changes, society scandals, all the tittle tattle of St. James's Street. Carlisle requests advice—whether it is better to come to town or remain in the country, the best method of saving money, information concerning gambling losses and philosophical reflections upon the same.

At times he has sense; at other times he most emphatically plays the fool, gambling away £10,000 in one evening. Of his life it is truly said that for many years it is nothing but a constant struggle between the temptations presented by the gaming table on the one hand, and warnings of conscience and affection on the other. There is talk of getting £200,000 from some soft hearted Christians; his lordship wants no dealing with the money lenders. Timber too is to be felled, and there are ominous consultations with stewards and lawyers as to ways and means. A year passes and there is evident embarrassment—the foreign valet is to be parted with, housekeeping is to be restricted. Castle Howard is endurable only because there his lordship can eat his own venison, burn his own firewood, and save in the course of two years enough to repair his disasters. The following year he is back again in town at White's and Almack's. "The hazard this evening was very deep," he writes to Selwyn, speaking of an evening at the latter, "Meynell won £4000 and Pigott £5000. I did nothing."

But a single month later comes a letter: "My dear George—I have undone myself and it is to no purpose to conceal from you my abominable madness and folly, though perhaps the particulars may not be known to the rest of the world. I never lost so much in five times as I have done tonight, and am in debt to the house for the whole. You may be sure I do not tell you this with an idea that you can be of the least assistance to me. It is a great deal more than your abilities are equal to. Let me see you, though I shall be ashamed to look at you, after your goodness to me."

After this there is remorse and dejection. At twenty-seven years of age the lord of Castle Howard is found telling his friend—"Except that the welfare and interest of others depend upon my existence, I should not wish that existence to be of long duration." Lady Carlisle and her children are forever in his thoughts. He will prevent "this man from setting ruin at her like a bulldog," will accept government employment anywhere, "let it tear me, as it will, from everything dear to me in this country."

Perhaps as a result he goes over to America as Chief Commissioner sent by Lord North in 1778 to reason with the rebels and agree upon the means of quieting the colonies—very fit, says Walpole, to make a treaty that will not be made. While there he becomes involved in a dispute with Lafayette, who, enraged at some strong expressions reflecting upon the conduct of the French, challenges Carlisle to a duel. Carlisle very properly declines the meeting and informs Lafayette in a letter that he considers himself solely responsible to his country and king and not to any individual for his public conduct and language.

From beginning to end, the embassy is a failure. But Lord Carlisle acts with dignity and courage. It is he who draws up the "last dying speech and confession" of the Commission before leaving America, in which the Commission sternly intimates that the limits of human endurance have been reached and that henceforth no mercy will be shown to the rebels. Having posted this proclamation, Lord Carlisle and his friends rather hurriedly sail away to England, perhaps to escape the annoying laughter of the rebels.

Lord Carlisle is a liberal patron of the fine arts with polished manners and a taste for writing bad poetry. He purchases a large part of the Orleans gallery and is one of the pallbearers at Sir Joshua's funeral. His letters are bright and lively.

He is a generous, open-hearted youth, a firm friend, impulsive and foolish at times but never wicked, anxious to do his duty as well as he knows how. He leaves behind him a noble race: "a man kind, accomplished, gentle, friendly and pure; and female descendants occupying high stations— some renowned for beauty and all for spotless lives and pious matronly virtues."

(Lord Carlisle has the reputation for several years of having an intrigue with his brother-in-law's wife, Lady Sutherland, the Marchioness of Stafford. Lord Stafford has long had a weakness in his sight which seems approaching fast to blindness and among the more common prescriptions is told by his physician that he must strictly abstain from all conjugal intercourse with his wife. This requirement he adheres to for more than a twelvemonth when, notwithstanding, her Ladyship proves with child. This occasions, of course, the sort of fracas natural under such circumstances. Meetings of friends and relations are held, and divorce, separation, exposure, etc. are threatened. But it soon appears that as his lordship has continued all the time to live and sleep under the same roof with her ladyship, no divorce can take place, and being of a cold, deliberate temper, and probably not entirely unapprised or unsuspicious of his wife's gallantries, Lord Stafford at last determines to hush the matter up and the birth of a male child in due time takes place. The boy is ushered into the world and christened Francis with the same giving and receiving of joy by his legal father as the rest of his children have been.

(There is scandal too about Lady Isabella, Lord Carlisle's mother. She begins by great strictness of conduct and principle and preserves an unspotted reputation throughout her married life. When her autumn season comes on, however,—that time at which most ladies who have been gay think it high time to draw in and become more grave—she surprises her acquaintances by seeming to relax and grow cheerful, reenters the world after quitting her weeds. Nobody can conceive the meaning of it till she takes the decisive step of marrying Sir William Musgrave, who is but three and twenty and not overrich. But in consideration of the match and of her having years to spare, she makes him a present of ten and calls him three and thirty. This for a pattern woman makes sufficient noise. It produces a comical dialogue between two ladies who have both taken second husbands—the blunt Dutch Lady Blandford and Lady Dalkeith.

"Well," says the former, "I have not patience with that woman. At her time of life, and with daughters grown or growing up round her, to go and marry a young fellow she must buy breeches for."

"But Ma'am," says Lady Dalkeith (a little sore), "does your Ladyship recollect that you married again yourself?"

"Aye! But *whom* did I marry? A *Sir William Wyndham.*"

"Ah, my dear Ma'am, we all think them Sir William Wyndhams."

However, Lady Carlisle's illusion does not last long. In a year or two her second mate and she fall out and part.

Then taking flight altogether she goes abroad, making acquaintance with one baron after another and gets into various scrapes about money.

George Selwyn is not on such good terms with Lady Isabella, but she never comes to a direct quarrel with him, hate him as she may, for she is always asking for money. The belle-mère like her son is forever scribbling verse.)

CHAPTER 21

SECOND SELWYN CIRCLE

SELWYN KNOWS EVERYBODY WHO IS WORTH knowing and many people who are not worth knowing. He keeps the friends of his youth—Lord March, Horace Walpole, Gilly Williams,—and he adds to them as the years go on, new friends of a younger generation. What is called the Second Selwyn Circle begins to be formed about 1760. Selwyn is then a man of forty. He is well known at the Clubs as a gossip and a wit, just the kind of person with whom young men fresh from the Universities wish to become acquainted. Accordingly this second circle is an ample one— besides Frederick, fifth Earl of Carlisle, there are Charles James Fox, Anthony Morris Storer, Richard Fitzpatrick, James Hare, Frederick, Lord Bolingbroke, and others.

Selwyn is an old friend of the Holland family. With Henry Fox, the first Lord Holland, he keeps up for many years a considerable correspondence. "Henry Fox: a bad black man, a dark and insidious genius, an engine of personality and faction," Lord Chancellor Hardwicke calls him. But he is nothing of the sort. He is straitforward and truthful. "I'll do him justice," says George II of him, "I don't believe he ever did tell me a lie. But if he did not," the King adds, "he's the only man that ever came into my closet and that did not." He is a sworn enemy of lawyers who have their seats in Parliament. He loves disputing as much as they do, but "he loves sense which they make a trade of perlexing." He is contemptuous of the masses. He is the most unpopular statesman of the age, not because he sins more than any of them, but because he cants less.

His contempt for appearances leads him to display much that others quite as unscrupulous as himself cover with a decent veil.

Henry Fox has great gifts and splendid opportunities. He fills high offices in the state. He helps to make and un-make ministries. Yet at the end of it all he is a disappointed man. Throughout all he says or writes runs a vein of bitter-ness—the humor of one who conceives that the world has not given him his due. He is always a little cynical about the gratitude of politicians, always teaching his sons the philosophy of a man who has been wicked but not quite wicked enough. "Aspire, Charles, to the first employments," he will say, "but don't ever *trust* as I did."

But it is *he* the world distrusts. The people trust Pitt, they do not trust Fox. For some years he holds the lucrative post of Paymaster of the Forces and is loudly accused of having enriched himself illegitimately at the expense of the state. "The public defaulter of unaccounted millions"—that fatal phrase hounds him until his death. But the Pay Office is an Eldorado, as the Paymaster is entitled to use the large sums passing through his hands as if he were a private banker. Not only is he entitled to interest on the balance in his hands, but to any capital profit he may make by its in-vestment. Nothing can be more candid than Holland's ex-planation: "The Government borrows money at twenty per cent discount. I am not consulted or concerned in making the bargain. I have, as Paymaster, great sums in my hands, which, not applicable to any present use, must either lie dead in the bank or be employed by me. I lend this to the government in 1761. A peace is thought certain. I am not in the least consulted, but my very bad opinion of Mr. Pitt makes me think it will not be concluded. I sell out and gain greatly."

Holland is Paymaster General almost throughout the Seven Years War. £49,500,000 pass thru his hands. Some of it is still in the hands of his executors nine years after his death and eighteen years after his resignation.

"'I cannot help sometimes asking myself, dear Selwyn," he writes, "why I am in such disgrace with the King? Have

I deserved it? I am now the only mark left of irrevocable displeasure, and I vow to God I cannot guess why." And again: "There is one question which, I hope, will not be asked: Has life no sourness drawn so near its end? Indeed it has; yet I guard against it as much as possible."

In his last years Holland amuses himself at a vast expense in building a fantastic villa situated in a dreary spot near Margate in Kent. Gray, a political opponent, writes:

> Old and abandon'd by each venal friend,
>   Here Holland form'd the pious resolution,
> To smuggle a few years and strive to mend
>   A broken character and constitution.

"Nobody," Holland says, "has been more hated in the world, but I flatter myself, nobody is more beloved in his own family than I am." His home life is an idyll.

He falls in love with Lady Caroline Lennox, elder sister of Lady Sarah, asks her, is refused, and steals her. His father is a footman, her great grandfather a King. (Fearing the result of a promised interview with her family suitor, Lady Caroline has her eyebrows shaved off to insure his defeat.) All the blood royal is up in arms to avenge what is esteemed an outrage upon the memory of his sacred Majesty Charles II. At the opera the news runs along the front boxes exactly like fire in a train of gunpowder. Newcastle treats the matter as an affair of state. "I thought our fleets or armies were beat or Mons betrayed into the hands of the French," he remarks in a special emissary to Lord Granville. "At last it came out that Harry Fox was married, which I knew before."

Henry Fox is a good husband, and Lady Caroline a kind and lovable companion. From first to last they are an enviable couple. They live together most happily for more than thirty years, and the wife survives her husband not quite so many days. He has so high an opinion of Lady Caroline's understanding that when discussing public measures he often says, "Well, I will go home and talk it over with Lady Caroline before I make up my mind."

His manner of educating his sons accounts for many of

their faults but also for some of their virtues. It is a system of the most unlimited indulgence of every passion, whim, and caprice. A great dinner is given at Holland House to all the foreign ministers. The children come in at the dessert. Charles, then in petticoats, spying a large bowl of cream in the middle of the table, has a sudden desire to get into it. Lord Holland insists he shall be gratified, and in spite of Lady Caroline's remonstrances, has it placed on the floor for the child to jump in and splash about at his pleasure.

Charles never fails to do what he has a mind to do, his father never checking him. One day standing by his father while he is winding up a watch, "I have a great mind to break that watch, papa," says the boy. "No, Charles," replies the father, "that would be foolish." "Indeed, papa," says he, "I must do it." "Nay," answers the father, "if you have such a violent inclination, I won't balk it." On which he delivers the watch into the hands of the youngster who instantly dashes it against the floor. Another time, when his father is secretary at war, having just finished a long despatch which he is going to send, Charles who stands near him with his hand upon the inkstand, says—"Papa, I have a mind to throw this ink over the paper." "Do, my dear," says the Secretary, "if it will give you any pleasure." The young gentleman immediately throws the ink, and the secretary sits down very contentedly to write the despatch over again.

The young Charles delights in arch tricks. In his walk one Easter Monday, meeting a blind woman who is crying puddings and pies, he takes her by the arm and says, "Come along with me, dame. I am going to Moorfields where, this holidaytime, you may chance to meet with good customers." "Thank you kindly, sir," replies the woman. On this Charles conducts her into Cripplegate Church and placing her in the middle aisle, he says, "Now you are in Moorfields." She immediately begins to cry: "Hot puddings and pies! Hot puddings and pies! Come they are all hot!" to the great entertainment of the Congregation. The sexton goes up to her and tells her she is in church. "You are a lying son of a bitch," the woman answers. The man enraged at this reply, drags her out of the church, she cursing him mightily all the way. Nor will she believe him till she hears the sound of the organ.

"There's a clever little boy for you," Lord Holland writes when Charles is little more than two and one half years old. "Charles is dreadfully passionate, what shall we do with him?" says Lady Caroline. "Oh, never mind," replies Lord Holland, "he is a very sensible little fellow and will learn to curb himself."

Though his over-indulgence of his children is a fault, yet Lord Holland partially atones for it by a rigid adherence to his word, teaching them, for example, the sacredness of a pledge. Once having promised Charles that he should be present when a garden wall was to be flung down, and then forgetting it, the wall is built up again that he may perform his promise.

He treats his children as men, introducing them as such into every company and accustoming them to deliver their sentiments on all occasions. His principle is to remonstrate with them but never to command or punish them. Seldom does he show the least displeasure at his sons' expensive luxury—gambling. His fortune is theirs—to save or to squander. He supplies Charles with a certain number of guineas every night for the purpose of speculating at the gaming table. On several occasions he buys in Charles's I. O. U.'s, and just before his death he satisfies his sons' creditors at a cost of £140,000. He invariably shields his favorite Charles. "Let nothing be done," he says, "to break his spirit. The world will effect that business soon enough."

Charles James Fox is short, fat, swarthy, and dark, and badly dressed. There certainly is something Jewish in his looks. In his youth he is a prodigious dandy, strutting up and down St. James's Street in a suit of French embroidery, a little silk hat, red heeled shoes, and a bouquet nearly large enough for a Maypole. He wears a hat and feather even in the House of Commons. Within a few years, however, his dress changes. He usually wears a shabby and threadbare blue frock coat with a buff waistcoat. Possibly this change is due to his gambling losses.

Lord George Germain asserts in the House of Commons: "Ministers have some property to lose as well as the gentlemen on the other side of the House." Fox replies with perfect truth, "It is well known that I have no stake to lose." In a short time his father's wealth vanishes over the faro tables of Mayfair and St. Jarmes's. His brother Stephen Fox sits down one evening with £13,000 to his credit and rises without a penny. Charles is equally unfortunate:

> At Almack's of pigeons I am told there are flocks,
> But it's thought the completest is one Mr. Fox;
> If he touches a card, if he rattle the box,
> Away fly the guineas of this Mr. Fox.
> In gaming, 'tis said, he's the stoutest of cocks—
> No man can play deeper than this Mr. Fox;
> And he always must lose, for the strongest of locks
> Cannot keep any money for this Mr. Fox.

He loses £20,000 in a night. Once he plays for twenty-four hours and loses £500 an hour. His father asks him how it is possible for him to sleep or enjoy any of the comforts of life when he reflects on the immense sums for which he stands indebted. "Your lordship need not be in the least surprised," answers Charles. "Your astonishment ought to be how my creditors can sleep."

When his brother Ste's wife is brought to bed of a son and heir, which cuts Charles out of the estate and title, he is called out of his Jerusalem Chamber (where sit his money lenders) to be informed of the circumstance. On his return, perceiving some disappointment in his countenance, they unanimously exclaim—"Vat is de matter? Vat is de matter, Master Fox?" "Bad enough, indeed," replies Charles. "Here is a second Messiah come to plague you all." (He has his jest and they have his estate.)

In the summer of 1773 his difficulties induce him to put his faith in an adventuress Mrs. Grieve who promises to procure him an heiress with £150,000. She informs him that Miss Phipps, a West Indian heiress, is in love with him. Sometimes she is not landed; sometimes she has the smallpox. In the meantime Miss Phipps does not like a dark haired man; Celadon must powder his hair and eyebrows white. He does and cleans himself. But the heiress is a myth.

A few years later he is reduced to the utmost distress owing to his gambling losses. He borrows money from the Club waiters. He lacks sufficient small change to pay the chairmen who carry him from house to house. His health is impaired—he suffers from acute pains which can only be alleviated by doses of laudanum. Yet he never loses his good spirits. After dropping large sums at hazard he goes home, not to destroy himself as his friends sometimes fear, but to sit down quietly and read Greek.

He once wins about £8000. One of his bond creditors, who soon hears of his good luck, presents himself and asks for payment. "Impossible, sir," replies Fox. "I must first discharge my debts of honor." The bond creditor remonstrates. "Well, sir, give me your bond." It is delivered to Fox who tears it in pieces and throws it into the fire. "Now, sir," says Fox, "my debt to you is a debt of honor," and he immediately pays him. (An incident of this kind is told of Sheridan.) But another run of ill luck leaves him penniless, and he is again in need of the smallest sums.

"Men of spirit," Ben Jonson tells us, "seldom keep earth long," and the acres of Fox's estate as well as the groves that stand upon them go the way of everything which Fox possesses except his public honor and his political conscience.

If it is not cards, it is chess. Fox goes chess mad. He is so taken up with the game that he wishes all the politics of Europe at the bottom of the sea and the politicians with them. He says on coming to breakfast one morning that he has not been able to sleep for thinking about some particular move.

His character is a mass of contradictions. He is a rake with a chivalrous respect for women (he marries his mistress Mrs. Armistead who has lived with Lord George Cavendish, Lord Derby, and Lord Cholmondely previous to her acquaintance with Fox. She has annuities from all three which she sells to pay some of his debts), a spendthrift who asks for little more than a crust, a terrific worker with extraordinary powers of dissipation, an idler equally at home in the Club room of St. James's or the open air of his beloved garden on St. Anne's Hill.

And he has a genuine delight in art and literature. His knowledge of the classics is sound. Passages from Virgil, Horace, Tacitus, Juvenal, and Cicero present themselves to his memory without effort. During a single winter, in addition to his private studies, he reads aloud to Mrs. Fox, Tasso, Ariosto, Milton, Spenser, Appollonius, Phodius, Lucretius, Virgil, and Homer. Cicero, Euripides, Virgil are his favorites, but Homer holds first place in his affections. He reads the *Iliad* and *Odyssey* every year, often more than once. He notes the minutest points in Homer, such as that he never mentions the singing of birds, and has an obvious dislike for the character of Heracles. Of Euripides he says—"He is the most precious thing left us—the most like Shakespeare." Of Virgil he says that he excels in the style which speaks to the heart. When he is suffering under the dropsy, his nephew Lord Holland to console him, says—*dabit Deus his quoque finem.* "Aye," says Fox, "but *finem,* young one, may have two senses." Though he is said to have gone through £16,000 in ten days in Naples, it is there that he conceives his passion for Italian poetry. His affection for poetry of all kinds is very remarkable for a politician. "If I had a boy," he says to Samuel Rogers, "I would make him write verse. It is the only way to know the meaning of words."

He is perfectly good-natured, eager, warm hearted and unselfish. He is all gifts and no stability. In London mixed society, he converses little, but at his own house in the country, with his intimate friends, he will talk on forever with all the openness and simplicity of a child. He continues talking to Rogers for half an hour after he has taken up his bedroom candle.

One morning at his own house, while speaking to Rogers of his travels, he cannot recollect the name of a particular town in Holland and is much vexed at the treacherousness of his memory. He has a dinner party that day, and just as he applies the carving knife to the sirloin, the name of the town suddenly occurs to him, and he roars out exultingly, to the astonishment of the noble company, "Gorcum! Gorcum!"

"Do you not hate that fellow?" he is once asked. "I am a bad hater," he replies. One night at Brooks's he makes some remark on government powder in allusion to something that has happened. William Adam, a supporter of Lord North, considers it a reflection and sends Fox a challenge. Fox goes out and takes his station, giving a full front. His friend Fitzpatrick says—"You must stand sideways." Fox says, "Why, I am as thick one way as the other." The order "fire" is given. Adam fires, Fox does not, and when they say he must, he says, "I'll be damned if I do. I have no quarrel." They then advance to shake hands. Fox says, "Adam, you'd have killed me if it had not been government powder." The ball hit him in the groin.

When Fox visits Voltaire at Geneva, the philosopher writes to Lord Holland, "Your son is an English lad and j an old frenchman. He is healthy and j sick. Yet j love him with all my heart, not only for his father, but for himself." Charles Fox is loved for himself despite his errors and weaknesses as few men of his age are loved.

George Selwyn is always at Holland House. He belongs to that pleasant Whiggish society, though he is not in any real sense a Whig. He watches the triumphs of Charles with as much pride as Lord Holland, mixed, perhaps, with some cynicism. Long before Charles begins to dazzle the House of Commons, he is on terms of close friendship with him. Charles's speeches in support of Lord North's government rejoice the heart of Selwyn. And in that very same year Charles pleases Selwyn immensely by his anti-popular attitude during the Onslow riots. Colonel Onslow moves in the House to commit the printers of certain Parliamentary reports, and a mob from the city marches to Westminster to protest. For about half an hour Charles leans out of a coffee house window in Palace Yard, shaking his fist at the people, and provoking them by all the reproachful words and menacing gestures that he can invent. George Selwyn stands behind, encouraging him and clapping him on the back, adds one newspaper, "as if he was a dirty ruffian going to fight in the streets." Fox, however, does not long retain Selwyn's approval of his political conduct.

But it is his private conduct which offends George in the first instance. Fox loses heavily at cards; he induces Lord Carlisle to join him in a bond of indemnity for £14,000, and then Fox-like, treats the whole matter in an airy and irresponsible way. Shortly after the bond is executed, he receives £50,000 from some quarter or other, and gambles it all away again without regard to Carlisle's agreement. This alienates from him the regard of George Selwyn. He writes angry and bitter letters to Carlisle. He has no mercy upon Fox or his family. In the end Carlisle escapes from the entanglement without loss.

Then Fox, still airy and irresponsible, takes the pernicious principles of the Opposition, nay, himself becomes the head and front of the Opposition. This is too much for George Selwyn, the King's friend.

It is, however, with many pangs that George ruptures this old friendship. "I am free to own," he writes to Carlisle, "that in speaking to you of Charles, who was perhaps your first and warmest friend, I suffer a great deal of perplexity. I have lived, notwithstanding the disparity of our years, in great friendship and intimacy with him. His behavior to me has always been kind and obliging. I have professed a regard to him and have had it." But henceforward Selwyn dissembles his love for Charles very successfully. "I saw Charles," he writes, "in a new hat, frock, waistcoat, shirt, and stockings. He was clean and smug as a gentleman, and upon perceiving my surprise, he told me that it was from the Pharo Bank. He then talked of the thousands it had lost, which I told him only proved its substance. He smiled and seemed perfectly satisfied with that which he had taken up. He was in such a sort of humor that I should have liked to have dined with him." A little later the bailiffs arrive. "You must know that for these two days past all passengers in St. James's Street have been amused with seeing two carts at Charles's door filling by the Jews with his goods, clothes, books, and pictures . . . Such furniture I never saw."

Why should Charles care? He and Dick Fitzpatrick and James Hare are holding the faro bank at Brooks's dealing by turns and winning thousands (40,000, Jack Manners says, but Jack exaggerates) while the money lenders are kindly removing his dirty furniture. At the faro table sits Charles Fox with his great black eyebrows and jolly round bibulous face, dealing out the cards with many a jest and many a loud guffaw. George Selwyn looks in and shakes his head virtuously as he crosses the street to White's where he himself is running a faro bank but not at the open window. On one occasion Selwyn calls at Brooks's and hints to Charles that he has a "suit to prefer." Charles guesses what it is and begs Selwyn not just then to speak to him about money as he is in the right. "I meant to have dunned him for yours [Carlisle's]. What pleases me," Selwyn confesses, "is that I may say anything to him, and he takes nothing ill, and by that and some other things, he does in a great measure disarm me, and I can never abuse him heartily but when I don't see him for some time."

He calls Fox a "field preacher," "a desperate rantipole vagabond," and after his accession to office, "the late Charles, now Mr. Fox (for I think that the other name has begun to sound obsolete already even at Brooks's) . . . I had no conversation with him or probably shall the rest of my life. I cannot gainsay, unthink, or repent of any one charge I ever brought against him." Of course not, and Selwyn nurses his resentment against the Secretary of State as long as possible. "Last night at supper with Charles, but not one syllable passed between us."

But Charles is invincible. Through all that difficult time when he is flouting the King and his ministers and bragging about the fine government he is on the point of forming, Selwyn never entirely breaks with him. He cannot do it. "Charles with all his insolence towards the King is very good-humored towards me." "I saw Charles last night," says Selwyn in another letter, "and by accident was alone with him. He stretched out his hand to me with great good humor." In spite of Selwyn's peevishness, Fox insists upon remaining friends with him to the end so that long afterwards Selwyn is still disposed to love Charles and to mount the rostrum in his favor.

An evening at White's. George is sitting among the old fellows by the fire grumbling at the insolence of the younger generation. Charles comes into the room with his patriots. He sees Selwyn at the fire and whispers to Hare and others that old George is there and in a deuce of a humor. "But observe," says he, "how I shall bring him round." He goes up to Selwyn, slaps him on the back, insists on shaking hands with him. George resists at first, keeps his sour looks for a while but thaws gradually under Charles's good humor. So they sit gossiping until midnight and separate after an "infinitely agreeable" time as Selwyn grudgingly admits next day to Carlisle.

One of Fox's earliest friends, whom he loves excessively, and a friend of Selwyn's too, is tall, distinguished Richard Fitzpatrick. Fox and Fitzpatrick have everything in common—pursuits, accomplishments, house, room, horse-flesh, money, and credit. Fitzpatrick is a man of wit, fashion, gallantry, one of the principal authors of the *Rolliad,* a constant attendant in the green rooms of the theatres and at Newmarket, and so noted for his fine manners and polite address that Old Q leaves him a considerable legacy on this account alone. He is constitutionally indolent, and habitual indulgence of his passions for women and play increases the infirmity. (However, he makes a flight in a balloon from Oxford, landing in a corn field). He is less remarkable for brilliant repartee than Hare. His conversation and writings remind his friends of Addison—leaving out the morality and piety.

Poor Ned Foley has many friends, all the wicked and witty satellites of Charles Fox. Lady Anne, his wife, a few days after one of her lyings-in, writes this short note and postscript to Dick Fitzpatrick—"Dear Richard, I give you joy. I have just made you the father of a beautiful boy. Yours etc. P. S. This is not circular."

Then there is James Hare, the "Hare of many friends," whose bow at the Opera is a more valued distinction than an invitation from the Prince of Wales. He is eager and impetuous, all fire and fancy. He dazzles and captivates women of beauty, talent, and condition by the brilliancy of his wit, the vivacity of his imagination. He has a natural, unaffected earnestness of manner in which there is not the slightest tinge of vulgarity or ill breeding. If, as Horace affirms, the favor and friendship of distinguished men constitute no slight commendation, no person in English society ever earns a larger portion of that reward. Hare is the son of an apothecary.

In politics he is a follower, almost a worshipper, of Fox. Indeed he measures all men's political merits and even talents by the degree of devotion they pay to Fox. This admiration is reciprocal. When Fox is complimented on the success of his maiden speech in the House of Commons, "Wait," is his reply, "till you hear Hare." However, the latter never attempts to speak in Parliament but once. It is on a point of order in which his friend has been attacked. Rage almost chokes his utterance, and on his sitting down, Fox greets him with a remark more frank than encouraging—"What a fine, passionate fellow you are."

Hare is extravagant, particularly at cards. In 1779 his losses are so great that he is anxious for either of the diplomatic posts of Munich or Warsaw. He vents his sense of the necessity but disagreeableness of the appointment extempore, in the following lines—

> Having been born to no land,
> 'Tis thought that I must go to Poland,
> So having long exhausted all tick,
> I soon, alas, must cross the Baltic.
> Of all the towns I read of or saw,
> I least expected seeing Warsaw;
> And now 'tisn't ten to one I a'nt sick
> Before I ever get to Dantzic.

With the exception of some very trifling jeaux d'esprit these are the only verses Mr. Hare ever writes.

But in conversation noone is wittier or more vivacious.

For instance, he is one day conversing with Fitzpatrick when the latter affects to discredit the report of General Burgoyne's defeat at Saratoga. "Perhaps you may be right in your opinion," says Hare, "but take it from me as a flying rumor." On another occasion he is dining with the Prince of Wales at the pavilion at Brighton immediately after the downfall of Fox's coalition ministry when the latter, who has also received an invitation to the Prince's table, arrives from London in informal dress and without powder. He is proceeding to make his excuses to the Prince for what is an unavoidable breach of etiquette, when he is stopped by Hare—"Make no apology. Our great guns are discharged, and we may now all do without powder."

Fox is one day sitting at Brooks's in a very moody humor, having lost a considerable sum at cards, and is indolently moving a pen backwards and forwards over a sheet of paper, when someone says to Hare, "What is he drawing?" "Anything but a draft," is the reply.

Breakfasting one morning at the house of Fox and looking out of the window, he sees a great number of the money hunters about the door, on which he calls out—"Pray, gentlemen, are ye fox hunting or hare hunting this morning?"

Hare's classical knowledge is considerable and he is well read in general literature. At Chatsworth he sits ready armed in a great chair, book in hand, with the other extended ready to discuss and pull to pieces any unfortunate author that falls under his look.

He has several natural children, a daughter by Miss Lucretia Payne, who is taken notice of by all his acquaintances, and a son by a person whom he debauches at Cambridge, and who, after he brings her to town, is kept first by him, afterwards by Sir Francis Vincent, and afterwards by Fitzherbert the contractor. The subject of Hare's money and children always produces a conversation after dinner—especially the conduct of his mistress Miss Payne in going abroad looking out for a husband as a model girl at the time that she has had more than one child by Hare.

Georgiana Devonshire hovers on the rim of Selwyn's circle. Perhaps the Duchess is the first to enjoy George's description of her kinsman Lord John Cavendish as "a learned canary bird." For Lord John is a fair-haired little prig who under an appearance of virgin modesty has a confidence in himself that nothing can equal and a thirst for dominion still more extraordinary.

Anthony Morris Storer is another of Selwyn's friends. He is at Eton with Carlisle and Charles Fox and like them afterwards comes under Selwyn's influence. He is a man who excels in everything he sets his heart and hand to, and who deserves the epithet Admirable. He is the best dancer, best skater of his time, and beats all his competitors in gymnastic honors. He excels too as a musician and disputant, and very early as a Latin poet. In short whatever he undertakes he does con amore and as perfectly as if it were his only accomplishment.

He is the Pylades of Lord Carlisle who brings him into Parliament (gratis), and is supercilious to all not of the ton. He is a dilettante, seized with a passion for collecting books and prints. These expensive tastes and the love of cards keep him in comparative poverty until his father's death. He lives at Portugal Street, Lincoln's Inn Fields, and to his rooms in that unfashionable locality come his friends, Carlisle, Fox, and George Selwyn. They come when they choose and dine informally, and are always sure of a welcome. If at any time he is rude, insolent, or overbearing, some allowance must be made for the state of his health which is highly bilious.

(The subject of Selwyn's want of appetite for women leads Storer to think of other instances. Storer says he is persuaded that Lord Henry Conway never was connected with a woman. He used to be often in love but would suddenly break off when he could no longer avoid coming to a denouement. It is known that he and the late Lady Holland were very much attached to one another. It is commonly supposed though, that after her husband Stephen, second Lord Holland's death, she gave him the last proof of love, and that remorse on that account produced or aggravated the illness of which she died. She certainly did not go out for two years before her death and showed the greatest anxiety during that time to see Conway, who never went near her. Storer says he is certain that her grief proceeded not from what had, but from what had not happened.)

Mr. James Crawford of Auchinames (the "Fish" of Selwyn's letters and the "Petit Crawford" of Mme. du Deffand) is the butt of the Selwyn circle. George (when talking good) tells the following story one day at Lord Macartney's. He and some other friends call upon Crawford just after he has won an enormous sum at Brooks's. They find a pretty boy playing about his room, and as he acknowledges him for his son, one of them says—"Well, now you are so flush of money, do make some provision for this poor child."

"Oh, aye, so I will in a little while—"

"Pshaw!" says Selwyn. "In a little while you will have lost it all again. Do it now directly while the money is there."

They prevail and a deed is drawn up, vesting a certain sum in George Selwyn's hands as trustee for the boy. According to their prediction, Crawford's winnings go back to the hazard table in a marvelously short time and presently considerable losses succeed. Crawford complains he has no money, nor anything now remaining of all his riches but bad debts. "So now," says Selwyn, "they have all set upon me to burn the trust deed and give up the money for Crawford himself. What signifies the child? But I am so hard hearted that I will do no such thing. I have accepted the trust, and I will give it up to nobody but the Lord Chancellor."

"Fish" Crawford never troubles his head much about the boy. The last we hear of him is his loitering about Richmond as cicisbeo to Lady Di Beauclerk when he is quite old enough to have done with that sort of thing.

There are many other members of White's and Brooks's who are also members of the second Selwyn circle: Topham Beauclerk, for example, who links Selwyn's circle to one far more important and distinguished—that of Dr. Johnson; and Selwyn's nephew, the politician Tommy Townshend. But of that astonishing crowd of rollicking gamesters who frequent Almack's and Brooks's and White's with Charles Fox as leader, George Selwyn is never an intimate part. He mixes with them but is not quite of them. He is older than they, graver, more responsible. Selwyn the middle aged seems out of place in St. James's Street which is an abode for young men. One finds him more at home farther west at Old Q's house in Piccadilly or still farther at Holland House talking politics with Henry Fox, chatting with "dear Lady Mary," or pacing the terrace between Charles and his young friend Carlisle.

CHAPTER 22

CLUBS AND GAMING

THE FOUNDING OF ALMACK'S IN 1764 IS AN important event for George Selwyn and his friends. The club is founded solely for the purpose of gaming and has twenty-seven original members. George Selwyn is not an original member, but he is elected in the same year on the introduction of Mr. Crewe, later Lord Crewe. Selwyn spends a good deal of time at the club in Pall Mall. Later a new assembly room of Almack's is opened in King Street, St. James's, and it is magnificent, but it is empty, for half the town is ill with colds, and many are afraid to go as the house is scarcely built yet. Almack (a Scotsman whose real name is Macall) advertises that it is built with hot bricks and boiling water. There is a ten guinea subscription for which you have a ball and supper once a week for twelve weeks. Both sexes are admitted as members, the ladies nom-inating the gentlemen and vice versa. It is a pretty sight: Almack's Scotch face in a bag wig waiting at supper, and his lady in a sack making tea and curtseying to the Duchesses.

The assembly soon flourishes. Mrs. Cornelys, the famous proprietess of Carlisle House, Soho Square, whose concerts and society nights have been so fashionable in the sixties, is ousted, and the enterprising cateress is reduced to providing asses' milk and occasional breakfasts in rural Knightsbridge. For years Almack's holds the reputation for exclusive and fashionable entertainment, and admission to the club is the height of achievement in the world of fashion.

If once to Almack's you belong,
Like monarchs, you can do no wrong,
But banished there on Wednesday night,
By Jove, you can do nothing right.

The rooms are lighted with wax; the branches for the candles, the urns for tea and coffee, and the baskets for cakes and macaroons are all of silver.

The original gambling club still continues in Pall Mall. Fox, Pitt, Burke, Reynolds, and Walpole are all members. No pack of cards is ever used a second time. At the end of a game the cards are thrown on the floor so that after a night of gambling the players sit knee deep in cards. Change is given in washed silver. The money is first plunged in hot water and cleansed after which it is placed in a wash leather bag. This is whirled around in the air at the end of a short cord till all coins contained in it are dry.

The gaming rules at Almack's are very strict: 1. No gaming in the eating room except tossing up for reckonings, on penalty of paying the whole bill of the members present.

2. That every person playing at the new guinea table do keep 50 guineas before him.

3. That every person playing at the 20 guinea table do not keep less than 20 guineas before him.

Generally there is as much as £10,000 in specie on the table. A thousand meadows and cornfields are staked at every throw and as many villages lost as in the earthquake that overwhelmed Herculaneum and Pompei. Mr. Thynne, however, having won only 12,000 guineas during the last two months, retires in disgust.

Almack's is not solely a gaming club; many eminent men who are not gamesters are members. But gaming is the chief interest. The rooms are full of players during any night of the London season. The gamesters begin by pulling off their embroidered clothes; they put on frieze great-coats or turn their coats inside out for luck. They then put on pieces of leather (such as are worn by footmen when they clean the knives) to save their laced ruffles, and to guard their eyes from the light, and to prevent the tumbling of their hair, wear high crowned straw hats with broad brims, adorned with flowers and ribbons—and masks to conceal their emotion when they play at quinze. They have small neat stands by them with large rims to hold their tea and wooden bowls to hold their guineas. Edward Gibbon finds life at Almack's very good. "The style of living," says he, "though somewhat expensive, is exceedingly pleasant, and notwithstanding the rage of play, I have found more entertainment and rational society than in any other club to which I belong." But Gibbon, to be sure, likes to be considered a man of the world.

The Macaronis are a singular company at Almack's. George Selwyn is no Macaroni—he is not youthful enough for that. The Macaronis burst upon the town as early as 1764, but they attain their zenith eight years afterwards. These extraordinary creatures render themselves conspicuous by their immense and glorious extravagances of dress. They wear great chignons of artificial hair with exceedingly small cocked hats, red-heeled shoes and eyeglasses, carry enormous walking sticks with long tassels, and have their jackets, waistcoats, and breeches cut close, the last being of striped silk with bows of ribbons at the knees. Sometimes they vary the fashion—dress their hair high or in long curls and blossom out in enormous nosegays. They are in the habit of carrying, with large bunches of seals and chains attached, two watches—one to indicate what the time is and the other to indicate what it is not. They add to their other accomplishments that of being able to whistle through their toothpicks.

They are indeed a kind of animal, neither male nor female, but of the neuter gender. They talk without meaning, smile without pleasantry, eat without appetite, ride without exercise, wench without passion. Blue is the macaroni's favorite color. For full dress he attires himself in a colored velvet coat of some delicate shade, lined with satin and faced with ermine. In cold weather he is never without his muff, hung round his neck and trimmed with a bunch of ribbons in the center.

> For I ride in a chair with my hands in a muff,
> And have bought a silk coat and embroider'd the cuff;
> But the weather was cold, and the coat it was thin,
> So the taylor advis'd me to line it with skin.

For a year or two London lives à la Macaroni. In the streets you can meet Macaroni divines and Macaroni scholars, Macaroni M. P.'s, turf Macaronis, Parade Macaronis, Macaroni artists, Macaroni actors and (for aught one knows), Macaroni chairmen and Macaroni linkboys. Macaroni articles abound everywhere. There is Macaroni music and there are Macaroni songs set to it.

> The world's so macaronied grown of late,
> That common mortals now are out of date,
> No single class of men this merit claims,
> Or high or low, in faith 'tis all the same.

But the fashion soon dies out.

Almack's is taken over by one Brookes, a wine merchant and money lender who moves the Club in 1778 to St. James's Street. The club does not prosper at first, despite its popularity and its brilliant list of members. Brookes himself retires from the club soon after it is built and dies poor. (Selwyn, however, says that Brookes is "the completest composition of knave and fool that ever was, to which I may add liar.")

Selwyn is a constant patron of Almack's before it is merged into Brooks's. He frequently dines and writes his letters there (he calls it "his bureau") and plays at quinze and faro and hazard—much more than is good for him. After 1778 he cultivates Brooks's for a few years with some regularity, though White's remains his favorite club. The politics at Brooks's is not to his taste and play is rather high for a poor man. "I have quite relinquished nasty Brooks's," he once says, "I am with the sexaginary at White's, et de cette manière je passe le temps assez tranquillement." "Brooks's," he says again, "is a precipice of perdition, upon which I have long stood, and now for fear that I should be abimé in it, I shall, I believe, strike my name immediately out of it."

When Lord North's government totters to its fall, Brooks's becomes a centre of feverish and liberal Opposition. Such an atmosphere is antipathetic to George Selwyn, yet a sort of fascination draws him again and again to the place. "Went last night to Brooks's and stayed with them all after supper on purpose to hear their discourse, which is with as little reserve before me as if I was one of their friends . . . I own that to see Charles closeted every instant at Brooks's by one or the other, that he can neither punt or deal for a quarter of an hour but he is obliged to give an audience, while Hare is whispering and standing behind him, with a pencil and paper for memo, is to me a scene la plus parfaitement comique que l'on puisse imaginer . . . I called in at Brooks's last night but avoided all conversation, and will for the future with anyone belonging to the party. Their insolence, vanity, and folly, and the satisfaction expressed in their countenances upon fancying themselves ministers . . . is no object to me now of mirth." "Stayed at Brooks's this morning till between two and three," he says again, "and then Charles was giving audiences in every corner of the room and that idiot Lord Derby telling aloud whom he should turn out, how civil he intended to be to the Prince, and how rude to the King."

It is no wonder that Selwyn retreats more and more to White's. "I like the Society better here," he writes. And he draws a picture of the old fellows around the fire. "The Pharo table had cards on it and four hundred guineas, but not a punter to be found. Such old birds are not to be caught with chaff." No, no! we shall leave play and politics to the youngsters, and sit by the fire and cough and tell stories.

Almack's, Brooks's, and White's are three of the notorious gaming clubs in London at a time when gaming haunts London society like a passion. It seems indigenous to the soil and the demon of play never runs his course more smoothly. People turn to it as they do to an ordinary recreation. It is not regarded as a vice. It is at worst regarded as an indiscretion. Few escape the infection. People of quality, lawyers, physicians, army and navy men, actors, politicians, even the clergy, gamble prodigiously and systematically. Society is one vast casino.

Venice alone can compete with London as a gambling center. White's is the bane of half the nobility, Haywood's a brothel. People continue to waste as much in one evening as a German prince in an opera for a season. Peers are impoverished and estates mortgaged in a single sitting, and the man who enters the room in a state of affluence rushes madly into the streets at night penniless and in debt to a large amount. Operas are infrequented, plays not in fashion, amours as old as marriages. The only token of the kingdom is a woman riding on a beast, which is the Mother of Abominations and the name on the forehead is Whist, and the four and twenty elders and the woman and the whole town do nothing but play with this beast.

The green rooms of the theatre, even, are the scenes of great doings in the gaming way. Thousands are frequently lost there in a night—rings, brooches, watches, stays, professional wardrobes, and even salaries in advance being staked and lost as well as money.

By some who haunt White's, six days' gambling a week is considered insufficient. Play becomes the business of the nation from the age of fifteen to fourscore. Old and young, married and single, assemble together and gamble away their nights and days. At midnight one third of London is wide awake and almost penniless. "Why, I hope, my lord, you would not think of abolishing gaming," cries Lord Merton in *Evelina*, " 'tis the very zest of life! Devil take me if I could live without it."

When Samuel Rogers is living in the Temple the chimney of one of his neighbors is to be swept. Up go two boys and at the end of an hour they have not come down again. Two other boys are then sent up, and up they remain also. The master of the boys is now summoned, who on his arrival exclaims, "'Oh, the idle little rascals! They are playing at all fours on the top of the chimney." And to be sure, there they are, trumping away at their ease. (We suppose spades are their favorite card.)

There are giants of play. Fox plays for twenty hours and loses on an average four hundred pounds an hour. He loses at Almack's one day £11,000. His brother Stephen loses £10,000 three nights afterwards and Charles £11,000 not a week later, so that in three nights the brothers, the elder not twenty-five, lose £32,000. Hare comes to town and for want of any amusement plays at hazard and loses £4000 in three nights to a set of fellows whom he has never seen before and never sees since. Fox is only one of the reckless gamblers. Lord Hertford, Lord Sefton, the Duke of York lose vast sums. The Duke of Portland is one of the fortunate ones and he and General Scott win £200,000. A lucky man, too, is Colonel Aubrey. He makes two fortunes in India, loses them both at hazard, and makes a third at play from five guineas a friend lends him. General Fitzpatrick and Lord Robert Spencer lose their fortunes at Brooks's, but the members not objecting, with borrowed capital they keep a faro bank. The bank wins and Lord Robert plays again. With his share of £100,000 he buys the estate of Woolbeding in Sussex.

Sir John Bland flirts away his whole fortune at hazard. When Lord Lempster is on his travels, he runs much in debt. His parents pay his debts; some more come out afterwards. He writes to his mother that he can only compare himself to Cerberus, who when one head was cut off had another spring up in its room. Lord Foley's two sons borrow money so extravagantly that the interest they contract to pay amounts to £18,000. The Duke of Devonshire loses his valuable estate of Leicester Abbey to Manners at basset. Harry Furness goes drunk from White's at six o'clock and wins the sum of 1000 guineas. Francis Charteris win £3000 from the Duchess of Queensberry by using a mirror which shows her cards.

Mr. O'Birne, an Irish gamester, wins £100,000 of a young Mr. Harvey of Chigwell, just fallen into an estate by his elder brother's death. O'Birne says, "You can never pay me." "I can," says the youth. "My estate will sell for the debt." "No," says O'Birne, "I will win £10,000—you shall throw for the odd ninety." They do and Harvey wins.

A gentleman whom ill fortune has hurried into a passion takes a box and dice to a side table and then falls to throwing by himself. At length he swears with an emphasis, "Damme, now I throw for nothing I can win £1000, but when I play for money I lose my all."

At a gambling party Lord Worthall loses every pound he possesses and in a fit of excitement stakes his whole estate against £1000 at cutting low with the cards, and in cutting exclaims—

> Up now Deuce or else a Trey,
> Or Worthall's gone forever and aye.

He has the luck to cut the deuce of diamonds. And to commemorate the serious event, he gets the deuce of diamonds cut in marble and has it fixed on the parapet of his mansion.

General Wade is at a low gaming house and has a very fine snuffbox which on a sudden he misses. Everybody denies having taken it. He insists on searching the company. He does. There remains only one man who has stood behind him, but this man refuses to be searched unless the general goes into another room alone with him. There the man tells him that he was born a gentleman, is reduced, and lives by what little bets he can pick up there, and by fragments which the waiters sometimes give him. "At this moment I have half a fowl in my pocket. I was afraid of being exposed. Here it is. Now, sir, you may search me." The general is so struck with the man's story that he presents the wretched gamester with a hundred pounds.

Englishmen are as reckless in playing abroad as they are at home. They assemble in great numbers at the Salle des Étrangers in Paris. Lord Thanet, who has an income of £50,000, loses every penny he has at the Salon. He will not stop playing when the public tables close and invites those present to remain and play hazard or écarte. One night he loses £120,000. His friends tell him he has most probably been cheated. "Then," he says with great coolness, "I consider myself lucky not to have lost twice as much."

"Englishmen," says Baron D'Holbach, "lose incredible sums in perfect silence. By thirty they have exhausted all the pleasures, even beneficence. Ennui conducts them to the Thames, unless they prefer a pistol."

There is a curious list of officers attached to every gaming house.

THE HIERARCHY OF GAMING

1. A director who superintends the room.
2. An operator who deals the cards at faro.
3. Two Crowpees (i.e. croupiers) who watch the cards and gather the money for the bank.
4. Two Puffs who have money given them to decoy others to play.
5. A Clerk who is a check upon the Puffs to see that they sink none of the money given them to play with.
6. A Squib who is a Puff of a lower rank. (He serves at half salary while he is learning to deal.)
7. A Flasher to swear how often the bank has been stripped.
8. A Dunner who goes about to recover money lost at play.
9. A Waiter to fill out wine, snuff, candles, and attend in the gaming room.
10. An Attorney, a Newgate Solicitor.
11. A Captain who is to fight any gentleman up and down stairs and gives the word to the porter.
13. A Porter who is generally a discharged soldier of the foot guards.
14. An Orderly Man who walks up and down the outside of the door to give notice to the porter and alarm the house at the approach of the constables.

And runners, link boys, watchmen, chairmen, etc.

Money lenders frequent the gaming houses in the morning for the express purpose of purchasing I. O. U.'s, for as they are given for debts of honor, their payment is considered sure. But in what manner are they generally paid? If an I. O. U. is for £500, a bond or some other solid security is given for £600. The money lender in order to purge the transaction of usury, sells the debtor some trifling piece of plate or an article of jewelry for the extra hundred pounds.

In the event of everything else failing, the choice of one of two alternatives lies open to a gambling gentleman. He may marry a wealthy woman if he gets the chance or importune his friends at Court to procure him some snug position under the government with plenty to receive and nothing to do. Of course there is the final resort: the pistol.

A certain young Lord loses to Nash at Bath at one sitting all his money, all his movables, all the title deeds of his large estates, the rings on his fingers and his watch. Nash gives them all back. On another ocasion Nash wins the whole fortune of a young man and gives it back with an admonition. It is wasted. The young man plays again, loses again, and blows out his brains.

A gentleman goes and insures his life, securing the privilege of a free dying Englishman. He carries the insurers to dine at a tavern where they meet several other persons. After dinner he says to the life and death brokers—"Gentlemen, it is fit that you should be acquainted with the company. These honest men are tradesmen to whom I was in debt, without any means of paying, but your assistance, and now I am your humble servant." And he pulls out a pistol and shoots himself.

The absorbing passion is not confined to the harsher sex alone. Coteries of ladies, young and old, have their regular nights of meeting and the household expenses are occasionally not a little increased by the loss in a single evening of three times the last night's winnings (already laid out in a new brocaded dress, stomacher, commode, or fan). So far the ladies carry this infatuation that women of fashion at length establish in their levées regular whist masters and professors of quadrille. They spend their mornings in counting their gains or lamenting their losses; they talk and think of nothing else. Some maids are so taken up with the passion of gaming that they have no time to devote to love.

"Oh, the damned vice," Steele bursts out. "That women can imagine all household care, regard to posterity and fear of poverty must be sacrificed to a game of cards."

"Don't talk to me about books," cries old Sarah Marlborough, "The only books I know are men and cards." The games principally played are bassett, ombre, quadrille, and faro. The four most notorious women to make a profit of the gambling craze are my Lady Buckinghamshire, my Lady Archer, Mrs. Sturt, and Mrs. Duncannon, who are known throughout the town as "Faro's Daughters." Frederick Reynolds' grandmother who resides in Montpelier Row reigns Queen of all the card players in that locality. Her infatuation is carried to such an extent that the four old maids of the Row, her principal subjects, are chiefly known in the neighborhood by the names of Manille, Spadille, Basto, and Punto.

So completely does gambling get the better of dancing that once at a private ball a gentleman asking a young lady from Bath to dance the next two dances, she very ingenuously replies, "Yes, if you will play two rubbers at Casino."

In the year 1776 a lady at the West End loses one night at a sitting three thousand guineas at loo. Again a lady having won a rubber of twenty guineas from a city merchant, the latter pulls out of his pocketbook and tenders her twenty-one pounds in bank notes. The fair gamestress with a disdainful toss of the head observes—"In the great houses which I frequent, sir, we always use gold." "That may be, Madam," says the gentleman, "but in the *little* house which I frequent, we always use paper."

Lady Buckinghamshire, a notorious gamester of St. James's Square, actually sleeps with a blunderbuss and a pair of pistols at her side to protect her faro bank.

Kate Clive alternately reddens and turns pale as she loses at play, and tears of rage start into her eyes. Once she shouts to a dowager (a starched old lady with a hoary head and white eyebrows as white as those of an albiness) who demands payment for the two black aces—"Two black aces— here take the money, though, instead I wish I could give you two black eyes, you old white cat." The starched old lady, who in her eagerness to receive her winnings has risen from her chair, astounded at her reception, sinks back into it as if she has received a blow. She literally closes her eyes and opens her mouth and for several moments thus remains fixed by the magnitude of her horror.

Lords Dillon and Bessborough playing at quinze one night with Miss Pelham, and happening to laugh, she flies into a passion and says—"It is terrible to play with boys!" And their two ages together make up about a hundred and forty.

Caroline Vernon, fille d'honneur, loses t'other night two hundred pounds at faro and bids Martindale mark it up. He says he would rather have a draft on her banker. "Oh, willingly," and she gives him one. Next morning, he hurries to Drummond's lest all her money be drawn out. "Sir," says the clerk, "would you receive the contents immediately?" "Assuredly." "Why, sir, have you read the note?" Martindale takes it. It is: "Pay the bearer 200 blows, well applied."

Not infrequently play affords Amazons an opportunity of avenging themselves upon their adversaries in a manner not likely to be forgotten. Jemmy Lumley has a party of whist at his own house with several combatant women. They play from six in the evening till twelve next day, Jemmy never winning one rubber and rising a loser of £2000. How it happened, he does not know, nor why his suspicions arrive so late, but he fancies himself cheated and refuses to pay. He promises a dinner at Hampstead. In the garden at Hampstead he finds the gentle conqueress Mrs. Mackenzy who accosts him in the most friendly manner. After a few compliments, she asks him if he does not intend to pay her. "No, indeed, I shan't. I shan't. Your servant, your servant." "Shan't you?" says the fair virago and taking a horsewhip from beneath her hoop, she falls upon him with as much vehemence as the Empress Queen would upon the King of Prussia if she could catch him alone in the garden at Hampstead.

Hollow eyes, haggard looks, and pale complexions are the natural indications of a female gamester. George Hanger is cross: "It is lamentable to see a lovely woman destroying her health and beauty at six o'clock in the morning at a gaming table. Can any woman expect to give to her husband a vigourous and healthy offspring whose mind night after night is thus distracted and whose body is relaxed by anxiety and the fatigue of late hours? It is impossible."

2.

There is a mania for betting not just confined to White's in St. James's Street. There is nothing however trivial or ridiculous which is not capable of producing a bet. Many pounds are lost upon the color of a coach horse, an article in the news, or a change in the weather.

A butcher in Leadenhall Market lays an ox to a shin of beef on the success of Sir John Barnard against the field. A reputed centenarian undertakes to walk ten miles on Hammersmith road in two hours and thirty minutes for a wager of ten guineas, and he accomplishes the task in two hours and twenty-three minutes. A nobleman and a gentleman in the army bet £500 between five turkeys and five geese to run from Norwich to London. Both sides begin training. Lord Montford is asked soon after his daughter's marriage if she is with child. He replies, "Upon my word, I don't know. I have not bet upon it." Even the King bets, going halves with Lord Orford who bets that he will have a child before Sir James Lowther, who is married the night before to Lord Bute's eldest daughter.

Sir George Beaumont is one day in the Mount (a famous coffee house in Mount Street, Grosvenor Square) with Harvey Aston. Various persons are seated at different tables. Among others present there is an Irishman who is celebrated as a duellist, having killed at least half a dozen antagonists. Aston talking to his acquaintances, swears that he will make the duellist stand barefooted before them. "You had better take care what you say," they reply, "he has his eye upon you." "No matter," rejoins Aston, "I declare again that he shall stand barefooted before you, if you will make up among you a purse of fifty guineas." They do so. Aston then says in a loud voice, "I have been in Ireland and am well acquainted with the natives." The Irishman is all ears. Aston goes on: "The Irish being born in bogs are every one of them webfooted. I know it for a fact." "Sir," roars the duellist, starting up from his table, "it is false." Aston persists in his assertion. "Sir," cries the other, "I was born in Ireland and I will prove to you that it is a falsehood." So saying, in great haste, he pulls off his shoes and stockings, and displays his bare feet. The joke ends in Aston's sharing the purse between the Irishman and himself, giving the former thirty guineas and keeping twenty.

"Sir G. Webster gives Lord Derby one guinea to receive one hundred guineas when Ld. Derby goes up in a Balloon one hundred yards from the surface of the earth.

"Mr. Fox bets Ld. Bolingbroke five guineas that America does not belong to the King of Great Britain this day two years.

"Mr. Sheridan betts Mr. Stepney an hundred guineas to five that the King of France is not absolute Jan. 1, 1791.

> "Won by Mr. Sheridan
> pd."

But this style of betting is harmless compared to that curse, betting upon horse racing. Lord Foley enters upon the turf with an estate of £18000 per annum and £100,000 ready money. He leaves with a ruined constitution, an encumbered estate, and not a shilling of ready money. Fox, on the other hand, wins £16000 at Newmarket by betting against the celebrated Puncher who loses the match by only half a neck. And at the spring meeting in 1789 he wins not less than £50,000.

Queen Anne is fond of racing and gives £100 gold cups to be raced for—nay more: she not only keeps race horses but runs them in her own name. The father of the turf is Tregonwell Frampton, Esq., the oldest and cunningest jockey in England. One day he loses a thousand guineas, the next he wins two thousand, and so alternately. He makes as light of throwing away five hundred or a thousand pounds at a time as other men do of their pocket money, and is perfectly calm, cheerful and unconcerned when he loses a thousand pounds as when he wins it. George III attends the Ascot Races and his uncle the "'butcher," Duke of Cumberland, is a great patron of the turf.

In this state of public feeling it is not to be wondered at that lottery schemes are received with favor. Legislators themselves fall victims to the craze. The people, they argue, patronize the lottery and why shouldn't they? Was it not by lot that it was determined which of the goats should be offered by Aaron? Was it not by lot that the land of Canaan was divided and by lot that Saul was chosen King? Anyway, the chance of a twenty or thirty thousand pound prize is too dazzling and the tickets are bought up almost as soon as they are issued—

> A lottery is a taxation
> Upon all the fools in creation;
> And Heaven be prais'd,
> It is easily rais'd,
> Credulity's always in fashion.

The rage for a ticket in the lottery is a species of monomania with which few people are not infected, from the nobleman who can afford to purchase a whole ticket to the servant who raises the sum (often by pilfering) necessary to purchase a sixteenth. Long and serious is the consideration in the choice of an agent. "Hazard" is a famous name, nay "Winpenny" is better—his office is in the King's Arms, but then "Good-Luck"—that has a more musical sound. The case is perplexing and the anxious speculator long wavers in doubt till a bill is perchance thrust into his hand with a doggerel song, ending in a chorus—

> For oh! 'tis Bish, 'tis Bish, 'tis BISH,
> Who sends the cash around,
> I only wish a friend in Bish,
> And 30,000 pound.

And to Bish's lottery office accordingly he hies. But now interposes another momentous question. What number shall he choose? Three is lucky—so is twelve—seven is decidedly unlucky—there must not be a seven in the number, nor must it be divisible by seven. Yes, it shall be twelve—no, he'll consult a fortunate friend. The friend is guided by the most frivolous reasons—the number of the year, the number of the Beast because the Devil certainly takes a hand in the lottery, the age of the purchaser, a number suggested in a dream, a number overheard in the street, a number which accidentally catches his eye in a book—anything will do.

From the commencement of the lottery until its conclusion, the lottery offices are illuminated with variegated lamps. Large flaming pictures or paintings depicting Dame Fortune in the act of showering guineas from a cornucopia into the laps of her votaries are exhibited in the show windows. Within Guildhall and overlooking the platform on which the numbers are drawn are galleries for people to see the drawing. For admission to these galleries sixpence is charged to each person and hundreds, after having spent all their money, will rake hell with a nail to secure another sixpence in order that they may ascend to the galleries and waste the day in idleness watching the progress of the drawing. Besides the crowds in the galleries, there is a large mob in the halls. Men with carrier pigeons wait to obtain the numbers. Often as many as a dozen are engaged on this errand. Generally the pigeon takes a turn or two and flies off home. Sometimes, however, it happens that one alights upon a house and when this occurs, the bystanders raise loud shouts and fling stones in all directions to cause it to wing its flight. Men on horseback also wait the drawing of the lottery and then gallop off to their confederates.

The bosom and sleeve of the Blue coat boy is closely buttoned, his pockets sewed up, and his hands examined. During the time of his being on duty, he keeps his left hand in his girdle behind him and his right hand open with his fingers extended. In 1777 two persons are brought before the Lord Mayor charged with counterfeiting a lottery ticket, but as they bring plenty of false witnesses, they are acquitted. (Sad to say, this year's lottery leads to at least one suicide, for in January, the body of a young man, clerk to a merchant in the city, is found in the river below the bridge. He had been dabbling in the lottery with his master's money and chose this method of settling his accounts.)

There is an ingenious set of lottery merchants—viz.: Lottery magazine proprietors—Lottery tailors—Lottery staymakers—Lottery glovers—Lottery hat makers—Lottery tea merchants—Lottery snuff and tobacco merchants—Lottery handkerchiefs—Lottery bakers—Lottery barbers (where a man, for being shaved and paying three pence may stand a chance of getting ten pounds)—Lottery shoe blacks—Lottery eating houses—Lottery oyster stalls—and Lottery sausages (or five shillings to be gained for a farthing relish).

"Advertisement: 27th Dec. 1797. Dr. B., a physician at Lune, Dorset, a few days since being under pecuniary embarrassment, and his house surrounded by bailiffs, made his escape by a window into a neighbor's house, from whence he fled to London. The furniture was seized, and the sale actually commenced, when it was stopped by a letter, stating that the Doctor upon his arrival in London found himself the proprietor of the £20,000 prize." *

"Notice: 19th March, 1798. The £20,000 prize, drawn on Friday, was divided amongst a number of poor persons: a female servant in Brook Street, Holborn, a woman who keeps a fruit stall in Gray's Inn Lane, a servant of the Duke of Roxburghe, a Chelsea carrier of vegetables to Covent Garden."

A lady residing in Holborn is presented with a ticket by her husband, and so anxious is she for its success that on the Sunday previous to its drawing, the clergyman gives out that "the prayers of the congregation are desired for the success of a person engaged in a new undertaking."

Lotteries still continue to hold their sway until a wave of virtue comes over the British nation. The House of Commons inquires into the evil attending lotteries and the sentence of condemnation is pronounced.

AN EPITAPH

In Memory of
The State of LOTTERY
the last of a long line
whose origin in England commenced
in the year 1569
which, after a series of tedious complaints
Expired
on the
18th day of October, 1826.

"(* We guarantee the truth of this fact.)"

During a period of 257 years, the family
flourished under the powerful protection
of the
British Parliament
the minister of the day continuing to
give them his support for the improvement
of the revenue.
His Majesty George IV
on the 9th of July, 1823,
pronounced sentence of condemnation
on the whole race
from which time they were almost
Neglected BY THE BRITISH PUBLIC.
Very great efforts were made by the
Partisans and friends of the family to
excite
the public feeling in favor of the last
of the race, in vain.
It continued to linger out the few
remaining
Moments of its existence without attention
or sympathy, and finally terminated
its career unregretted by any
virtuous mind.

3.

Selwyn has the reputation of being a most reckless gamester but he never really is a "deep" player. His gains and
losses at play are not considerable. For this there are many
reasons. In the first place Selwyn is a duffer at the principal
games—hazard, quinze, and faro. He is a tolerable whist
player and could make a fair income from cards if he confined his attention to the game. But again, he is a poor man;
at best his income is well under £3000 a year. He is a sporting man who plays for a win and if he loses, mysterious
bonds make their appearance and tide the loser over until
the next win. But here the second reason begins to operate.
Selwyn comes of a family noted for its shrewdness and care-
fulness in all matters relating to money. And George inherits
a share at least of this family virtue. He never loses his head

at cards or plunges wildly on the turf or books extravagant wagers. Behind all his passion for play is a shrewd estimate of the ways and means, a calculated finance. Thus, through all the extravagant gaming of the period, George arrives at a comparatively unembarrassed old age.

But he has his experiences. "I am sorry," writes Lord March, "that you have lost your money: it is unpleasant. In the meantime, what the devil signify *le fable de Paris* or the nonsense of White's? You may be sure they will be glad you have lost your money, not because they dislike you, but because they like to laugh . . . all that signifies nothing: the disagreeable part is having lost your money. Almack's or White's will bring all back again." This £1000 is lost at Paris but in the same year Mr. I. Shafto duns him for the same amount. "I intended to have spoke to you last night in regard to the one thousand pounds you owe me . . . I hope it will not be inconvenient to you to leave the money for me at White's either tomorrow or next day." Selwyn pays Mr. Shafto with money borrowed from Lord March. But lenders are not all so accommodating. Richard Fitzpatrick, applied to for assistance, is "heartily sorry for your *malheur,* though it is some satisfaction to me to find the resolutions of others are not more binding than my own." He promises to speak to Stephen Fox, and can give Selwyn no other hopes. The banker Drummond is "heartily sorry I cannot comply with your request, having determined to lend no money on personal security, and hope therefore you will excuse, sir, your most obedient humble servant."

Selwyn is often hardly pressed. The Earl of Derby writes him—

MY DEAR GEORGE,—Nothing can equal what I feel at troubling you with this disagreeable note, but having lost a very monstrous sum of money last night, I find myself under the necessity of entreating your goodness to excuse the liberty I am taking now of applying to you for assistance. If it is not very inconvenient to you, I should be glad of the money you owe me. If it is, I must pay what I can, and desire Brookes to trust me for the remainder. I repeat again my apologies, to which I shall beg leave to add how very sincerely I have the honour to be, my dear Sir, your most obedient humble servant,

DERBY

Of course there are many other ways of raising money besides that of borrowing. Thus in 1758 George mortgages the parsonage of Whitchurch in Hampshire, part of the family property. He has other mortgages, but in 1782 he has a grand financial clearing up.

He makes efforts to abandon the gaming table but never succeeds. True, he limits his play. "Leave off play," writes Lord Holland, "You are a fool at it." He apologizes to Carlisle for his lapses and allows that the comparison of him to Arlequin is just. But as he approaches the age of sixty and finds his household cares and anxieties increase, he gradually gives up the gaming table. The first time Wilberforce is at Brooks's, scarcely knowing anything, he joins from mere shyness in play at the faro table where Selwyn keeps bank. A friend who knows Wilberforce's inexperience and regards him as a victim decked out for the sacrifice calls to him—"What, Wilberforce, is that you?" Selwyn resenting the interference turns and says in his most expressive tone, "Oh, sir, don't interrupt Mr. Wilberforce; he cannot be better employed."

Selwyn's faro bank at White's in 1781 is his last venture in play and it is not successful. He then becomes quite virtuous. "I hear no news," he writes to Carlisle. "The gaming world would afford a great deal, but I hope it will never any more be interesting to either of us." And again: "Pharaon [faro] s'empare de tous les quartiers de la ville. It may approach me under any guise it pleases but it will never succeed with me for any time . . . It is time in my sixty-third year to know what I am worth and can count upon." He gives up play entirely—except for trifling sums. "It is one of the greatest consumers," he says, "of time, fortune, constitution, and thinking."

CHAPTER 23

MIE MIE

"HEAVEN IS REMARKABLY INDULGENT TO
you," writes Gilly Williams to Selwyn, "to secure you a
nursery in perpetuo. The moment the old one is fledged, and
takes to wing, you have another with clouts and a pap-
spoon to which you are equally attentive." "What stuff is
this!" is George's half angry comment, but it is the truth,
nevertheless. For George takes an affectionate interest in
children. For a long time he directs his affection to the
Coventry children, at another time to the Carlisle children,
who look upon him as a good-natured and benevolent uncle
and call him "Coffee." But the real love of his life is given
to Mie Mie—Maria Fagnani, afterwards Marchioness of
Hertford.

Maria is born on the 25th of August, 1771. Her mother
is the Marchioness Fagnani, wife of an Italian nobleman
whose family belongs to Milan. Whoever Maria's father is,
he is not the Marquis Fagnani. Some say Lord March, some
George Selwyn; probably it is the former. Lord March does
not care very much about the child. True when she is
grown up, he does protect her and take the authority of a
parent, preventing her from marrying a worthless Frenchman. He leaves her his wealth too, but then he cannot carry
it with him.

Selwyn, on the other hand, takes an absorbing interest in
the child from her very early days. When she is eleven
months old, he reports to her mother on the great teething
question. When she is less than three, he determines to lose
no time "in settling for my dear Mie Mie that which may

be the only thing done for her"—in other words, in making his will in her favor. "My affection and anxiety about her are beyond conception." March and Selwyn compete at first in their attention to this young lady of four. March thinks of sending her to boarding school while Selwyn takes her to Richmond for a few weeks of change and fresh air—"writing in my garden, and Mie Mie at work in it and I have ordered them to bring my dinner here, which I shall have on my grass plat under an apple tree." In London he sits on his doorstep, the pretty foreign looking child in his arms, pleased at the attention she attracts.

Soon March places himself *hors concours*, and Selwyn proudly assumes entire control of the infant. She never goes out to air in the coach, never eats or does anything without Selwyn attending her. He decides to send her to school and selects Mrs. Terry's establishment at Kensington. Here he watches over her with the most assiduous care. He calls every day, sends anxious notes to inquire how the dear child is and was, whether she sleeps well or is ill.

"Mrs. Terry presents her compliments to Mr. Selwyn: has the pleasure to assure him that dear Mademoiselle Fagnani is as well today as her good friend could possibly wish her to be. She is this minute engaged in a party at high romps."

"Mrs. Terry presents her best compliments to Mr. Selwyn: is very sorry to find that he is so uneasy. The dear child's spirits *are not* depressed. She is very lively, ate a good dinner, and behaves just like other children."

When the holidays come, Selwyn takes Mie Mie to "Brighthelmstone" for the bathing or to Chislehurst for the fresh country air. These are halcyon times for Selwyn and his little maid.

But they do not last long. Madame Fagnani hints to Selwyn that he must soon give her up to her parents. They have been separated from her long enough. They will shortly be returning to Italy and the dear child must return with them. Her grandparents particularly desire it. Selwyn is in despair. He has an interview with Madame Fagnani when a compromise is arrived at. Madame agrees to leave

Mie Mie in England under his care for a year, but after that she is to be sent home to Milan. Selwyn is satisfied for the time being. He has a year before him. His friends entreat him to make the best of it. But Selwyn cannot make the best of things; he cannot enjoy the moment; he is always anticipating misfortune. The shadow of parting with Mie Mie hangs over him during that grace of twelve months. Madame Fagnani never fails to impress upon him the absolute finality of her decision. Selwyn asks Lord March to use his influence with Madame for him, but March has "no opinion of his credit there." Meanwhile Selwyn is sombre.

To his niece Mary Townshend: "I thank you very much for acquainting me with my mother's being so well. I hope to hear that she continues to be so, and excepting this absence of six weeks, shall hereafter be at no great distance from you, and ready to give you and the family as much of my company as you will be troubled with. I beg my best love to them all and my duty to my mother. I should be glad to make my visits to her more frequent, but I would never come to her but when I was as cheerful as possible, and I am very much afraid that she will perceive that I cannot be so, and shall be very awkward in assuming the air of it. I ask pardon for this little épanchement d'un coeur qui est fort gros et triste. But I cannot help speaking of what is constantly the subject of my thoughts, and I believe when I am speaking to you of what I feel, it is to one whose natural sensibility will encline you to pity me as much as the regard which you have always expressed to one who is ever most affectionately yours."

He appeals to the Count Fermian, the Governor of Milan, but in vain. He negotiates with everyone. He writes a wild letter to Madame Fagnani and she replies—"You have decided, then, in order to secure your own happiness, to accomplish our ruin by embroiling us with our family while at the same time you destroy the reputation of the child you pretend to love. Learn, then, the result of your imprudent conduct. Our parents (more irritated than ever by your insulting offer of giving our daughter a dower, and at the same time very angry with us on account of the bad faith we have kept with them) have forbidden our writing to them again until we have Mie Mie in our charge . . . We do not really know, sir, what devilish idea has seized you. Was it to reward us for our own good nature in leaving you Mie Mie, contrary to the advice of our parents, or because you doubted our word? In any case you were wrong. I repeat to you that Mie Mie is not an object of pity as you endeavour to make out. Thank heaven! she is in want of nothing; she belongs to a very great house; she has fortune enough to be independent of everyone, and I can assure you that no greater misfortune could befall her than that of living in a strange country separated, like a foundling, from her family, maintained by a person who does not belong to her, and in regard to whom, the world would always question by what title he adopted the child."

This letter brings Selwyn to reason and by the end of August, 1777, he is preparing busily for the departure of Mie Mie. He has some idea of traveling as far as Paris with her, but is induced by his friends to give it up. He finds his greatest distraction in work. He personally superintends all the details of the child's journey, he even makes a memorandum of the inns at which she is to stay.

PLAN OF STOPS FOR MIE MIE
De Londres
À Dartford, à la Couronne;
à Rochester, à la Couronne;
à Canterbury, aux Fontaines;
à Douvre, chez Brochon, King's Head;
à Calais, chez Dessein, Hôtel d'Angleterre;
à Boulogne, Ville de Londres;
à Montreuil, la meilleure auberge, je ne me souviens pas;
à Abbeville, à l'Ecu de Brabant;
à Amiens, les Bons Enfants;
à Chantilly, à la Poste, etc., etc.

He finds time to bring Mie Mie to Sir Joshua's studio to have her portrait painted. By the third week of September everything is ready for Mie Mie's departure, and on the 22nd she leaves Cleveland Court for Dover in Selwyn's traveling carriage, accompanied by Selwyn's faithful valet,

Pierre Michalin. Selwyn runs away to Frognal two or three days before: he cannot bear the pang of actual parting. Reports reach him from various points on the outward journey. From Dover his agents have the pleasure to acquaint him that "the little lady you recommended to us sailed this morning, with very fine weather and a favorable opportunity. We provided her with a very good vessel and an exceedingly careful Captain." From Paris Madame Fagnani reports Mie Mie "perfectly well. She has not suffered the least from the journey." There are notes from the young lady herself, short but to the point. Under one brief epistle she scrawls the figure of a woman with an immense head and headdress and a very diminutive body, with the words subjoined—"This great woman, she is my gouvernante." In another:

My Dear MONSIEUR SELWYN—God bless you and preserve you, with all my heart, and let me see you as soon as I can. I am your

MIE MIE

Selwyn spends a melancholy winter after Mie Mie's departure. To add to his sorrows his good old mother dies at the age of eighty-five. Lord Carlisle advises him to vary the scene and invites him to Castle Howard. He reaches that hospitable place in December and his health and spirits begin immediately to improve. The society of the two Carlisle children, George and Caroline, keep him "from the *regno Hispaniae et fatalibus arvis.*" But another circumstance helps to make him cheerful. He decides to visit Milan in the spring and to make another effort with Mie Mie's parents and still more with her grandparents to recover possession of the child. This gives him something to look forward to during the hard and bitter winter of 1777 when the snow lies piled high on the roads of England.

It is neither Rome nor Florence nor Naples which attracts him. His escapade perplexes his friends. He is not concerned with pictures or statues; he goes to see a little girl whom he loves to distraction and who is only seven years old. He speaks of her with tenderness, with tears in his eyes.

CHAPTER 24

IN QUEST OF MIE MIE:
MILAN AND CORRESPONDENCE

"I EMBARKED YESTERDAY ABOUT FOUR IN the morning," Selwyn writes to Mary Townshend from Calais on April 22,* "and having but little wind, it was near ten before I could land. My stomach and head were so out of order when I embarked that I endeavored by going to bed on board the ship to avoid, what we imprudent people generally do, what would have done me the most good; so for fear of being sick one hour, I have been squeamish 24. This morning I am much better both in my health and spirits, and if I had more years to expect, should find myself very happy in being once more in this country, and with this people, but as it is, I must be contented with my own country, which altho' I am told will not be long our own, yet while it is, I may be permitted to have a penchant to it. . . .

"I have as yet seen nothing like invasion, or even a disposition to carry hostilities further than we invite them.

"The Duchess of Kingston** is here, in a house which she has purchased and furnished magnificently. She has had the singular good fortune to obtain from the government an Act of Parliament to naturalize her to a certain degree. She can now purchase and bequeath. Her ship is returning

---

* The letters quoted are addressed either to his niece or nephew, Mary or Charles Townshend.
** The famous bigamist Miss Chudleigh.

from Russia into this port, after it has been put in perfect repair at the expense of the Empress of Russia, with whom she has made a treaty offensive and defensive. She has une forte petite sante, had an attack of paralysie, has a fine vis-a-vis and four handsome dun horses—que n'a-t-elle pas? She has two characters in Calais, altho' she may have but one in her own country. Une Dame Dominicaine told me yesterday that she performed great acts of charity, and seemed to entertain a very good opinion of her . . .

"Adieu, my dear Mary, most affectionately. Aimez moi toujours un peu, as they say here, and let me hear from you often.

"I hope six months hence, at all events, to have interest enough with the Court of England to get me a ship for my return, for I will not embark either at Ostend or Helvoet-sluys, if I stay here till there is a peace.

"I forgot to tell you that the Duchess sails to Rome in October, where her faith is to be confirmed, unless she is taken by an American Privateer, in provision of which she has got Berkley's Book in Defence of the Quakers . . ."

Paris. May 10, 1778. "I was some hours last night, before I went to supper with the Duchess of Gainsbro et son Mari, I do not know if he is a clergyman, but I thought he was, and I expected to find a little grey parson and I found with her a gentleman in scarlet and gold embroidery, whom I under-stood to be Mr. Pygloz. They say here that he is a good sort of man: he may be so, for anything they know, for they seem to know nothing of the English, but that they read in books, misrepresent their characters, and are employed the whole day in copying their dress and equippage of which they have made a strange mode. I wish people would con-fine themselves in all things to the ways of their own coun-try which generally points out what is most convenient and ornamental, and each will have something belonging to them that is superior, but they mix them both together, that is like the language of the refugees, a Patois, that if you understand is horrible to hear. . . .

"I shall apply myself to Italian for the next five or six months. I believe Warner [Selwyn's companion on the trip to Milan] is further advanced in that than I am. Dr. Gemm [Selwyn's physician] is superior to us both as I imagine. I am in hopes that my poor Mie Mie has not forgot her English, I believe that I shall apply more to that than to anything else that is personal to myself. . . .

"At present I have no notion of anything they have but Opera singers, Parmezan cheese, and Italian flowers. . . ."

Lyons. May 20, 1778. "I have now performed two parts of my journey, but the third I am afraid will be worse than the other two, on account of the Mauvais gites et mauvaise chose. I have a cook and a bed, but they will not, I am apprehensive, be of so much use as I wished them to be. The Bed it is difficult to carry, and the cook can dress nothing on the road, so how I shall do, I know not; Michelet* assures me very well. I wish at all times to see you, and here as well as in other places. The manufactures and stuffs and embroideries are mighty pretty, le choix embarrasse. But things are monstrously cheap.

"I beg my Love to all the Family. I am very impatient to hear something of you. [Walpole often thinks of posterity; Selwyn always of his friends.]

"Everything now begins to look to Italy, houses, sky, etc. The journey hither is really nothing if you send on anybody before for your Rooms and your Dinner, and the country delightful. I met Peas and Strawberries here for the first time. I have passed through all the vineyards and had my choice of wine, as I hardly drink any but with water. There is a very good theatre and troupe, but the occupation of the English is choosing cloaks from morning to night because the fancy is new, and the commodity cheap. I never was before so far from home, and therefore like a Badaud de Paris 'le monde me passit bien grand,' as Mme. de Chatelet (?) said when she went to the South with the P. du Maine . . ."

Milan. May 31, 1778. "I got hither last Tuesday the 26th to dinner. . . . I feel myself quite forgot, which perhaps may not be the greatest misfortune which can happen

---

* His valet. The name is spelt "Michalin" in Selwyn's will.

to me, and yet it would mortifie me too, to a certain degree. Whether any letters have been detained or miscarried I know not, but it has been very unpleasant to me, and till Friday night I was in pain to know whether Lady Carlisle was alive or not from the account which I had of her in Paris. I was to such a degree uneasy about it, that when I had found means by great accident to gett some English newspapers, and they came to me at a house while I was at dinner, I was obliged to make Pierre go into another room to read them to see if her name was mentioned in them before I could eat my dinner with satisfaction. I am now satisfied upon that point because when Ld. M[arch]'s steward called at her house, she was gone out.

"I shall stay here till I find the weather cool enough for traveling in September, for as I shall be three weeks on the road to Calais, so I shall be afraid of delays or the falling of the snow, and in regard to poor Mie Mie, I shall have done all that I could have expected or do expect to do for her benefit, and when that is over, I must leave her with the frail hopes of seeing her again in England, which perhaps, best for her sake and my own had better not happen. She is in regard to her health I think, well, but I must own that I am in constant pain for it, from the extensive liberty which is allowed her to eat or to do whatever she likes. Everybody seems very fond of her and she has always had (indeed, very luckily for herself) as I told her grandmother last night, an uncommon attention and desire to please, and to be acceptable to the people she is with, especially if they behave in any manner agreeable to her . . .

"She has a grandfather, the old Marquis Fagnani and his wife, who was the Maréchal Clince's sister. These are people, I see, of great rank, and living in a great style; the fondness which they express for this little girl, is more than I suppose you would have expected. They are constantly finding out amusements for her, but what she learns, or what she forgetts, except her religion, they do not seem much to care. Their civilities to me are as great and assiduous as can be, and their remercimens also. She is, in a manner, delivered up to me here, but what I can do, with the impediments I have, will signify nothing, and if it did, when I am gone will be lost. I am now aiming but at one thing, which is preserving her English, of which she has forgott more than I could have imagined, and I am in Hopes to obtain of her Mother permission to have some English maid about her and if possible one who can read it with her. They all desire this, and if this maid is a Catholick, I suppose Monsr. le Cardinal will not oppose it . . .

"The house which they have taken for me is a very large one built around a Court à l'Italienne. The Venetian Resident occupies one part of it, and I the other. They are as distinct in all respects as if we were separated by two streets. Everything is new and clean, as much as brick floors will permitt. But I shall never be able to reconcile myself to them, although there are no other in their finest palaces. The houses here are indeed magnificent, and with all kinds of accommodations, every sort of Apartment, court, and Garden. But there is not a workman in the town that knows how to hang a door. Their ceilings are well painted, and mine among the rest, but it is the painting of a Green House, or an Orangerie. Paintings they have without end, and some of them I believe fine, but the subjects are either uninteresting or horrid. I have a certain number in my House which would bear a price, I suppose, at Mr. Christie's, and receive from him a panegyrick. It has been with great good luck I have found a carpet, for the Marquis happened to have sent one, and a large one from England. My windows are directly over against Mie Mie's so I have as much of her company as if she was in the House with me. With her French governess she speaks French, with the other maids a patois of the Milanese, which she has learnt the quicker as all children will because it is bad, and with me it is a ragoût melé of them and English. But she is now so much with me, and I send her governess away so, it may be for the present that she will recover her native language. I can never dine at home, because I must not refuse invitations. . . .

"I was told by all who have been here that they spoke French here, and that it was like a French town; point du tout; many do speak it and some very tolerably, but they are in this respect as we are in London. French is a talent which some have acquired and some have not. They do not choose to talk it, and I find I change the language as much as a foreigner would at London, and that they speak it before me because they think, and with reason enough, that my conversation in Italian would be très bornée . . . but I must do all these Italians here the justice to say that there is as much empressement in them to be civil to me as it is possible. . . . The shops and the shopkeepers here with whom I have, both in London and Paris, a great connection, afford me here no amusement. Three shops out of four sell nothing but saints and ornaments for the Church, and they talk a jargon to understand which if I understood Italian ever so well it would avail me nothing. . . .

"The weather will soon grow so hott that I shall be able to stir very little out, but to dinner. But my house I can keep cooler than most others. There is a Picture done of me here, which is said by everybody to be the likest which ever was, and the painting is good with a verité that I seldom see in Pictures painted in England. It has gained the man, who is a Piedmontois, great reputation, the pains he has taken about it are infinite. The Fagnanis have desired it. Adieu."

Milan. June 13, 1778. "Everyday I stay at Milan convinces me more that if I mean to give Mie Mie every possible succour which I can give her, I did right to come. Her situation and connections here are great, and may hereafter make her happy, but Education is my favorite advantage, because it is the foundation upon which every good superstructure must be raised. I am sure that that would have been better in England than anywhere else, and all over England better with me, unless she had been the object of your care or Lady Carlisle's. You will think this presumptuous in me to say, but I know it to be true, for besides being a little of a Connoisseur myself in Education, I think noone would have equalled me in attention and assiduity, because I believe noone ever equalled me in affection. Parents who would leave their daughter in a foreign country, and in such hands as they left this poor child for six years, and who would then have given her up to me, if family pride and convenience had not intervened were not the persons to whom I could wish to have placed á dépôt une bien si precieuse . . . They now and then give me hopes that she shall come again to England to see me. L'ultima che si perde è la Speranza. I do not however build upon it, and shall acquiesce if it does not happen. . . . Mie Mie and I are to go this afternoon to see a very fine procession at St. Antoine at the Marchesa Leta's. . . ."

They also go to see the body of Cardinal Borrimeo which lies in a crystal coffin with six candles lighted and placed before the coffin to enable them to see the body. The face is black and shrivelled like the face of a mummy, the body dressed in scarlet and gold, with a collar of rich jewels hanging from the neck, white sleeves, white gloves, with a ring over one glove on the fourth finger . . . The women of Milan sit at the doors and windows without veils. They are tolerably handsome.

Milan. June 15, 1778. "The life at Milan is not only dull to me, but seems to be so to those who from habitude only lead it. It seems to be an established system of ennui. It is totally different either from that in France or England, as much as the language that they speak, so that my being constantly with Mie Mie is a sacrifice of nothing, supposing myself to have any pleasure preferable to it . . .

"Poor Lord H[olland?]. need not have employed his talents building *Ruins*, when he had children who could do all that so much better. . . .

"It is surprising to me that I am still to ask whether we shall go to war with France, but if I do I do not suppose my question can be yet resolved.* I wish that if occasion offer, you will ask somebody that is likely to know in case of a war how I am to come from Calais, for I do from hence protest against returning either from Helvoetsluys or Ostend. . . .

---

* In fact England and France were then at war, following upon the Treaty between France and America, signed May, 1778.

"I suppose that I shall be abused for seeing in Italy nothing but Milan and in Milan nothing but the Child, which will be very near the case, but I cannot help it. I believe if Rome was but the journey of one day, I should not go there, so little curiosity have I left."

Milan. July 28, 1778. "I have done inquiring about the degrees of heat, for it surpasses all common barometers. I am in a constant sweat which they tell me is wholesome. Warner eats notwithstanding comme quartre.

"I beg my kind compts. to Mr. Townshend and tell him that I saw the other day a letter from the Professor of Modern Languages at Cambridge to the Comte Fermian, and of three French words in the superscription of his letter he contrives to spell two of them wrong. He says that the place he holds is one which the son of the first nobleman in the land might have accepted of. It is all in what he calls English and is full of such slip slop as a laundry maid would be ashamed of. It would have diverted me much if I had not seen it in the hands of a foreign Minister.

"Mie Mie thanks you for your kind mention of her and so do I. What is to become of us? Are we to have war? If we have will it last long? What is to be the state of our funds? What changes are there to be in Administration? These are my chief points of inquiry. Bankruptcy and separations etc. may come in by way of episodes."

Milan. Saturday, August 1, 1778. "I continue well but cannot stir from my couch till the evening from the excessive heat. But then Mie Mie and I go out airing, and we have a kind of Vauxhall now for her amusement, which is about as good as Marybone. But they admire it, and think it quite à l'angloise. There is musick, Rafraîchissement, and marionettes, and the Archduke walks about like the Duke of York, so I say that with a prince or two more, it would be as good as Marybone.

"Who is the Lady who intended to hang herself for Lord Tyrconnel? What Beauclerk is it who is gone off? How many more are undone? When shall you return to town? Is there to be a change of administration? Will the Americans treat? Will the Stocks arise? Can you answer any of these ques-

tions? . . . If I can do anything for you in Paris pray let
me know."

Milan. September, 1778. "The Duchess of Parma had
been here to whom I was presented, and with whom I afterwards dined, and her brother the Arch Duke and Arch
Dutchess at Comte Fermian's. She received me with the
greatest affability imaginable and seems a very sensible
woman, with some singularity of dress and amusement. She
is tall and well shaped but seemed to be big with child,
so I could not very well judge of that . . . Before she went
away, she was to see all that Milan could show her, and
when she was at the Opera, she went into the rooms of the
Ridotto, before the Opera began. I had leave to carry Mie
Mie there, and Mme. Crevelli, one of the dames d'honneur,
presented her to the Duchess. The Arch Dutchess spied her
out first, and said je ferai venir ma belle soeur pour lui
parler; she did so, and it gave me great pleasure to see how
well the child acquitted herself. She spoke to her in French
sans confusion, et avec beaucoup de grace, then in Italian
to some of the Ladies who asked me if she spoke English
as well. I said pas le moins. They were mightily pleased
with her, and the Cardinal Dorini, whose mother is Mie
Mie's great aunt, by her father's side, talked to her a great
deal. I assured his eminence que pour avoir été six ans en
Angleterre elle n'en était pas moins bonne Catholique. Oh,
je le crois bien, Monsieur, me dit-il, et mille fois plus spiri-
tuelle, j'en suis persuadé; la réponse fut jolie et honnête. I
like that Cardinal much, but on account of some coolness
in the family, altho' I was then at Gennetto, but four miles
from him, I could not continue to improve our acquaintance, and Mme. Mellario, Mie Mie's G. Mother, carried us
there but once.

"I long for some house out of town, and if these are not
to be had, or upon too high terms for me, I must have a
less: but the best and the cheapest thing for me is to be
as much out of London as I can. You know too well, among
my other foibles, my ungovernable passion for play, and I
want to put an entire end to it, for many reasons, if more
than one was necessary. Here I have been very discreet,

for altho' in these Ridotto rooms there were no less than twelve Pharo tables, each covered with 1200 sequins, and this very night, and all night I believe, I have ventured but one Guinea since I have been here, and for a few times at Paris with the Pope's Nuncio at Loto—which is a game not very likely to tempt or to ruin me. In short I hope to do at least what a great many do, which is to die corrigé, if not before. It is a pity that we are all so mistaken as to the period, and defer acquiring any prudence till it becomes almost of no use to us."

Gernetto. September 8, 1778. "Mie Mie and her grandmother and I have been chiefly together at this place about three weeks, and I have had some very interesting conversations with the old lady on the subject of her Grand-daughter, whom she seems really to love, and whose welfare she would be happy to procure. We are much more agreed upon the Nature of the disease than about the Remedy. I believe that if I was a Catholick, there would be no difficulty in obtaining what I desire; and even that might be remov'd if it was not for the obstinacy of those whose Religion I am as yet to learn . . . However, before I leave Milan, I shall have settled, or not settled, something concerning her education, with those of her family.

"On Sunday Me. la Comtesse, Mie Mie, and I dined in a Convent of Benedictines a few miles from hence, two of the religieuses are sisters to la Comtesse. It was the best dinner I have had since I came into Italy, for it was the least nasty. We dined in a large salon, which is a kind of parlour near the Grille; on the other side dined the nuns, waited upon by the soeurs converses. Mie Mie not being seven years old, had permission to run in and out the Convent the whole day. Before dinner we sate upon the landing place of a large stone stair case and the great doors of the Convent were open. One side of the threshold sate the Abbesse, and some of the nuns, on the other Me. la Comtesse and I. I received a great many compliments on Mie Mie's account, some of which were really more due to her than to myself . . . They made her a present of a basket of all kinds of toys and sweet meats made in the Convent and she was very happy the whole day. The heat was excessive. It was 23 degrees by Reaumur's Thermomètre, as I have been told, and we have half a degree more to expect. After dinner I went into an appartement which is for the use of the Cardinal Archevécque upon his visitation, and lay down on his Eminency's bed till the cool of the evening and it was time to return home . . .

"Lady Middleton is a better manager of money than I am and for the future I shall ask her advice. You ask me about the poor Rena,* which looks as if you was more sentimental than I am. That I cannot allow although I know que vous avez le coeur très bon: no, I have not seen her, nor made any enquiries after her. Have I not had assez de separations? assez de regrets? assez de congés? desormais il me faudra plutôt des détachments, que de nouvelles occasions de renouveller des liaisons que ne peuvent me procure que du chagrin ou du ridicule. The last thing I heard of her was that she was well, e Ricca, ma molto invecciata; jugez don du reste."

Milan. September 16, 1778. "I have had a slight degree of fever this week, I suppose arising partly from the change of weather, and partly from the agitation de mon départ. But I am now well; and perfectly satisfied with everybody here, as they profess to have been with me. I have obtained the points I wanted to carry, in the only mode which reason could well fortify . . . I shall leave the country without being either poisoned or pillaged; all those from whom good treatment could be expected, I have experienced as much as possible. So, whatever disagreeable feelings I may find for the moment, upon leaving Mie Mie, things are now in so good a tract both for her and for my own peace of mind that I am quite at ease, hoping that no accidents will happen, which it is not my temper to anticipate unnecessarily by imagination."

Selwyn leaves Milan on September 17, travelling homewards by way of Genoa, Nice, and Aix. Like Horace Walpole and the rest of his circle he is a great admirer of

* March's Mistress.

Madame de Sévigné. On his way through Provence he cannot resist the temptation to visit her home at Grignan.

Lyons. October 5, 1778. "Monsieur le Bouilli has made me a present of a little ebony cabinet, le dernier des meubles qui restait, which was in Mme. de Sev.'s appartement, and where, he says, she kept her bijouterie. It was preserved by an old man who waited on her, and as he pretended, qui taillent ses plumes. Mais c'est un pais de superstitition et de l'égotisme de sorte que tout m'est suspect et apocriphe.

"But if there should be any historical doubt about it, Horry shall clear it up for us. . . .

"The sight of our countrymen prisoners at Aix me fit faire mauvais sang, and the wound in my leg [he mentions in a letter of Sept. 27 that he hurt his leg] is but just healed. I would have no chirurgien, and so I had no help but from one I found with them. Adieu."

Selwyn arrives in Paris early in October with his "cabinet d'ébène" and duly reports himself at the Convent St. Joseph.

Paris. October 14, 1778. "I have received today an account of Lady Holland's death, which has so much dispirited me that I believe that you will quit this time for a very short letter. I had really so little hopes myself that although by those letters which I found on my arrival here, there seemed to be a great alteration for the better, as they called it, I never allowed myself to rejoice at it. Noone I believe ever yet recovered from the state in which she was represented to be. I hear also that the D. of Queensberry is extremely ill, so there may be a revolution in the affairs of my friend March. I am told that you expect peace in England; to tell you the truth, my hopes of that have diminished much since I came here. In short I am today quite out of sorts . . . I am now plagued with Abbesses. Those who are people of distinction, have a mixture of all the nonsense, pride, commesage, bavardise, etc., and the devil knows what, that they exercise my patience beyond conception. They seemed to have carried into their convents all the imperfections of the world, and dressed them up in the habits and delusions of their religion, and if I was not too old to be so tartuffi'd by them I should never gett out of them one word of truth. But they are the heifers that I am to plough (as the phrase is), so I must submitt. Mr. Boone has been here and placed his daughter in the Abbayé of Panthement, where I want to place Mie Mie, that is the convent which I shall recommend, if she is not placed with our English nunns."

Paris. October 30, 1778. "I must own that London has lost its charms to me, in a great measure, and that is why I wish for a place near it, because it may be more convenient than to be at a great distance, especially in the beginning of the spring or summer. Je me trouve blazé sur trop de choses, à vous dire la vérité. I have been often told there are some pleasures for every season of life. I wish I could find out what I had now to choose out of. I only know at present what I have lost. But I will make the experiment if Mie Mie comes to me; and if she does not, I shall be plus endeffant que jamais. I am very unfortunate to have placed my happiness so much upon one bottom. But it is as you may say a scrape, a labyrinth, out of which I may perhaps find my way, but I have gone a great way to search it. . . I hear now and then of peace being in a state of negotiation. I hope that it is true. Why should it not be so, when so many of both countries wish it? . . . Me. de Sévigné, Cabinet d'Ébène, is arrived and deposited dans la communauté de St. Joseph. . ."

And Selwyn adds on the wrapper: "You may gett your leg of pork and pease-pudden ready by the 29th of next month."

During the winter of 1778-79 Selwyn is very much troubled that he will not see Mie Mie in Paris in the following spring. Will her parents keep their half promise or not? "Soyez sûr," Madame writes, "que vous aurez ce printemps notre chère Mie Mie, et qu'elle se porte bien." But Selwyn cannot trust Madame. However, a second daughter is born to that lady in December, which perhaps makes her more willing to part with her first. At all events Mie Mie is despatched to Paris in April, and Selwyn hurries there to meet her. When he arrives he finds that the Fagnanis expect him to go as far as Lyons. On April 18 Selwyn writes to Carlisle: "This afternoon I find tous mes projects pour le présent sont suspendus. I am obliged to set out tomorrow for Lyons. It is so unexpected that it is by much the greatest *embarras* I ever felt, and a monstrous exercise of expense for me. Mie Mie will be there tomorrow. . . God knows how much further I would go to conduct her safely. . . Ma patience et ma persévérance sont inépuisables sur ce qui regarde Mie Mie."

And Mme. du Deffand writes to Walpole on the same date: "I believe if they refuse Lindor his Mimie, he will kill himself: it is a folly without precedent." On the next day: "The head of this poor man is turned; his economy yields to the passion which he has for his *Marmotte;* but there is sorrow in this, too."

Selwyn duly travels to Lyons, finds Mie Mie awaiting him, and returns with her to Paris, "drunken with joy." Immediately he is engaged in the harassing occupation of finding a school for a small child.

May 4, 1779. To Mary Townshend: "I perfectly agree with you that the History of Mie Mie and Yan Yan, as she used to call me when she began to speak, is an extraordinary one, et j'avoue aussi que j'y fais un Personage assez singulier . . . But I do not desire either to write or to talk of it. I wish only to breed up Mie Mie in such a manner as to make her beloved and respected, and to supply the want of feeling in other people. It would have been unfortunate enough for me if I had had only the usual degree of sensibility on such an occasion, but to have added to that la tendresse de père, et les entrailles de mère, is an insupportable burthen to my mind, and at my age. But I have endeavoured as yet with so much perseverance and patience to get out of this labyrinth, or what you properly call a scrape, I have had so much more success than I expected that I still flatter myself that I shall at last succeed . . . We are now in my hotel at Paris, but Mie Mie will go this week to her Convent, and I to my Boudoir . . .

"Mme. l'Abbesse and I are in pretty good humour with

one another, and she will humour me, who am much more an enfant gâté than Mie Mie. So I am to have her here to dine, and to read English with Mrs. Webb as often as I send my coach for her. We were in the parlor last night for the first time. Mie Mie's physiognomie, son charactère d'esprit, et ses manières, et ses graces, strike everybody as well as her being able to express herself so well in different languages. She has so much penetration that elle vendra Mme. l'Abbesse et toutes ses religieuses en fort peu détours. But that I cannot help . . .

"My return to England is uncertain, for I will not venture to carry Mie Mie from hence without the consent of her parents, and when I shall obtain that, I do not know.

"Mie Mie desires to be remembered to you all most kindly. I am, for my part, endeavouring to make her remember and forgett, but to do both c'est un ouvrage."

Paris. May 20, 1779. To Mary Townshend. "This writing an hour after the post is gone out seems odd, but if I do not write when my eyes do not pain me, I shall have no power to write at all. It is one of my grievances, which I am afraid that time will not assist. I will consult an oculist when I return to England, but it is everybody's interest here to blind me. I am here l'ennemi tout court; I am the only English person they see, and last night, when they were talking of their expeditions and hostilities, they asked me if I would acquaint the Government of England with anything which I heard in their company. There was a ready answer to that. Our Government, I hope, wants no instructions from me, and I was not sent here as a spy. Indeed I am nothing less than suspected and I pass my time at least as well among them as in a profound peace. . . .

"Mie Mie is the most tractable little creature in the world. She gains herself and me reputation every day, for they see that she is not spoiled. She is going on with her reading, both in French and English, but her Anglomanie, her desire to return to England, and to go to Matson is prodigious; in that we are very much of a mind . . .

"Monsieur le Marquis de la Fayette talks to me much of Lord Cornwallis and of the esteem which he has for him.

I have promised through your means to make his compliments . . . When does the Parliament rise? are there to be any new arrangements? . . I cannot tell you how near you are all to your destruction. But you deserve it . . .

"I have done thinking of a country house near London, while my foreign negotiations go on, and till I can force people to pay the shot they owe me, which noone will do, if they can help it. I must retire to the sabine farm and be as frugally blessed there as any of my ancestors. I can really reconcile myself at present to no other sort of life; and my succession of suppers here are worse to me than the vue de la plus affreux would be. While I have Mie Mie with me I do very well. . . ."

Paris. May 30, 1779. "Mie Mie is in her convent and contented there, upon the terms I have obtained for her, which has as much reason in them as gratification to myself. As Mrs. Webb cannot go into the Convent, Mie Mie is permitted to come to us three days in the week on which days she reads, dances, and perfects herself in her English with us. The other days she reads and talks French and writes . . . She has infinitely more reason and information than are usual dans l'enceinte de ces murailles. She sings them Italian songs and diverts them. She says that I let her do anything. But that Mrs. Webb controls her in everything, which is exactly true, and as I intended it. To act a part which you are not fitt for, you will act ill and be of no use. So I give it quite over to Mrs. W. I never interfere in the least thing . . . Mme. Fagnani's caprice, ill humour, and deceit are the torments of my life. She contrives even at a distance of 300 leagues to disgust me. For lett me do what I will, I know that she will never be satisfied . . ."

True Madame is causing Selwyn great unhappiness. He neither eats nor sleeps. "He will fall ill or go astray in the mind. I really think this, and I am very sorry for him," writes Mme. du Deffand to Horace Walpole. However, Selwyn's torments are ended in June by receiving permission from the Fagnanis to bring Mie Mie to England. As soon as the letter arrives from Italy, he hastens to Mme. du Deffand to ask her to obtain a passport for him. It comes on the morning of June 15, and he leaves at once with Mie Mie for England.

After all these excursions and alarms he brings her to Matson. His troubles with reference to the young lady are nearly over. Thenceforward until his death he never parts from her, although he has periodic panics on the subject. That dreadful "Madame F." haunts him in his dreams.

Tunbridge Wells, July 14, 1780. To Mary Townshend. "I am much obliged to you for your letter, as well as Mie Mie who is so kindly made the chief subject of it. I am in hopes that the worst part of the worst disorder is over, and that her cough will now grow less violent, and less painful to her every day. I have been assured that there was no appearance of its having any bad consequences, and I am disposed to hope, that by the efforts made to discharge the bile, her constitution may be mended. As to my own case, I can only say, that it is like everything which ever happened to me, very extraordinary, to have the hooping cough, which I have très décidément at 61. Seems as now as if I had been seized with the gum fever and the rickets, or was cutting my teeth for the third time. I shall not despair of appearing next winter with a coral and an anodyne necklace. It is a most horrible disorder. I lose my senses with it some times for a minute, and dropt this morning in the Child's room, which frightened her excessively, but what diverts me is their calling it a bastard hooping cough . . . Mie Mie, as the people who are about her tell me, has not had it so violent as other children generally have. We are here more for the air than anything else, and therefore might as well be where we should pay no rent as hire a bandbox at eight guineas a week. I think that when our Lease is expired, which will be in less than three weeks, we shall change the air again."

He tells Carlisle that he is much too happy with Mie Mie, but not one word comes to him from her Italian parents and the silence is terrible to him because it is so unnatural. He takes Mie Mie to see her first play. It is *Dissipation* and *Robinson Crusoe*, the farce. Then there is a New Year's party where young George Howard is King, Mie Mie, Miss

Hoyden, and Selwyn, Sir Tunbelly Clumsy. Miss Townshend dines with them and cuts the cake and they play
at whist and are all as happy as possible. Everybody in
the Selwyn circle is kind to Mie Mie. The Reverend Dr.
Warner, Selwyn's faithful henchman, addresses affectionate
notes to his "sweet little Queen," signed "Your loving Snail."

My Sweet Little Queen,—I shall be au désespoir if I have
not a letter from you and Miss Selwyn on Monday morning. An
ugly, envious cloud hid the moon from me last night at nine
o'clock. I hope for better luck tonight. You, perhaps, might see
the moon, as the sky looked clear toward your quarter, but you
could not see your poor Snail, as he was under a cloud. Matson
House, you know, bears directly S. W. from Scrivelsby Parsonage, or if you don't know it, you presently may, if our best
friend will get you a pretty plaything, which will amuse you
into the knowledge of the geography of your native country.
We always drink your health at Scrivelsby. I am, your loving

SNAIL.

When Selwyn finally gets Mie Mie, the reverend doctor
bursts into triumphant song:

> The morn that gave to Mie Mie birth
> Provokes the dullest son of earth,
> Provokes a snail, prosaic creature!
> To try for once to crawl in metre.
> Her rising virtues to salute
> And wish the blossom into fruit,
> Sure that his effort can't offend
> His fair, good humored little friend,
> Who praised him erst, by candour's rule,
> Playing for her as now the fool.

(At the commencement of the French Revolution this jolly
wordling of a parson hastens to France to enjoy the promised Utopia. The scenes of blood and horror, however,
speedily disgust him, and he gladly returns to enjoy his
liberty at home. A book, a pipe, and cheerful conversation
are his supreme delights.)

Old Q's visit to his Scotch estate at Drumlanrig where
he seldom goes is as much to escape from Selwyn's recital

of the merits and beauties of Mie Mie as for any other purpose. From that safe retreat he sends a letter to his friend, asking how Mie Mie is. To the learned clergyman's story of Mie Mie and the little flannel petticoat, the hardened sinner only says pick and damn.

It is a great occasion when Mie Mie is presented at Court. She is seventeen then and is beginning to be called Miss Fagnani. She is "very splendid," says Storer, but George is "most magnificent and *new* in every article of dress." Romney paints her portrait, full of lightness and grace. Mie Mie is popular in the Regent's circle. One summer afternoon, she and Selwyn are dining by the open windows in Cleveland Court when His Royal Highness, Prince Florizel, passes by in his chaise and makes a most gracious bow to Mie Mie. "And if he could have been sure of my not being in the room," says Selwyn, "it may be he would have stopped to have told how much he liked Castle Howard."

Looking at Mie Mie one day Selwyn says to Storer: "What a pleasure it is to love that girl so tenderly without having had the trouble to get her."

CHAPTER 25

LAST YEARS

THE FAMILY MANSION IS FOR SOME YEARS
Selwyn's headquarters in London. But it is much too large
for a single gentleman and accordingly Selwyn lets it to his
nephew Tommy Townshend who has a family. He acquires
for himself instead the lease of a house in Chesterfield
Street, Mayfair. But about 1781 he comes back to Cleveland Court.

During this time he alternates between London and
Matson with occasional visits to Bath and Tunbridge Wells.
When Mie Mie begins to grow up, he wishes to have a villa
somewhere near London to which he can retire in the summer and autumn months. He wants the fresh country air
for Mie Mie, but for his own comfort it must not be too far
from the flags of Piccadilly. In the end he takes a house—
"the warmest and most comfortable of any"—near Old Q
at Richmond.

Richmond is a pleasant little town: Queen of the vale
and empress of the hill: the Thames with its shelvy
banks and charming lawns rising like an amphitheatre, with
here and there a white house to pierce the dark foliage of
surrounding trees. All is green, a soft green; at the horizon
whitish mists in floating layers, a darkened cloud, or a violet
patch of a shower. Once in Richmond men and women stay
there, walking, talking, and calling on each other, sometimes driving into London, but delighting in it as a residence, not as a mere resort for an evening's pleasure.

Selwyn enjoys his last few years at Richmond with the
Walpoles and Queenberrys. There are card parties, dinners,

balls, assemblies, not to speak of the theatre in which Lord Barrymore plays to admiring audiences. "The Duke dines with me when he is here a little after four," says Selwyn, "and when we have drunk our wine, we resort to his Great Hall, bien éclairée, bien échauffée, to drink our coffee and hear quintettos." The Great Hall, the Great Gallery, the eating room and the corridor of Old Q's red brick villa are covered with whole or half lengths of the royal family, favorite ministers, peers and judges of the reign of Charles I—not one an original. Here come the distinguished members of Richmond society—the Penns, the Onslows, the Douglasses, the Keenes, Lady Mount-Edgecumbe, Lady Diana Beauclerk, and Horace Walpole. Selwyn is a kind of standing dish—the concierge, Walpole calls him. Suppers are fine but not tedious. When they are over, there is music, and dancing. The company is waited on by servants in their green and silver liveries.

When the revolution breaks out in France, many of the emigrés settle in Richmond, and the Duke, who loves the society of foreigners, is wont to throw open his house twice a week to such of them as choose to come. Mme. du Barry, apparently, comes to England in order to recover some of her jewels of which she has been robbed by certain money lenders who are caught and lodged in Newgate. Old Q receives her with empressement, and at one entertainment, the Comtesse de Boufflers plays on the harp and the Princess di Casteleiglia, the Neapolitan minister's wife, dances one of her country dances with castenets, very prettily, with her husband.

Selwyn is thoroughly happy at Richmond despite indifferent health and other anxieties. Mie Mie is old enough to be a companion to him. She treats him with kindness and consideration. When he is ill, she nurses him, and he for his part watches anxiously over her. To Lady Carlisle: "Caroline [Lady Carlisle's daughter, married to Mr. Campbell] is perfectly well. I have not seen her today . . . At present I only know that about 12 o'clock last night she ate plumb cake and drank wine and water in my parlour— she, Mr. Campbell, and Mie Mie, and who besides I have not yet asked. I was in bed when she came; it was an *heure perdue* but not lost upon me, for I was not asleep, nor could sleep till I heard that those two girls were come home safe. From what, in the name of God? you will say. From seeing that étourdi Lord Barrymore play the fool in three or four different characters upon our Richmond theatre. Well, but what did that signify? Nothing to me! let him expose himself on as many stages as he pleases . . . but he comes here and assembles as many people ten miles around as can squeeze into the Booth . . . I did not expect them to be clear of the House till near twelve, so went into my room, and soon after to bed, but I slept well, for I had heard of them. They were all, I tell you, before twelve in my parlour, eating cake and chattering, talking the whole farce over *comme a la grille du couvent.*"

About this time Selwyn strikes up an intimacy with his fireside "to which perhaps in the course of the winter I may admit that very popular man Mr. Thomas Jones. He also proposes to read Dr. White's Hampton Lectures. "I have a design upon Botany Bay and Cibber's Apology for his own life, which everybody has read, and which I should have read myself forty years ago if I had not preferred the reading of men so much to that of books." He buys Johnson's *Lives of the Poets.* "I repent of it already," he says. And he has this to say of other people: "Parsons, University men, and Templars, renvoyent bien loin la simplicité, and when they would talk agreeably or write to obtain approbation, give you such a hash of all their reading and such quaint compliments as make me sick." He has only one genuine literary enthusiasm—that is, for the letters of Mme. de Sévigné. He likes her common sense, her vivacity, her worldly wisdom.

He moves from Richmond to Cleveland Court for some weeks in the winter so that Mie Mie may have all the advantages of life in town. Once he gives a Drum at his house which is not altogether a success. He is not at his ease a moment. He has a Commerce table and one of whist. His company are the Middletons, Bostons, Townshends, and Selwyns. Old Q comes to the door at eleven, but hearing that supper is served, and almost over, and perhaps hearing of the company too, he goes away. They are all good people who have conversation enough in their own families, but, although they are related, not one word to say to one another. The cook, the housekeeper, and Maître Jacques all exert themselves and do their parts tolerably well, but nothing puts Selwyn at his ease, and the more he tries the more he is "désorienté; so I believe I shall try some other kind of party for the future."

In July, 1788, Selwyn is confined in town by a fever which "I thought was going away with my last fee to Dr. G. Baker, but point du tout. It pretended to take leave and then had encore un petit mot à l'oreille and so came back et menace encore, but I think it will pass; and without young Duchesses, young Lords, and young ministers, to which I might add young Tricks of my own, I may do well and boast on a few years longer and even without much labor and sorrow."

During the same month he is obliged to go down to Matson since His Gracious Majesty, King George III intimates that he will honor Mr. Selwyn with a visit. Selwyn is prodigiously delighted. The King and his party come on July 30, and spend a few hours. They partake of a cold collation and receive the compliments of the neighboring gentry, take a view of Selwyn's elegant park and mansion, and leave. Boys climb the elm trees near the Church and watch their Majesties drive up the road. (Selwyn bottles up some relic of the royal visit. His label to a certain *patera* of *La Reine boit* far outgoes Walpole's imagination. It is apparently not to be quoted in a letter to a lady.)

In October Selwyn returns to Richmond. Later on in the year he is much agitated over the insanity of the King. "It is a sad time, indeed," he says. It is a sad time in other respects. He is in poor health and is continually subject to coughs and colds. These grow more frequent and troublesome. "My cough must be attended to or it will increase and perhaps destroy me," he says. Meanwhile he has plenty of society at Richmond. "It is no solitude, this place," he remarks. The French emigrants are there in large numbers.

"If this winter does not make a perfect Frenchman of me, I shall give it up." Once his garden is as full as it can hold of foreigners and their children. There are Warenzow's boy and girl and the Marquis de Cinq Minutes, who of all infants is the most completely spoiled. His roars and screams, if he has not everything that he wants in an instant, are enough to split your head. His menace is: "Maman, je veux être bien méchant ce soir, je vous le promets."

The curious thing is that with all his ailments, Selwyn never lives the life of an invalid. He keeps his place in society to the end. He continues in it until, as Wilberforce says, "he looks really like the wax work figure of a corpse." Thus in one week in August, 1790, he dines with the Duke of Queensberry at Richmond, travels to Fulham, and from thence to London, dines with the Duke and Duchess of Devonshire at Devonshire House, returns to Richmond in Old Q's coach and dines at Richmond Castle with Madame la Comtesse Balbé and her French friends.

He often visits Horace Walpole and they talk of Paris and of the fate of mutual old friends there. The Bastille has fallen, the Guillotine is running patrician blood; we are filled with abhorrence at these crimes. Is not Grenier's hotel more like a hospital than anything else? "Such rooms, such a crowd of miserable wretches, and Mme. de Boufflers among them . . . altogether a piteous sight," says Selwyn. But why linger on these things? It is more pleasing to go down the river to Isleworth and pluck roses in the Duke's garden or to go up the river to Twitn'am and take tea with Horry. We shall not have many opportunities.

In November Selwyn writes a pathetic letter to Lady Carlisle with an account of his troubles. He is perishing with cold and the reason is plain. He has no clothes, his stockings are of a fine thin thread, half of them full of holes. He has no flannel waistcoat, which everybody else wears. In short he has been shivering in the warmest room without knowing why. As a result there is a committee at the Duke's upon his drapery and a tailor is sent for. He is to be flannelled and cottoned and kept alive if possible. "But if that cannot be done, I must be embalmed, with my face, mummy-like, only bare, to converse through my cerements. It is amazing to what a degree I am become helpless. Nothing can account for it but extreme dotage or extreme infancy."

Later: "Sir L. Pepys was with me in the morning and thought my pulse very quiet, which could only have been from the fatigue of the day before—juste Dieu! fatigue of going eight or nine miles, my legs on the foreseat and reposing my head on Jones's shoulder. Sir Lucas pronounced no immediate end of myself, but that I should continue the bark with hemlock. I'll do anything for some time longer, but my patience will, I see, after a certain time be exhausted."

This is on December 9, 1790. Selwyn returns to London shortly before Christmas in a very serious condition. On January 25, Walpole writes to Miss Berry: "I am on the point of losing or have lost my oldest acquaintance and friend, George Selwyn, who was yesterday at the extremity. These misfortunes, though they can be so but for a short time, are very sensible to the old; but him I really loved, not only for his infinite wit but for a thousand good qualities."

In fact this is the day of Selwyn's death. He dies at his house in Cleveland Court on January 25, 1791, in his seventy-second year and is buried in the family vault at Matson.

A few days afterwards, Walpole writes: "I have had another grievous memento, the death of poor Selwyn. From eight years old I had known him, intimately without a cloud between us. Few knew him so well and consequently few knew so well the goodness of his heart and nature." And again: "Poor Selwyn is gone to my sorrow, and no wonder Ucalegon feels it."

No wonder, indeed. But Ucalegon, gouty and old, must not dwell upon it. Agitation must be avoided at his age. Here is a good story about Caroline Vernon, fille d'honneur, who lost £200 at faro t'other night. And don't you notice that the evenings are lengthening and the spring coming on? Soon it will be lilac-tide again, when we may leave

Berkeley Square for Strawberry and wander in the pleasant river garden, companioned by the ghosts of those who were once our friends. . . .

A Georgian house in St. James's Street. Warm mellow brickwork fronted by dingy iron railings with stands where the flares are put and cups in which linkboys extinguish their torches. The house is filled with a merry company— ladies in their extravagant flowered gowns and high dressed hair, the gentlemen in their velvet coats, lace ruffles, satin breeches and stockings, wigs and swords. After a night of cards and scandal and wine, the company breaks up, crowding to the door. Linkboys light their torches and run hither and thither, sedan chairmen waken from their slumbers, expectant of vails, flunkeys shout for carriages. There is a general uproar and confusion. In the midst of it all, there is a cry of Mr. Selwyn's carriage, and from the crowd of revellers at the door, a man emerges and comes slowly down the steps, a man with a parchment face and grey hair showing under his bob-wig. He enters the carriage, waves his hand to the people at the door, who are laughing heartily at something he has just said, and drives off into the night. We cannot follow him; he disappears in the darkness, and even as we linger, the whole scene shifts and changes. The crowd melts away before our eyes—the fine ladies and gentlemen, the torches, linkboys, chairmen, flunkeys, vanish utterly. Nothing is left but an old shabby house in a shabby street in a shabby world.

BIBLIOGRAPHY

I owe a very large debt to S. Parnell Kerr's scholarly volume, *George Selwyn and the Wits*, Nicholas Amhurst's *Terrae Filius*, and Horace Wyndham's *Blotted 'Scutcheons*. Much of the dialogue in the incident of the Swearing Beau comes from Fielding's *Covent Garden Journal*.

I also wish to thank the Yale University Press for permission to quote from *The Yale Edition of Horace Walpole's Correspondence*, Vol. XX, ed. by W. S. Lewis, Warren H. Smith, and George L. Lam (New Haven, 1960).

Professor Robert B. Hennion of the Classics Department of The City College of New York has kindly and expertly translated some of the Hell Fire Club Mottoes.

Allen, J. W., "Simon Fraser, Lord Lovat," in *Lives of Twelve Bad Men*, ed. by Thomas Seccombe (New York, 1894).

Almack's, Vol. III (London, 1857).

Amhurst, Nicholas, *Terrae Filius* (London, 1754).

Andrews, Alexander, *The Eighteenth Century* (London, 1856).

Angelo, Henry, *Picnic or Table Talk* (London, 1840).

Angelo, Henry, *Reminiscences*, 2 vols. (London, 1828).

Ashton, John, *Social Life in the Reign of Queen Anne* (London, 1925).

Ashton, John, *A History of English Lotteries* (London, 1893).

Ashton, John, *The History of Gambling in England* (London, 1898).

Benson, A. C., *Fastes Etonenses* (Eton, 1899).

Besant, Sir Walter, *London in the Eighteenth Century* (London, 1902).

Bleackley, Horace, *The Story of a Beautiful Duchess* (London, 1907).

Bleackley, Horace, *The Hangmen of England* (London, 1929).

Boswell, James, *Private Papers of James Boswell from Malahide Castle in the Collection of Lt. Colonel Ralph Heyward Isham*, prepared for the press by Geoffrey Scott and Frederick A. Pottle (Mount Vernon, New York, 1928-1934).

Bradby, Godfrey F., *The Great Days of Versailles* (London, 1927).

Bradford, Gamaliel, *Portraits of Women* (Boston, 1916).

Bradford, Gamaliel, *Bare Souls* (New York, 1924).

Bradford, Gamaliel, *Daughters of Eve* (Boston, 1930).

Bradstreet, Captain Dudley, *Life and Uncommon Adventures of Captain Dudley Bradstreet*, ed. by G. S. Taylor (London, 1929).

Brisay, A. C. de, "Oxford University in the Eighteenth Century under the Hanoverians," *French Quarterly*, Vol. VI (Manchester, 1924).

Brodrick, George C., *A History of the University of Oxford* (London, 1886).

Buckley, Eric R., *A Lily of Old France* (London, 1926).

Burke, Edmund, *The Correspondence of Edmund Burke*, Vol. I, ed. by Thomas W. Copeland; Vol. II, ed. by Lucy S. Sutherland (University of Chicago Press, 1958, 1960).

Burney, Frances (Madame D'Arblay), *The Early Diary of Frances Burney*, 1768-1778, ed. by Annie R. Ellis (London, 1889).

Chancellor, E. Beresford, *The History and Antiquities of Richmond, Kew, Petersham, etc.* (Richmond, 1894).

Chancellor, E. Beresford, *Memorials of St. James's Street and Chronicles of Almack's* (New York, 1922).

Chancellor, E. Beresford, "The Hell Fire Club," in *Lives of the Rakes*, Vols. II, V, VI (London, 1925).

Charlotte, Catherine, Lady Jackson, *The Old Régime* (New York, 1882).

Charlotte, Catherine, Lady Jackson, *The French Court and Society*, Vol. I (Boston, 1897).

Chesterfield, Earl of, *Letters*, ed. by John Bradshaw, 3 vols. (New York, 1892).

Chidsey, Donald Barr, *Bonnie Prince Charlie* (New York, 1928).

Churchill, Charles, *Poetical Works*, with life of the author by W. Tooke, Vol. III (Boston, 1854).

Clergue, Helen, *The Salon* (New York, 1907).

Clinch, George, *English Costume* (London, 1909).

Coit, Charles W., *Charles I* (Boston, 1926).

Cole, Reverend William, *A Journal of My Journey to Paris in the Year 1765*, ed. by Francis G. Stokes (London, 1931).

Colman, George and Thornton, Bonnell, *The Connoisseur*, 4 vols. (London, 1784).

Covent Garden Journal, The (No. 33, April 23, 1752).

Craik, G. L., "The House of Commons," in *London,* ed. by Chas.
Knight, 4 vols., Vol. II (London, 1841).

Crisp, Richard, *Richmond and Its Inhabitants* (Richmond, 1866).

Cumberland, Richard, *Memoirs,* 2 vols. (London, 1807).

Cust, Lionel, *History of the Society of Dilettanti* (London,
1914).

D'Auvergne, M. Nelson, *Tarnished Coronets* (London, 1914).

Deffand, Madame du, *Lettres de Mme. du Deffand à Horace
Walpole,* 3 vols., ed. by Mrs. Paget Toynbee (London, 1912).

Delany, Mrs., *Autobiography and Correspondence of Mary Granville, Mrs. Delany,* 6 vols., ed. by Lady Llanover, first and
second series (London, 1861).

Dictionary of National Biography, ed. by Sir Leslie Stephen and
Sir Sidney Lee (1917).

Dobson, Austin, *Eighteenth Century Vignettes,* first series (New
York, 1892).

Dobson, Austin, *Horace Walpole* (London, 1927).

Doran, Dr. John, *London in the Jacobite Times,* Vol. II (London, 1877).

Ducros, Louis, *French Society in the Eighteenth Century,* tr.
by W. de Geijer (London, 1926).

Farmer, James E., *Versailles and the Court of Louis XIV* (New
York, 1905).

Fielding, Henry (Drawcansir, Sir Alexander), *The Covent
Garden Journal,* ed. by Gerard E. Jensen, 2 vols. (1915).

Fielding, Henry, *The Works of Henry Fielding,* ed. by James
P. Browne, Vol. X (London, 1871).

Fitzgerald, Percy H., *Dukes and Princesses of the Family of
George III,* Vol. I (London, 1882).

Funck-Brentano, Frantz, *The Old Régime in France,* tr. by
Herbert Wilson (New York, 1929).

Garrick, David, *Diary,* ed. by Ryllis C. Alexander (New York,
1928).

George, M. Dorothy, *England in Johnson's Day* (London, 1928).

Gibbon, Edward, *Memoirs* (London, 1891).

Glenbervie, Sylvester Douglas, Lord, *Diaries,* ed. by Francis
Bickley, 2 vols. (London, 1928).

Godley, A. D., *Oxford in the Eighteenth Century* (London,
1908).

Goncourt, Edmond and Jules de, *The Women of the Eighteenth
Century,* tr. by Jacques Le Clerq and Ralph Roeder (New
York, 1927).

Gooch, George P., *Catherine the Great and Other Studies* (London, 1954).

Grant, James, *The White Cockade* (London, 1867).

Graves, Richard, *Recollection of Some Particulars in the Life of William Shenstone* (London, 1788).

Green, Frederick C., *Eighteenth Century France* (New York, 1931).

Green, John Richard, *Oxford Studies* (London, 1901).

Greenwood, Alice D., *Horace Walpole's World* (London, 1913).

Grego, Joseph, *A History of Parliamentary Elections* (London, 1892).

Grenville Papers, The, Being the Correspondence Between Earl Temple and George Grenville, Vol. IV (London, 1853).

Grimm, Baron Frederic Melchior de, and Diderot, Denis, *Memoirs and Anecdotes,* 2 vols. (London, 1814).

Guerard, Albert, *The Life and Death of an Ideal* (New York, 1928).

Gwynn, Stephen L., *Life of Horace Walpole* (Boston, 1932).

Hamel, Frank, *An Eighteenth Century Marquise* (London, 1910).

Hamilton, C. J., *Notable Irishwomen* (Dublin, 1904).

Hamilton, Sidney G., *Hertford College* (London, 1903).

Harper, Chas. G., *Half Hours with the Highwaymen,* 2 vols. (London, 1908).

Havens, Munson Aldrich, *Horace Walpole and the Strawberry Hill Press* (Canton, Pa., 1901).

Hawkins, Miss Laetitia, *Gossip About Dr. Johnson and Others,* being chapters from the *Memoirs of Miss Laetitia Hawkins,* ed. by Francis H. Skrine (London, 1926).

Headlam, Cecil, *Oxford and Its Story* (London, 1904).

Headlam, Cecil, *France* (London, 1913).

Herbert, A. P., "The London of *The Beggar's Opera,*" in *The London Mercury,* Vol. V (Nov. 1921–April, 1922).

Hervey, John, Lord, *Memoirs of the Reign of George II,* Vol. I (London, 1848).

Hickey, William, *Memoirs,* ed. by Albert Spencer, Vol. II (New York, 1921).

Hill, Cecilia, *Versailles* (London, 1925).

Hill, Georgiana, *A History of English Dress,* 2 vols. (New York, 1893).

Hitchcock, R., *The Macaroni* (Phila., 1774).

Hobhouse, Christopher, *Fox* (Boston and New York, 1935).

Hodgson, F. C., "Horace Walpole," *The Gentleman's Magazine,* Vol. 286 (London, March, 1899).

Holland, Henry Richard Vassall, 3rd Lord, *Further Memoirs of the Whig Party,* ed. by Lord Stavordale (London, 1905).

Huish, Robert, *Memoirs of George IV,* Vol. I (London, 1831).

Hunt, William, *The History of England, 1760–1801, The Political History of England,* ed. by William Hunt and Reginald L. Poole, Vol. X (New York, 1905).

Hutton, William H., *Burford Papers* (London, 1905).

Ilchester, Earl of, *Henry Fox, First Lord Holland,* 2 vols. (London, 1920).

Ilchester, Earl of, and Langford-Brooke, Mrs., *Life of Sir Charles Hanbury Williams* (London, 1929).

Jebb, Camilia, *A Star of the Salons* (New York, 1908).

Jennings, George H., *An Anecdotal History of the British Parliament* (New York, 1881).

Jesse, John Heneage, *George Selwyn and His Contemporaries,* 4 vols (Boston, 1843).

Jesse, John Heneage, *Memoirs of Celebrated Etonians,* 2 vols. (Boston, 190–?).

Jesse, John Heneage, *Memoirs of the Pretenders and Their Adherents,* 2 vols. (London, 1845).

Jesse, John Heneage, *Memoirs of the Life and Reign of King George III,* 5 vols. (Boston, 190–?).

Johnes, Merideth, *Prince Charlie* (New York, 1860).

Johnson, Capt. Charles, *The Lives and Actions of the Most Noted Highwaymen, Street Robbers, Pirates, etc.* (London, –?).

Johnson, Reginald Brimley, *The Undergraduate,* revised from Dr. Christopher Wordsworth's *Social Life at the English Universities in the Eighteenth Century* (London, 1928).

Johnstone, Charles, *Chrysal or the Adventures of a Guinea* (New York, 1816).

Jones, Louis C., *The Clubs of the Georgian Rakes* (New York, 1942).

Kavanagh, Julia, *Women in France During the Eighteenth Century* (London, 1864).

Kerr, S. Parnell, *George Selwyn and the Wits* (London, 1909).

Ketton-Cremer, R. W., *Horace Walpole* (London, 1946).

Kielmansegge, Count Frederick, *Diary of a Journey to England in 1761–1762* (New York, 1902).

Koven, Anna de, *Horace Walpole and Mme. du Deffand* (New York, 1929).

Lacroix, Paul, *The Eighteenth Century, France 1700–1789* (London, 1876).

Latour, Thérèse L., *Princesses, Ladies, and Salonnières of the Reign of Louis XV* (New York, 1928).

Lecky, William E. H., *A History of England in the Eighteenth Century*, 8 vols. (London, 1887).

Lennox, Lady Sarah, *Life and Letters*, ed. by the Countess of Ilchester and Lord Stavordale, 2 vols. (London, 1901).

Leslie, Charles R., and Taylor, Tom, *Life and Times of Sir Joshua Reynolds*, 4 vols. (London, 1865).

Letters on the French Nation by a Sicilian Gentleman Residing in Paris (London, 1749).

Lewis, Wilmarth S., *Horace Walpole*, The A. W. Mellon Lectures in the Fine Arts (Bollingen Series, Vol. IX, 1961).

Lives of the Most Remarkable Criminals, ed. by Arthur L. Hayward (New York, 1927).

Lockitt, C. H., *The Relations of French and English Society* (London, 1920).

Lucas, William, *A Five Weeks' Tour to Paris* (London, 1754).

Macaulay, Thomas B., *Critical and Historical Essays*, Vol. I (London, 1916).

Mackenzie, W. C., *Simon Fraser, Lord Lovat* (London, 1908).

Magnus, Sir Philip, *Burke* (London, 1939).

Mallet, Charles E., *A History of the University of Oxford*, Vol. III (London, 1927).

Mason, Alfred B., *Horace Walpole's England* (Boston, 1930).

Mason, Amelia G., *The Women of the French Salons* (New York, 1891).

McCarthy, Justin, *History of the Four Georges*, Vol. II (New York, 1885).

McCormick, Donald, *The Hell Fire Club* (London, 1958).

Mead, William E., *The Grand Tour in the Eighteenth Century* (Boston, 1914).

Melville, Lewis, *Farmer George*, 2 vols. (London, 1907).

Melville, Lewis, *Horace Walpole* (London, 1930).

Melville, Lewis, *The Star of Piccadilly* (London, 1927).

Melville, Lewis, *The First Gentleman of Europe*, 2 vols. (London, 1906).

Memorials of Brooks's (London, 1907).

Miller, James, *The Humours of Oxford* (London, 1730).

Mitchell, William, *Prince Charles Edward Stuart of Scotland and the Rising of 1745* (Edinburgh and Glasgow, 1930).

Mme. du Deffand and Her Friends, *The Edinburgh Review or Critical Journal*, Vol. 193, no. 395 (London, 1901).

Mrs. Montagu, *Mrs. Montagu, Queen of the Blues, Her Letters and Friendships*, 2 vols., ed. by Reginald Blount (London, 1923).

Morgan, John, *Journal of Dr. John Morgan of Philadelphia from the City of Rome to the City of London* (Phila., 1907).

Moritz, Carl Philipp, *Travels of Carl Philipp Moritz in England in 1782* (London, 1924).

Murray, Robert H., *Edmund Burke* (Oxford University Press, 1931).

Musée Carnavalet, *The Great Literary Salons*, tr. by Mabel Robinson (London, 1930).

Namier, Lewis B., *Structure of Politics at the Accession of George III*, 2 vols. (London, 1929).

Nevill, Ralph, *London Clubs* (London, 1911).

Notes and Queries, Series 9, Vols. IV, VI, VIII, IX, X, XI (London, 1899-1903).

Palgrave, Reginald F. D., *The House of Commons* (London, 1869).

Payne, Francis L., *The Story of Versailles* (New York, 1919).

Pearson, Norman, "Some Neglected Aspects of Horace Walpole," *Fortnightly Review*, new series, Vol. 86 (September, 1909).

Perkins, Clarence, "Electioneering in the Eighteenth Century," in *The Quarterly Journal*, University of North Dakota, Vol. XIII, no. 2 (January, 1923).

Perkins, James B., *France under Louis XV*, 2 vols. (Boston, 1897).

Plaisted, Arthur H., *The Manor and Parish Records of Medmenham* (London, 1925).

Postgate, R. W., *That Devil Wilkes* (New York, 1929).

Power, William, *Prince Charlie* (London, 1912).

Pückler-Muskau, Hermann Ludwig Heinrich Fürst von, *Tour in England, Ireland, and France* by a German Prince (Phila., 1833).

Rae, W. Fraser, *Wilkes, Sheridan, Fox* (London, 1874).

Reynolds, Frederick, *The Life and Times of Frederick Reynolds*, 2 vols. (London, 1826).

Riker, Thad W., *Henry Fox, First Lord Holland*, 2 vols. (Oxford, 1911).

Robertson, John M., *Bolingbroke and Walpole* (New York, 1919).

Robinson, C. Grant, *England Under the Hanoverians*, in *A His-*

tory of England, 7 vols., ed. by Charles Oman, Vol. VI (London, 1911).

Rogers, Samuel, *Recollections of the Table Talk of Samuel Rogers,* 2 vols. (London, 1856).

Roscoe, E. S., and Clergue, Helen, *George Selwyn, His Life and Letters* (London 1899).

Rudder, Samuel, *A New History of Gloucestershire* (Cirencester, 1779).

Saint-Amand, Imbert de, *The Court of Louis XV* (New York, 1900).

Sala, George A., *The Strange Adventures of Captain Dangerous,* Vol. II (London, 1863).

Sedgwick, Henry Dwight, *France* (Boston, 1929).

Sergeant, Philip W., *Gamblers All* (London, 1931).

Seymour, Charles, *Electoral Reform in England and Wales* (New Haven, 1915).

Sherson, Erroll, *The Lively Lady Townshend and Her Friends* (London, 1926).

Sichel, Walter, *Bolingbroke and His Times,* 2 vols. (London, 1901).

Sidney, Philip, "The Executioner of Charles I," *The Gentleman's Magazine,* Vol. 299 (September, 1905).

Skottowe, B. C., *A Short History of Parliament* (New York, 1887).

Smith, G. Barnett, *History of the English Parliament,* Vol. II (London, 1894).

Steinmetz, Andrew, *The Gaming Table,* 2 vols. (London, 1870).

Stokes, Hugh. *The Devonshire House Circle* (London, 1917).

Strachey, Lytton, *Books and Characters* (London, 1922).

Street, G. S., "The Betting Book at Brooks's," in *The North American Review,* Vol. 173, no. 1 (New York, 1901).

Stryienski, Casimir, "The Eighteenth Century," *The National History of France,* ed. by Fr. Funck-Brentano (New York, 1916).

Stuart, Dorothy M., *Horace Walpole* (New York, 1927).

Stuart, Lady Louisa, Notes on John H. Jesse's *George Selwyn and His Contemporaries,* ed. by W. S. Lewis (New York, 1928).

Sydney, William C., *England and the English in the Eighteenth Century,* 2 vols. (Edinburgh, –?).

Synge, Margaret B., *A Short History of Social Life in England* (London, 1922).

Taine, H. A., *The Ancient Régime,* translated by John Durand (New York, 1896).

Tait, J. H. M., "William Boyd, Fourth Earl of Kilmarnock," *Transactions of the Glasgow Archeological Society,* Vol. VII, new series, part I (Glasgow, 1916).

Tallentyre, S. G., *Madame du Deffand,* in *Living Age,* Vol. 225, series 7 (April–June, 1900).

Tallentyre, S. G., *The Friends of Voltaire* (London, 1906).

Terry, Charles S., *The Forty-five* (Cambridge, 1929).

The Complete Newgate Calendar, collated and edited by J. L. Rayner and G. T. Cook, 5 vols. (London, 1926).

The Criminal Recorder or Biographical Sketches of Notorious Public Characters, 2 vols. (Nottingham, 1815).

The History of White's, 2 vols. (London, 1892).

The New Foundling Hospital For Wit, 6 vols. (London, 1784).

Thomson, Mrs. Katherine, *Memoirs of the Jacobites,* Vols. II, III (London, 1846).

Thoughts of a Citizen of London on the Conduct of Dr. Dodd in His Life and Death (London, 1767).

Tilley, Arthur A., *The Decline of the Age of Louis XIV* (Cambridge, 1929).

Timbs, John, *Clubs and Club Life in London* (London, 1902).

Tinker, Chauncey B., *The Salon and English Letters* (New York, 1915).

Tornius, Valerian, *Salons* (New York, 1929).

Trevelyan, George O., *The Early History of Charles James Fox,* (New York, 190–?).

"Trial of Lord Lovat," *Notable Scottish Trials,* ed. by David N. Mackay (Edinburgh and Glasgow, 1911).

Walpole, B. C., *C. J. Fox* (London 190–?).

Walpole, Horace, *A Description of the Villa of Mr. Horace Walpole at Strawberry Hill* (London, 1842).

Walpole, Horace, *Horace Walpole and His World,* ed. by L. A. Seeley (New York, 1895).

Walpole, Horace, *Reminiscences,* with notes and index by Paget Toynbee (Oxford, 1924).

Walpole, Horace, *Letters,* ed. by Mrs. Paget Toynbee, 16 vols. (Oxford, 1903).

Walpole, Horace, *The Yale Edition of Horace Walpole's Correspondence,* Vol. XX, ed. by W. S. Lewis, Warren H. Smith, and George L. Lam (New Haven, 1960); Vol. XXX, ed. by W. S. Lewis and Robert A. Smith (New Haven, 1961).

Ward, Edward, *A Compleat and Humorous Account of the Clubs and Society in the Cities of London and Westminster* (London, 1745).

Ward, Mary E., "Horace Walpole and the Strawberry Hill Press," *The Printing Art*, Vol. XXXII, no. 1 (September, 1918).

Ward, W. R., *Georgian Oxford* (Oxford, 1958).

Warton, Grace and Philip (Thomson, Katherine B., and John C.), *Queens of Society*, Vol. II (London, 1840).

Wechter, Dixon, *Edmund Burke and His Kinsmen* (University of Colorado Studies, 1939).

Weiner, Margery, *The French Exiles, 1789–1815* (London, 1960).

Williams, J. B., "Who Beheaded Charles I?" *The Month*, vol. 135, no. 672 (June, 1920).

Wordsworth Christopher, *Social Life at the English Universities in the Eighteenth Century* (Cambridge, 1874).

Wraxall, Nathaniel W., *The Historical and Posthumous Memoirs of Sir Nathaniel W. Wraxall*, ed. by Henry B. Wheatley, 5 vols. (New York, 1884).

Wright, Thomas, *Caricature History of the Georges*, 2 vols. (London, 1904).

Wrong, Edward M., *History of England* (London, 1927).

Wyndham, Horace, *Blotted 'Scutcheons* (New York, 1926).

INDEX